★ ★ ★ ★ ★ ★ ★ ★ ★ ★

INSIDE
CONGRESS

★ ★ ★ ★ ★ ★ ★ ★ ★ ★

Books by Ronald Kessler

Inside Congress*
The Sins of the Father
Inside the White House*
The FBI*
Inside the CIA*
Escape from the CIA*
The Spy in the Russian Club*
Moscow Station*
Spy vs. Spy*
The Richest Man in the World
The Life Insurance Game

*Published by POCKET BOOKS

★★★★★★★★★★★★★★★★★

INSIDE
CONGRESS

The Shocking Scandals, Corruption,
and Abuse of Power
Behind the Scenes on Capitol Hill

★★★★★★★★★★★★★★★★★

RONALD KESSLER

POCKET BOOKS
New York   London   Toronto   Sydney   Tokyo   Singapore

POCKET BOOKS, a division of Simon & Schuster Inc.
1230 Avenue of the Americas, New York, NY 10020

ISBN: 978-1-4767-4661-6

First Pocket Books hardcover printing June 1997

10 9 8 7 6 5 4 3 2 1

POCKET and colophon are registered trademarks of
Simon & Schuster Inc.

Printed in the U.S.A.

For Pam, Rachel,
and Greg Kessler

★ ★ ★ ★ ★ ★ ★ ★ ★

Contents

★ ★ ★ ★ ★ ★ ★ ★ ★

Contents

$\star$ $\star$ $\star$ $\star$ $\star$ $\star$ $\star$ $\star$ $\star$

Acknowledgments

$\star$ $\star$ $\star$ $\star$ $\star$ $\star$ $\star$ $\star$ $\star$

This book was the idea of my agent, Robert Gottlieb, executive vice president of the William Morris Agency and head of its Literary Department. I am indebted to Robert for sharing the fruits of his genius with me, and for his support.

My editor, Paul D. McCarthy, senior editor at Pocket Books, immediately recognized the importance of the idea, encouraged me throughout, and brilliantly edited the final manuscript. This is my fifth book with Paul. An author could not hope for a better editor.

More than a decade ago, I decided to take the risky step of leaving the *Washington Post* to write books. My wife, Pamela Kessler, encouraged me to make that decision. Pam perceptively edited the book initially and shared her good judgment with me throughout. A former *Washington Post* reporter who is the author of *Undercover Washington*, a book on the spy sites of Washington, she also applied her unique writing talent to help describe the Capitol. She is my best friend and trusted adviser. Without her, there would not have been a book.

My grown children, Greg and Rachel Kessler, were sources of loving support, encouragement, and pride. Their devotion means everything to me. My stepson, Mike Whitehead, cheered me on with his usual charm.

Friends and experts read the manuscript and offered helpful suggestions. They include Dr. Bertram S. Brown, Daniel M.

Acknowledgments

Clements, and former Senate staffer Martin Lobel, as well as my daughter, Rachel Kessler. Others from the Congressional Research Service, the Capitol Police, and the executive branch also read the manuscript for accuracy.

I am fortunate to have so many talented supporters and thank them for their help. Those who were interviewed or helped in other ways include:

Former senator James G. Abourezk, Charles D. Akins, Steve C. Alder, Ariadne Allan, McGeary Allison, McCoy Ancrum Jr., Donnald K. Anderson, Richard A. Arenberg, Trevor Armbrister, Henry F. Arrett, Joseph A. Attig, David D. Aughtry, Brian Auth, Patricia Bario, Knox M. Barnes, Michael F. Barrett Jr., Martin D. Baumgart, Daniel P. Beard, Wayne N. Beckett, former representative Anthony C. Beilenson, Brian S. Benninghoff, David K. Berry, Gaston Bethea Jr., Jerome Beuchert, Mario R. Bignotti, Linwood T. Binford Jr., Jack A. Blum, Lloyd E. Bond, Werner W. Brandt, John Brautigam, Sen. John B. Breaux, and Dr. Bertram S. Brown.

Sen. Hank Brown, Brian M. Bruh, Kenneth J. Burney, Sen. Conrad Burns, Dean J. Burridge, Johnny A. Byrd, Joseph A. Califano Jr., Sen. Ben Nighthorse Campbell, Bobby L. Canard, Robert G. Cantor, Margot D. B. Carlisle, Raymond L. Carson, James J. Carvino, Daniel P. Casserly, John T. Caulfield, David W. Clements, Donald F. Cline, Floyd F. Cline, Sen. Thad Cochran, William M. Cochrane, Edwin H. Cockshott, Kenneth Derreck Cohen, Thomas A. Connaughton, Jay Constantine, Matthew T. Cook, Richard K. Cook, David L. Coon, Terry D. Coons, Joseph R. Crapa, John Cronin Jr., Wilbert N. Croom, John L. Crowl, Joshua Crupi, and Frank Cullen Jr.

Isabella S. Cummins, Bruce A. Currie, David A. Curry, John E. Daniels, Darvin L. Davis, Steven E. Dekelbaum, Roger L. Derflinger, former representative Butler C. Derrick Jr., Robert E. Devine, Douglas S. Dibbert, Raymond I. Dingle, Dennis G. Doherty, David Donnelly, Lenore F. Donnelly, Jerry O. Duke, Joseph M. Dungan, Reginald A. Dunkins, Rodney C. Eades, James D. Early, Dr. Terry Eisenberg, Roy L. Elson, Rep. Anna G. Eshoo, Frederick W. Faerber, Charles E. Farmer, and Dave Farrell.

Acknowledgments

Scot M. Faulkner, Gabriele J. Fedele, Sen. Russell D. Feingold, former representative Eric D. Fingerhut, David J. First, Heather Forsgren, Thomas W. Fox, Bruce F. Freed, Charles W. Funkhouser, James J. Furey, Al Gammal, Charles F. Gardner, Theodore M. Gardner, Joe P. Gear, Robert Gellman, Robert E. Glessner, Ashton Gonella, Jamie S. Gorelick, John A. Gott, Ed Greelegs, Sen. Judd Gregg, Harold M. Gross, Rep. Lee H. Hamilton, Michael R. Hanneld, Kenneth R. Harding, Greg C. Harness, Terri Hasdorff, Sen. Orrin G. Hatch, Mark D. Hauglie, Christopher A. Heil, Paul Hendrie, Gail F. Henkin, and Paul Z. Herman.

William F. Hildenbrand, John L. Hitzel, Charles L. Hoag, Carol Hoffman, George L. Holmes Jr., former representative Larry J. Hopkins, Howard R. Horowitz, Michael E. Hupp, Frank C. Hutto III, Rep. Bob Inglis, Meldon R. Jackson, Rita Jenrette, Robert Jones, Paul Joyal, Ginny Kass, Patrick J. Keniston, Frank A. Kerrigan, Robert W. Kieliger, David S. Kiernan, John W. Kifer, J. Stanley Kimmitt, Charles T. Kindsvatter, Sean Kirkendall, Rep. Scott L. Klug, Arthur S. Knoller, Rep. Jim Kolbe, Laura Kopelson, former representative Peter H. Kostmayer, Daniel J. Kreitman, Andrew Kruk, Eugene J. Kuser, William D. Lackey Jr., Gregory M. Lacoss, Thomas E. Ladd, David Ladenburg, and Terry Lamberton.

Rep. Jim Leach, Michael R. Lemov, former representative Mel Levine, William Lightfoot, Charles B. (Chuck) Lipsen, Jason E. Livengood, Rep. Robert L. Livingston, Martin Lobel, Douglas B. Loon, Larry F. Loughery, Dr. Mark M. Lowenthal, James E. Mack, Mary Ann Mahoney, Stephen Mahoney, Amy Mall, Neal Manne, Wilbur Marceron, Frank J. Marchone, Grant C. Massey, Dan Mattoon, Rudy Maxa, Steve Mayer, former representative Romano L. Mazzoli, Larry J. McCune, Scott McGeary, Paul R. McGill, Wilbur R. Mead, Rep. Martin T. Meehan, Julie Chatterjee Mehta, Carl J. Merz, Lawrence G. Meyer, Richard W. Micer, Charles R. Midgette, Ellen S. Miller, Morton Mintz, Clark Mitchell, and Claudia Molloy.

Rep. Constance A. Morella, Mathew H. Moser, former representative John E. Moss, James L. Muldrow, Sen. Frank H. Murkowski, Thomas F. Nairn, former senator Gaylord A.

Acknowledgments

Nelson, Daniel R. Nichols, John R. Niston, Sylvia Nolde, Douglas W. Norris, William G. Norton, Morgan H. Norval, Alan S. Novins, Walter Oleszak, Bob Pack, Melvin F. Parker, Gary L. Parks, Stephan Pashkovsky, David R. Peebler, Edward P. Percival, Rep. Collin C. Peterson, Kenneth L. Pittman, Robert G. Plato, Howard F. Pond, Dean Popps, Jack W. Pridgen, former senator William Proxmire, Richard R. Pulliam, Joe T. Quattrone, Charles H. Raines, Carl B. Raupe, Joel C. Raupe, Richard L. Rausch, and William L. Rawls.

Matt Raymond, Harper T. Redden, Aubrey C. Redling, Talmadge (Tom) W. Reed, David K. Rehr, Raymond H. Reisig, Diane Rennert, Patricia Reuss, Robert R. Reuss, Spencer Rich, Vincent A. Richardson, Judge Charles R. Richey, William R. Ricker, Floyd M. Riddick, Ernest M. Riddle, Donald A. Ritchie, Jeffrey T. Robinson, Peter D. Robinson, Amy Rosenbaum, Carl T. Rowan Jr., Eugene J. Rucchio, Dale R. Ruffaner, Howard R. Ryland, Arthur C. Sampson, Paul A. Samuelson, Frédérique J. Sandretto, Charles L. Scala, Joseph R. Schaap, Frederick Schauer, Robert F. Schiff, Lee A. Schmalbach, Marvin Shadman, Rep. Christopher Shays, Franklin C. Shelton, Robert L. Shipe, the late Carl M. Shoffler, Paul E. Sigmund IV, William P. Siko, Frank Silbey, Victor E. Siler, and Don Simon.

Marcus J. Singleton, Leo Skenyon, Paul Smith, Edward E. Smolarsky, L. Britt Snider, William C. Soderberg, John F. Sopko, Nelson C. Sours, Adolph Spagnoli, Rep. Floyd D. Spence, Lawrence V. Spillers, Jeffrey B. Staser, Carley J. Stedman, Rickey L. Stephens, Carl Stern, Steven F. Stockmeyer, Peter D. H. Stockton, Herbert Strongin, Thomas M. Strzemienski, Pamela B. Stuart, Rep. Bob Stump, Barry Sussman, Lennart P. Swanson, Robert M. Swart, Bill Tate, Steven H. Taubenberger, David L. Teichert, Len Tepper, Robert Thomas, James E. Thorndike, Barbara Timmer, Leroy Tolbert, Debbie Tomasko, Kenneth A. Tomlin, Walter J. Trohan, James T. Trollinger, William H. Tucker, and Vernon L. Vail.

Steven R. (Rick) Valentine, Thomas L. van der Voort, Virgil L. VanFleet, David Vienna, Scott M. Waitlevertch, John T. Walker, former representative Robert S. Walker, Harry I. Wall, Vern B.

Acknowledgments

Wallace, Douglas F. Wallick, Mark A. Watkins, Amanda Whee-ler, William E. Wickens, Stephan A. Wido, Sterling Willhoit, Noah Wofsy, Barbara A. Wolanin, Lisa Wolfington, Paula G. Wolfson, Mark Wyn, Richard F. Xander, Richard P. Yeatman, Jimmie G. Young, Lenvil D. Young, Jay Youngclaus, Ronald A. Yudd, and Murray Zweben.

INSIDE CONGRESS

Prologue

Now more than ever, Congress runs America. It is no accident that the founding fathers enumerated Congress's powers in Article I of the Constitution, saving the president's powers for Article II. Aware of the British Parliament's struggles with the Crown, they expected Congress to be the chief policy-making body.

Beyond ordering military strikes, the president can do little unless Congress passes a law. Only Congress can make legal what is illegal. Even if the Supreme Court finds a law unconstitutional, Congress can still pass a new law or ask the states to ratify an amendment to the Constitution. As voters have opted for passive, undistinguished presidents, Congress has assumed even more power.

As the final authority, Congress is the grand know-it-all, holding agencies and executive branch officials to microscopic scrutiny in hearings and General Accounting Office reports. Yet if Congress found in the executive branch the kinds of abuses it engages in, it would demand investigations, firings, and criminal prosecutions. Only the denizens of the Hill—the Capitol Police officers, doormen, elevator operators, waiters, clerks, pages, professional staffers, and members of Congress themselves—know the difference between the facade and the reality.

"If the American people found out what was going on there, they would tear it down brick by brick," said Howard R. Ryland, a Capitol Police officer for sixteen years.[1]

For this book, more than 350 insiders like Ryland talked for the first time. This is their eyewitness account.

★ ★ ★ ★ ★ ★ ★ ★ ★ ★

1

★ ★ ★ ★ ★ ★ ★ ★ ★ ★

Hideaways

The Capitol sits on land once known as Jenkins' Hill, which rises eighty-eight feet above the Potomac River in Washington. Bathed in light at night, the Capitol's white dome is a symbol of America—strong, dignified, and pure. But the impression is misleading. First occupied on November 17, 1800, the nineteenth-century neoclassical building has over the years been burned, bombed, rebuilt, extended, and restored. "Part of it was sandstone, part of it was marble, the dome is cast-iron. It's all painted white to make it look like one unified building," said Donald A. Ritchie, associate historian of the Senate. "It's really a hodgepodge."

If the white paint masks the turbulent history of the Capitol, so does the labyrinthine Capitol conceal what goes on inside Congress. For in the 540-room Capitol, and in the surrounding House and Senate office buildings, on the manicured grounds, and in secret hideaways and tunnels, the most shocking, outrageous, and often corrupt activities take place. The activities highlight not only the hypocrisy of members of Congress and their staffs, but also what is wrong with the political system Congress itself has fashioned.

Each year, 3 to 5 million Americans traverse the corridors of this mosaic-lined treasure box, wearing out the Minton tiles underfoot. Yet the tourists never see large portions, which are roped off or closed to the public. These areas include nearly one hundred hideaway offices that the congressional leadership and more senior members maintain for themselves in the Capitol. Marked only by door numbers, the hideaway offices are often fabulously appointed rooms with gilded crystal chandeliers, ornate floor-length mirrors, working fireplaces, and frescoed walls and ceilings. Some of the first hideaway offices were carved out of the chambers of Supreme Court justices when the court met in the Capitol.

Ostensibly, the offices allow members to escape the demands of their regular offices so they can think, or to save time getting to a vote on the floor of the House or Senate. But Daniel Webster used his hideaway—S-326-A—to store his wine. More recently, hideaways have often been used for "hideaway honeys."

Capitol Police officer Gregory M. Lacoss will never forget turning the doorknob to one of Lyndon B. Johnson's seven Capitol hideaways when LBJ was majority leader of the Senate. It was 3 A.M., and Lacoss was making his rounds, checking to make sure all offices were locked. Lacoss opened the massive door and gasped. On the sofa, Johnson was having sex with Carole Tyler, a blond, curvaceous secretary.

"There was LBJ on top of Carole," Lacoss recalled. "I said, 'Excuse me.' He said, 'You son of a bitch.' He jumped up. I took off running because I knew that man's temper. I ran to the other end of the Senate building, down the marble stairway, past the Ohio clock. I ran through the Rotunda. He was running after me. I ran to the House wing, down to the terrace level, and to the chief's office."[2]

"I just caught LBJ on top of Carole," Lacoss shouted at the desk officer on duty. "He's threatening to kill me."

The desk officer told Lacoss to hide in a locker. "Those lockers were little," Lacoss said. "I had a gun and flashlight, and

I crammed myself in. I could hardly breathe. LBJ came flying in. I could hear him slam the door. I thought it would break. He said, 'Where is that officer?' " The desk officer said, "Who are you talking about?" Johnson replied, "That son of a bitch who came in here. I'll kill him."

Eventually, Johnson tired of the hunt, and the desk officer extricated Lacoss from the locker. "He had to pull me out," Lacoss said. "I couldn't open it myself."

James T. Trollinger, a former deputy chief of the Capitol Police, said that one night one of his officers told him he had found the door to a Capitol hideaway unlocked. Said Trollinger, "The officer told me there was trouble in this one room. He was checking to make sure things were locked up. This door was open, and somebody yelled at him. There were no lights on. . . . He said something was wrong there."

A real police officer would have demanded that the individual come out with his hands up. But over the years, Capitol Police officers have been so repressed by their masters—members of the U.S. Congress—that they do not think like real police and often defend practices that other law enforcement officers would consider scandalous. So the officer in this case simply told his supervisor, who was Trollinger.

"I went there and opened the door," Trollinger said. "I flicked on a light. It was a senator with his secretary," a pretty brunette. "I knew them both. He was a big man. Everyone in the country knew his name. He was a statesman. But he did like his secretary. . . . They were naked and having sex. He said to get the hell out of here and close that f------ door."[3]

"One secretary had her hair in a swept-up hairdo pinned with a couple of pins," a former congressional aide said. "She used to whip over to Sen. Joseph M. Montoya's hideaway and screw him or give him [oral sex], and then she'd be back in thirty minutes with her hair back up."

Some members use their regular offices for similar purposes. "I've seen a lot of members falling-down drunk, and pretty girls going into their offices at two A.M.," said George L. Holmes Jr., a former Capitol Police officer. "This goes on all the time."

"I think everybody [in the Capitol Police] came across members or staffers having sex in their offices at one time or another," said Charles T. Kindsvatter, a retired Capitol Police captain who was in charge of training and research until 1991. "It was hard to find somebody who hadn't had this experience."[4]

"We checked the doors, and if they were unlocked, we would open them and see who was in there," David A. Curry, a former Capitol Police captain, said. While Curry was patrolling the Cannon House Office Building, the first congressional office building, at 2 A.M., he "walked in" on Silvio O. Conte from Massachusetts. "He had a girl with him. They were on a couch and had no clothes on," Curry recalled.[5]

Later, Curry served as bartender at parties given by Congressman Kenneth J. Gray on his houseboat. "Ken Gray would have wild parties," Curry said.

Richard F. Xander, a Metropolitan Police sergeant who was detailed to the Capitol Police, recalled that long before Rep. Wilbur D. Mills began consorting with stripper Fanne Foxe in 1974, he saw Mills in the Silver Slipper, a strip joint, getting drunk. "They had a dark place where the girls gave guys a bottle of cheap champagne and charged them for Dom Pérignon," he said. "They played with them. An old codger was half-drunk, and the girl would run her hands up his leg a few times, and then she would leave and he would go home horny and broke. Mills was in there."[6]

According to a Metropolitan Police informant in Washington, Mills—then considered the most powerful member of Congress because of his tight control of the House Ways and Means Committee—regularly received oral sex from a transvestite. When he finally found out the transvestite's true gender, he was devastated. But Mills, who was married, also regularly had sex with secretaries in his hideaway office. Wayne N. Beckett, a former Capitol Police officer, recalled surprising Mills there around midnight one night.

"I saw the secretary bent over the desk," he said. "He looked up, and I got the hell out of there. I couldn't tell what she looked like. All I saw was that naked butt. . . . I just left there kind of embarrassed. I went to the basement. The phone rang. The sergeant came back and said, 'Were you just upstairs? Were you in his office?' I said yes. He said, 'Then get the hell out of here. You weren't working tonight.' I said, 'What?' He said, 'Do you want your job or not? Just go home.' They wouldn't tell him who I was."[7]

"I walked in on a member having sex," said Jimmie G. Young, a former Capitol Police officer. "The senator is still there. It was in his personal office. It was around eight P.M. when we were doing building checks. . . . He was having sex with one of his secretaries on the couch. . . . She was a beautiful young girl in her early twenties."[8]

The senator asked if the door was locked. "My partner said if the door was locked, we wouldn't be in here," Young said.

Rodney C. Eades, a former Capitol Police officer, recalled that former House Speaker Carl B. Albert, who was a "very heavy drinker," would "come in on Saturday mornings just blasted away. He couldn't walk. He had a white Thunderbird. He would bang [the car] into the wall or the steps [of the Capitol]."[9]

"Carl Albert was always drunk," said Raymond L. Carson, a former Capitol Police lieutenant.[10] Albert has long denied he had a drinking problem.[11]

"There's a room behind where the Speaker sits," former officer Beckett said. "The members rest there. They had high-backed chairs and a fireplace. There was a door to the balcony. Wilbur Mills and this sergeant would get drunk. To sober them up, the Speaker [Albert] would tell us to put them out on the balcony and lock the door. Sometimes it was ten degrees out. Carl Albert was drunk, too. They would play pranks on each other. They would lock each other in the bathroom. Albert was in a stall and Mills took Super Glue and glued him in."

Like Albert, Sen. Edward M. Kennedy in the 1980s "had a serious drinking problem" and was "arrogant," Eades said. One morning, Eades was patrolling the steps of the Capitol and saw Kennedy in his car "flying across the plaza at a very high rate of speed. A member came out and was going to jog down the steps and go directly across the street. I saw Kennedy coming. I know he would not have hit him. The congressman probably would have stopped. But Kennedy might have swerved around and hit someone else. I put my hand up to stop him. He came within

7

inches of me in his car. He said, 'You know you are a stupid son of a bitch.'"[12]

Nelson C. Sours, who retired from the Capitol Police in 1992, said Kennedy would arrive "inebriated" at the Dirksen Senate Office Building at 1 or 3 A.M. On one occasion, even though several entrances to the building were open, Kennedy demanded that the Capitol Police open the one nearest his office. "We got the keys from the superintendent and opened the door for him specifically. He wouldn't walk thirty yards to the other door," Sours said.[13]

Richard W. Micer, a Capitol Police inspector who retired in 1995, said Kennedy often made such demands. "Ted Kennedy was drinking a lot," Micer said. "He would like to go in the door closest to his office, which was locked. He would rant and rave. They would unlock it."[14]

"We have found members literally lying in the gutter," former deputy chief Trollinger said. "One time, we had real deep snow. I was working midnight. The scout cars were having difficulty even with chains. I used my own car, and I found this member of Congress fallen in the street. He was bleeding and drunk."

"A member had had a snootful and had fallen asleep on the street," Joseph R. Schaap, who retired from the Capitol Police in 1992 as a lieutenant, said. "We picked him up. He was a mess. He had vomited on himself. He was a conservative Republican. I put him in the car. . . . We took him to the Cannon Building and washed him off with a hose in the car wash. Then we put him in his office."[15]

One night, the Capitol Police received a call to pick up a powerful congressman from Texas who was drunk. "We picked him up and asked his address," Schaap said. It turned out the address, which was in northern Virginia, was wrong. "We pulled into a filling station. A county police car pulled up. They said, 'What are you guys doing down here?' We said, 'We're trying to find his home.' They said, 'That drunken son of a bitch.' So they told us his address," Schaap said. "His wife called him every name under the sun."

Several times, Eades learned from women he was dating that members of Congress ranging from Wayne Hays to Sen. John G.

Tower had made passes at them. "I was dating a secretary who worked for Hays," he said. "He was a vicious manipulator. He would say, 'When are you going to have Uncle Wayne over for dinner?' "[16]

One afternoon, Eades was called to Hays's hideaway office in the Capitol. Elizabeth Ray, the voluptuous former beauty queen who could not type and later claimed that Rep. Wayne L. Hays, the Ohio Democrat, had hired her to have sex with him, had called the Capitol Police for help. At the time, she had not yet begun working for Hays, who later admitted having a "personal relationship" with her.[17]

"Her blouse was slightly torn," Eades said. "Hays was in one room, she was in another. She didn't say he was trying to rape her. She said, 'He put his hands on me.' She looked disheveled."[18]

On another occasion, a Capitol elevator operator told Eades that Senator Tower, the Republican from Texas, had attacked her. "He felt her up one time when she was operating the elevator," Eades said. "She was a knockout—gorgeous, blond, well built. She was in college at the time. . . . He was half-drunk. There was alcohol on his breath. She said, 'Please don't touch me again.' "

If the elevator operator was unwilling, many other women were.

"One woman tried to bed every member of the Senate," said Martin Lobel, a Washington lawyer who was formerly an aide to Sen. William Proxmire, the Wisconsin Democrat. "She almost had a majority. The word got out she was available and terrific."[19]

A former congressional aide recalled how, in pre-AIDS days, he participated in a monthly "gang bang" with a shapely twenty-five-year-old blonde who worked for Sen. Alan Cranston, the California Democrat. "The Dirksen Senate Office Building has an attic," the aide said. "The word would spread that the girl was out, and guys would go. You'd go up there and join the end of the line. She was very pretty. She would be sitting in a chair, and you'd either stand there and stick your [penis] in her mouth or sit in the chair and she would sit on you."

The woman became known as the Attic Girl. The former aide said, "A dozen would do a gang bang. She did it about once a month. She just got horny. . . . She would do it in the morning around coffee hour." Occasionally, the Attic Girl got down on all fours and took on two male staffers at once. Dave Curry, the Capitol Police captain, said senators participated in the ritual. "She was a regular with senators in one of the attics," he said.

A female aide on the House side would stay late almost every night, leaving the door to her congressman's office unlocked. Capitol Police officers would go in to see if everything was all right. "She would come on to them," a former officer said. "She had sex with them there in the office every night."

"If you wanted to have a good time, you'd go up there," said Wayne Beckett, the former Capitol Police officer. "She would leave the door open purposely so the officers would find her. It was a little game."

In a variation on that theme, David S. Kiernan, another former Capitol Police officer, said that a female House staffer regularly showed up late at night at the Cannon House Office Building. Wearing a tight skirt and sweater, she would claim she had forgotten her keys and would ask that someone from the building superintendent's office let her in.

"Later the guys would say, 'I was glad to be of service,'" Kiernan said. "They told me that the woman would ask them to come in and would stand over her desk and invite them to 'make sure everything is okay' or to 'check things for me.' They would proceed to have sex on the desk."[20]

Of all the perquisites available to members and their staffs, none is more precious than parking. Carson, the former Capitol Police lieutenant, was assigned to make sure only members or— if there was room—staffers parked on the Southeast Capitol Drive. "This beautiful blonde, a House staffer who was well built, came up in a convertible," Carson said. "She said, 'You got a place for me, big guys?'—real flirtatious. We said, 'No, ma'am, we're full.' She said, 'Well, I bet if I showed you something, you could get me a parking place.' I said, 'Well, I don't know.' So she lifts up her dress, and she is wearing no underwear. She flashes us. I said, 'That's very nice, but we still have no parking places.'"[21]

A legendary female staffer on the Senate Judiciary Committee was even more accommodating. She regularly drove to the plaza at the west front of the Capitol at night and asked Capitol Police officers if they wanted oral sex. She quickly got the name Blow Job Jane.

"Her ambition in life was to give every policeman on Capitol Hill [oral sex]," said Wayne Beckett, the former Capitol Police officer. "She'd walk up to you or drive up to you and would say, 'Do you want [oral sex]?' . . . She was proud of it."

"She would drive across the plaza and take officers in her car and give them a blow job," Carson, the former Capitol Police lieutenant, said.[22]

Members of Congress were even more brazen. When blond, buxom Rita Jenrette revealed that she had had sex on the steps of the Capitol with her husband, Rep. John W. Jenrette Jr., a South Carolina Democrat, it sounded to outsiders like an aberration. "It was behind the columns at the east front," said Jenrette, who later posed for *Playboy.* "I had on a full-length coat that enveloped him. We were standing."[23]

In fact, outdoor sex was common but not publicized. "A lot of stuff went on in the parking lots with the young girls," Linwood T. Binford Jr., a former officer, said. "They pulled in the parking lot. They were congressmen, and you didn't bother them. [After they had had sex inside their cars,] they would stand outside the car, kiss, and one would go one way and the other went another."[24]

"One time a member from Texas was having sex right in front of the Capitol in his car," Paul R. McGill, a former officer, said. "We tried to get him to move his car out of the way. He told us basically go to hell. It was on the east front of the Capitol. It was oral sex to each other on the backseat. . . . You could tell they were having sex. The car was rocking."[25]

McGill said he left the Texan alone. "Whatever they did was never wrong," he said. "They make the laws for everyone but themselves."

$$\star \quad \star \quad \star \quad \star \quad \star \quad \star \quad \star \quad \star \quad \star$$

2

$$\star \quad \star \quad \star \quad \star \quad \star \quad \star \quad \star \quad \star \quad \star$$

No Bullets

Until the 1970s, Capitol Police officers were appointed strictly through patronage bestowed by members. They were given no training. "I went in probably on a Monday morning in June 1964," said Talmadge W. Reed, a former Capitol Police officer. "They gave me a uniform and they found a hat that fit and a gun with no bullets. They said put all this on. They said, 'Go out on that corner and direct traffic.' No training, no bullets. They said, 'We're scheduled to go down to the FBI range next Thursday, and we'll take you along. If you can hit anything, we'll give you bullets.'"

Reed performed passably and was given bullets—but only five. The chamber under the hammer was supposed to be kept empty in case the revolver was set off by accident. Two other recruits failed the test. "They walked around with no bullets for a while," Reed said.

None of the officers was given any books of parking tickets. "We didn't know what we were doing anyway, but there was a fear that we might give a ticket to the wrong person," Reed said.

"The theory was everyone who walked on the Capitol grounds had a congressman. So if we gave someone a ticket for parking, the lieutenant would get a call from an irate congressman saying, 'What do you mean by giving John Smith a ticket?' So they said, 'If you want to give a ticket, you call us, and we'll decide.' I never called. We had people parking in front of fire hydrants." When Reed asked headquarters to tow a car blocking a driveway, he was told, "They'll be out soon."

Nor were the Capitol Police about to ticket members for drunk driving. Quite the contrary. The job of the Capitol Police was to escort drunk members to their cars. "I remember helping drunken members find their cars and making sure they got started and out of the parking lot," Reed said.[26]

The role of the Capitol Police has expanded since it started as a one-man guard force in 1801. That was when Congress assigned one man, John Golding, to security duties at the Capitol. In the argot of the day, his job was to "take as much care of the property of the United States." Golding had no legal authority. If he wanted to detain a suspect, he had to call on the marshal of the District of Columbia.[27]

In 1828, farmers broke through a fence around the Capitol so their cattle could graze. Alarmed members enacted legislation allowing the federal commissioner of public buildings to assist Congress in maintaining order at the Capitol. By then, the force had grown to a handful of watchmen. The first mention of the Capitol Police as a congressional expense appeared in the 1852 appropriations act. By 1960, the Capitol Police numbered 216 officers.

Today, the Capitol Police force has 1,076 officers, 260 support personnel, and a budget of $74 million a year, but it is only a small part of Congress's operations. With 33,396 employees and an annual budget of $2.5 billion, the legislative branch is a self-contained mini-city that sprawls over 274 acres. On this turf Congress has established its own police department, barbers, restaurants, health spa, public works department, office buildings, subway, post offices, parking lots, printer, travel agencies, florist, and power plant—all subsidized by taxpayers. The tentacles of Congress are connected by miles of subterranean tunnels and subways that allow members of Congress and their staffs to travel from one building to another without ever emerging.

Subway cars have shuttled from the Senate wing of the Capitol to the Russell Senate Office Building since 1909. A line has run to the Dirksen Senate Office Building since 1960, and to the Hart Senate Office Building since 1982. Another subway operates between the House wing of the Capitol and the Rayburn House Office Building.

Congress consists of the House and Senate, which are further subdivided into members' offices, committee offices, and an infrastructure to maintain both houses. The legislative staff includes 10,372 employed by the House; 7,194 employed by the Senate; and 2,127 employed by the Architect of the Capitol, who runs and maintains the buildings.[28] Within the legislative branch, Congress runs the Library of Congress, which employs 3,902 and has a copy of every book copyrighted in the United States; the General Accounting Office, which employs 4,408 and is the audit arm of Congress; the Government Printing Office, which employs 4,158 and prints the *Congressional Record*, records of congressional hearings, and other government publications; the Congressional Research Service, which employs 775 and does research for Congress; the Congressional Budget Office, which employs 218 and analyzes budget requests; and the National Botanic Garden, which employs 51 and provides flowers and plants to Congress.

Capitol Police now have full law enforcement powers. They are no longer selected by members, and they receive first-rate training at the Federal Law Enforcement Training Center in Glynco, Georgia. But they are as subservient as ever. Congress loves to castigate the FBI and other federal law enforcement agencies when it perceives political favoritism or cover-ups. Yet as a matter of policy, the Capitol Police have long maintained a double standard—one for members of Congress and their staffs, the other for the rest of the public. In the topsy-turvy world Congress has created for itself, Capitol Police officers who try to enforce the law or protect themselves are punished.

Ernest M. Riddle, a former Capitol Police officer, said he was guarding the old Democratic Club in the Congressional Hotel. "There had been some thefts inside the building," he said. "They told us to stop anyone coming out of the garage at night. The door opened up—it was raining. This gentleman who turned out to be a congressman came out. He had his hands in his pockets. He just stood there and smiled at me. He was drunk. When I asked him to take his hands out of his pockets, he wouldn't do it. So I turned him around and put handcuffs on him. I called my superiors. That was a no-no."[29]

Called to headquarters, Riddle was asked what he would do if the same kind of incident occurred in the future. "I said to protect myself, I would do the same thing if someone won't take his hands out of his pockets. . . . So I ended up patrolling the sub-basement of the Rayburn Building for six months."

Former officer George Holmes recalled that six years ago, he was directing traffic at Independence and New Jersey Avenues. "It was around two A.M. Congress had been in late. I held up my hand to stop the cars coming off the Capitol parking lot and was directing them down Independence Avenue. This congressman decided he didn't want to wait," Holmes said. "He pulled out, and this guy from North Carolina whacked into him." The congressman said to Holmes, " 'You directed me forward, didn't you?' I said, 'No, I didn't, Congressman.' He said, 'Yes, you did.' I said, 'No, I didn't.' "

The next morning, a lieutenant called Holmes in. "I was told I would sign a sheet saying the congressman was not at fault," Holmes said. "I refused. Originally, I had made out a report saying the congressman was at fault. I never knew what happened to it. But I knew my ass was in a sling from then on. I just got lousy posts."[30]

Paul R. McGill, a former officer, said he was directing traffic on Independence Avenue when a member of Congress ran a red light. "They figure they can go through any intersection," McGill said. "He ran a red light and had an accident. I wrote up the report, and they [the Capitol Police] changed it. He didn't like the idea of being charged with the accident. Other officials over me changed it."[31]

"You couldn't write a parking ticket to a congressional aide or secretary without its being fixed," Holmes said. "So the police came up with what was known as an Alabama parking ticket. You just let air out of two of their tires. There was no sense in writing a ticket."

"It was understood you didn't write tickets or arrest people," Howard F. Pond, a former Capitol Police sergeant, said. "If they were not powerful, then you did."

Pond recalled what happened when he caught a young woman entering a House office building carrying a pistol in her purse in the early 1980s. "I asked what she was doing with the gun," Pond said. The young woman explained that she was from Georgia and had just begun working for Newt Gingrich. "The girl said her mother gave her the gun because there are a lot of coloreds up in Washington," Pond said.

To carry a gun in Washington, District of Columbia law requires a permit, which is almost impossible to obtain. Every year, the Capitol Police arrest nearly a hundred people for carrying a gun without a permit. In nearly every case, the gun is seized and melted down. It took a court ruling to save the .38-caliber Colt Cobra that Jack Ruby used to kill Lee Harvey Oswald. On March 28, 1992, the Capitol Police seized the gun from Robert Luongo. Luongo had brought it to Washington for an appearance on CNN's *Larry King Live.* Luongo represented Florida real estate developer Anthony V. Pugliese III and a consortium that had bought the gun at auction for $220,000. Because Luongo was merely acting as an agent, and District gun registration laws provide an exception for an agent carrying an unloaded gun, charges against Luongo were dismissed. If convicted, he could have been sentenced to up to a year and fined up to $1,000.[32]

In the case of the young woman from Georgia, Gingrich intervened, giving the Capitol Police a letter claiming *he* owned the gun. Even if Gingrich had owned the gun, it would not have meant he could carry it legally. Under an exception in the federal law, members and their staffs may carry a gun, but only if it is wrapped securely away from ammunition. The young woman's gun was loaded and was not securely wrapped. Yet on the basis of Gingrich's letter, Pond said, the Capitol Police released the young woman.[33]

"Of course, it wasn't true [that Gingrich owned the gun]," Pond said. The woman had already told him that she owned the gun. But it made no difference. If Gingrich had owned the gun and had brought it in himself, he would have been in violation of the D.C. law. Thus, Gingrich had gotten the Capitol Police to ignore a felony that would have landed any other citizen in court and possibly in jail. If the young woman had not worked for Gingrich, "it would have been U.S. Attorney time," Pond said. "But all was forgiven. . . . I guess it's okay for congressmen [to waive the laws]."

Those who brought weapons into congressional buildings were routinely arrested, "but they were not prosecuted depending on who they were," former officer Wayne Beckett said. If a suspect called a prominent member, the Capitol Police "would package up the weapon and send it back to him in his state. Other people without connections are put in jail."

Similarly, within the force, Beckett said, "Promotions were based on whether you could do favors for people and if they [members of Congress] liked you. The more favors you did, the more power you had. If you took a congressman's son home when he was drunk, the congressman owed you a favor. . . . If you took care of someone, they took care of you." The favors Capitol Police officers performed included "keeping people out of jail, keeping things hush-hush, bringing them booze or girls," he said.

Bruce A. Currie, a former officer, recalled what happened when he gave a ticket for jaywalking to the brother of an aide to Jimmy Carter, who was then president. "I explained that if he did that, others would follow, and someone would get hit. He flew into a rage," Currie said. "On Monday morning, I wasn't on the roster. I was told for my own benefit, I should work inside. For me that was bad because I didn't like to work inside. A few members knew me, and one raised hell a few weeks later. So I was back on the street, but they said they wouldn't give me a ticket book. I said, 'Then I'm not going on the street.' So they gave me a ticket book."[34]

In the late 1970s, Rep. William D. Ford, a Democrat from Michigan, drove his car into a parked Capitol Police motorcycle on New Jersey Avenue around midnight, according to David Curry, who was then a Capitol Police sergeant and was called to investigate. "He hit the bike and dragged it seven blocks," Curry said. "We followed him to his apartment and stopped him. He was drunk."[35]

A captain who was the night supervisor arrived on the scene. "I said I was going to charge the congressman with leaving the scene and destroying government property," Curry said. "He [the captain] said, 'No, you're not.' I said, 'Are you going to take responsibility for this?' He said, 'I sure will. As a matter of fact, I want to see your ass in the chief's office tomorrow morning.'"

The next morning, James M. Powell, who was the first Capitol Police chief, called Curry to his office. "I went in, and he said, 'Well, we're going to smooth this out. You shouldn't have wanted to charge the congressman.'"

In July 1983, Congressman Ford this time crashed his car into the rear of a parked car on Southwest Capitol Drive. Kevin G. Caulfield, a Capitol Police officer on the scene, instructed him to stop. The congressman drove another thirty yards, according to what an officer on the scene told a *Washington Post* reporter. The officer said he smelled liquor on Ford's breath from several feet away.[36]

After the story hit the papers, the Capitol Police claimed they had investigated and found that Ford had not been drinking and had not intentionally tried to leave the scene of the accident. "The evidence shows no indication that the congressman was intoxicated or impaired," then lieutenant Robert Howe of the Capitol Police inspections and internal affairs section, said. "Likewise, there was no indication that he tried to leave the scene of the accident."

While the *Washington Post* story did not mention him as a source, the Capitol Police reprimanded Caulfield for violating police regulations by discussing "police department business" without prior approval of superiors.[37]

Terry D. Coons, a former officer, said he was assigned to the Capitol that night. He heard a crash. Over his radio, Coons heard Kevin Caulfield report what had happened. "I could hear him on the radio asking for backup because he had a drunk driver," Coons said. "He didn't know he was a congressman until the night supervisor came on the scene and recognized him. I wasn't there, but it's my understanding [from Caulfield] that he said, 'Uncuff him.' Kevin said, 'The guy is drunk.' But the night supervisor said, 'It doesn't make any difference.' He let him get back in the car. He [Ford] got back in the car and drove off. And do you know they wrote Kevin up?"[38]

Because of the leak to the press about the accident, "They took eighty hours away from his vacation time," Coons said. "I went to the supervisor of the night detail. I said, 'This is not right. You had a police officer doing his job, doing what he was sworn to do, and then you guys undo everything and punish him for doing it. In my book you are nothing but a bunch of goddamn worms.' He just looked at me."

Steven E. Dekelbaum, a former Capitol Police officer who is a Metropolitan Police detective in Washington, said that one night when he was crossing a street near the Capitol on the green light, Ted Kennedy went through a red light and almost ran him over.

"He was speeding. The speed limit was twenty-five, and he was well over that," Dekelbaum said. "I jumped out of his way. I guess he looked in his rearview mirror and said, 'I almost hit a cop.' He stopped. I approached the car. He reeked [of liquor]. . . . I said, 'Look, Senator, you're pretty drunk, and you almost ran me over.' I said, 'I don't want you to get any bad publicity.' I was pretty diplomatic for a dumb twenty-two-year-old. I knew I would get in trouble otherwise."[39]

Dekelbaum suggested that Kennedy park his car and take a taxi.

"He said, 'You know, you're right.' I said, 'I don't want you to kill anybody or kill yourself.' By this time, the sergeant saw what was going on. He sees whom I've stopped. The sergeant literally grabbed me by my shoulder. He gave [Kennedy] his keys back. He said, 'Do you know who that is?' I said, 'Yes.'"

The sergeant turned to Kennedy, apologized for the "inconvenience," and told him to get back in his car.

"The senator took off, and the sergeant started yelling at me, cussing me out," Dekelbaum said. "I said, 'You're a f------ asshole. What happens if he goes down the street and kills somebody or kills himself? They're going to see a cop stopped him. They can make me an accessory."

"Too f------ bad," the sergeant said. "Don't ever do it again."

"It was common practice to 'unarrest' people because they were powerful or someone powerful intervened," Terry Coons said. "You always considered what you were going to do. 'If I arrest this person, what will happen later? What will the consequences of an arrest be on me?'"

"If you find a member doing something wrong, you unarrest him," said Edward P. Percival, who retired from the Capitol Police in October 1995. "It happens all the time."

"Congress never wanted the Capitol Police to be so professional that they would have the ability to investigate [the members]," said Capitol Police sergeant John A. Gott. "If they kept us as their little private guards, we would never be a threat."

At one point, Coons was ordered to ticket cars parked illegally on New Jersey Avenue. "So after an hour and a half, the inspector comes down in a squad car and calls to me. He said, 'What in the hell are you doing?' I said, 'I'm doing what you told me to do.' He said, 'Man, there are people who have been parking here for years. You're telling them they can't. We're getting call after call about it.'"

That was the end of that ticket-writing campaign. Even if a ticket is written, "more tickets got fixed there [on Capitol Hill] than anywhere else in the world combined," Coons said. "You basically did nothing because chances were good it would be undone later anyway." Coons said he tried to sleep on duty "as much as possible." Indeed, he boasted, "I acquired a knack for sleeping while being aware of what was going on. I got so good at it that I only needed a couple of hours of sleep at home."[40]

As a Capitol Police officer, Harper T. Redden was assigned to maintain liaison with prosecutors and courts. In fact, "twenty-five percent of my time was occupied fixing tickets [for members of Congress and their staffs]," Redden said. Redden said he fixed tickets given to members by all police forces in the Washington metropolitan area.

On July 23, 1976, the Justice Department said that members of Congress were no longer immune from arrest by any police force. The department said a previous policy of releasing members who had been arrested was based on a misinterpretation of the congressional immunity clause in the Constitution. The Justice Department issued the statement after the Metropolitan Police in Washington arrested Rep. Joe D. Waggonner Jr., a Louisiana Democrat, for allegedly soliciting a District of Columbia policewoman who was posing as a prostitute. When police identified him as a member of Congress, he was released. The Justice Department said he should not have been.[41]

The only exception, contained in District law, was for parking tickets issued to cars bearing congressional plates, but only if a member is on official business. Even then, members may be issued tickets if they park illegally during rush hour or at a fire hydrant or loading zone. Redden said the overwhelming majority of tickets he fixed from 1981 to 1986 did not fall within the legal exemptions.

"I fixed fifteen hundred to two thousand tickets a year," Redden said. "I used to keep a record of all the different congressmen whose tickets I fixed. They were not just Capitol Police tickets but tickets from police all over the Washington area. It's well-known that congressmen are exempt from parking tickets while on official business, but that doesn't mean that they are exempt from tickets when they're at a nightclub at two A.M. I took care of all kinds of tickets like that."

According to Redden, one of the "champions" was David E. Bonior, the Michigan Democrat who is minority whip—a lieutenant of the party leadership. "I fixed hundreds of his tickets each year from all over the place," Redden said. Other major violators were Senators Robert C. Byrd, the West Virginia Democrat, and Ted Kennedy.[42]

If the Capitol Police help members evade the law, they also look the other way when thefts occur. Sgt. John Gott said he is constantly asked to certify that a stolen computer or other piece of office equipment is "missing" instead of stolen. "It seemed every time they did an audit and they couldn't find equipment, they had us do a police report on lost property," he said. "It was conveniently lost. Bullshit. . . . I would have a stack of reports I had to fill out. It was kind of sickening to think that most people can't afford a computer, and these members were walking out with them at the end of every Congress."

"This guy who was one of the maintenance crew came out of the Dirksen Building garage with his pickup truck with a new boxed refrigerator in the back," said Mathew H. Moser, a former officer. "All the garage doors are guarded. You have to sign in and out, except for members, of course. He didn't slow down. I got my sergeant. They had surveillance cameras in the area where they were stored. Sure enough, one [refrigerator] was missing. Normal police procedure is you get a warrant and lock the guy up. The superintendent of the building said he admitted to it and brought it back, and so we'll just fire him. He brought it back after we caught him."[43]

The Capitol Police are so brazenly averse to enforcing the law that they even ignore criminal violations by ordinary citizens. Former Capitol Police officer Steven Dekelbaum said he was stunned when his superior ordered him to "unarrest" a man who matched a description of a rape suspect.

"I heard a radio broadcast about a guy wanted for a violent rape with scratches on his hands and face," Dekelbaum said. "I walked up to the guy and that was him. The rape had just happened an hour before right off the Capitol. The D.C. police initially got the call. . . . I put cuffs on him. I got on the radio and said I had an arrest. These sergeants and lieutenants showed up. I said, 'He fits the description of the rapist.' They said, 'Let him go.' I said, 'No, I'm not letting him go.' A couple of scout cars from the patrol division of Metropolitan Police showed up. They said, 'That's the dude right there.'"

The D.C. police officers took the man into custody. Later, the victim identified the suspect as her attacker. Yet the Capitol Police "didn't want any waves. They wanted you to look the other way," Dekelbaum said. Knowing Dekelbaum liked to be assigned outside, "they kept me inside for two months," Dekelbaum said. They told him not to lock up anyone anymore.

"They wanted to do forty hours a week with no headaches, don't make waves. If you do police work, you're causing havoc." The Capitol Police, he said, are "a joke, a total joke. It's embarrassing."

Former officer Riddle will never forget what happened when he heard a woman screaming near the Senate side of the Capitol. Riddle was assigned to the House side. Then, as now, the Capitol Police have two payrolls. One pays officers who began guarding the House; the other is for the Senate. Despite the two payrolls, Capitol Police are often transferred from one side to another. They continue to receive paychecks from the side on which they started.

"I crossed the street to see what was happening," Riddle said. Pulling up in a cruiser, another officer asked what he was doing. "The lieutenant will hang you. They don't allow that," he said. "The House side takes care of the House; the Senate takes care of the Senate." Riddle told the other officer, "I heard someone holler. I was a policeman before I came here. I guess they'll hang me."

As it turned out, the woman had screamed as a joke.

Similarly, Paul Z. Herman, an officer who retired in 1992, said that when a deranged man assaulted a charwoman working for the House side, "the House officer made an arrest, and a lieutenant told him to turn him loose. He had beaten her. I couldn't tell you what his thinking was. A lot of them don't want their people to get involved. It's that simple."[44]

"They brainwash you to not see things you saw," Dekelbaum said. "You might have thought you saw that, but you actually didn't. . . . I've seen guys who were bright and motivated, and their brains went to mush. They didn't use their brains eight hours a day. They became stupid, lazy, complacent. They have a lot of educated, bright guys up there. But if they want to make good money for doing nothing, that's what it's all about.

"If I were back in that situation, I'd probably be making calls to the Justice Department biweekly," Dekelbaum said, "because there was always something going on there—always a cover-up. It's obstruction of justice. . . . I would say when I was there [from 1980 to 1987], a little more than a third of the

Capitol Police were guilty of obstruction of justice. I've been there, seen it, done it. They violate every law known to mankind. . . . It's see no evil, hear no evil, speak no evil."[45]

In one of the more shocking examples of how irresponsible the Capitol Police can be, they make it a practice when confronted by mentally unbalanced individuals seeking access to the Capitol to recommend that they go to the White House instead. "Every nut who came to Washington went to the Capitol or the White House," said Richard Xander, the Metropolitan Police officer detailed to the Capitol Police. "Some weirdo came up, and the best we could do was escort him off the Hill. Normally, we send them to the White House. Then the Secret Service would do the paperwork [to have them committed to St. Elizabeth's Hospital for observation]. So many people come to the city and believe the president lives in the Capitol. If it wasn't a flaming mental case, and we didn't think he was going to hit someone right then and there, the best thing would be to say, 'Go west to 1600 Pennsylvania Avenue.' "

"We would send nuts to the White House," confirmed Capitol sergeant John Gott. "That's pretty much routine. I think the uniformed Secret Service would do the same thing, sending them to the Capitol."[46]

"That always goes on," former captain Dave Curry said. "We send them to the White House, and they send them to the Capitol."

Indeed, said Paul McGill, "We would put them in a taxi, give them a dollar, and send them to the White House. The White House would do the same thing."

But a Secret Service agent disputed that claim: "We would never send them to the Capitol. The Secret Service is more competent at getting mentally disturbed persons admitted to St. Elizabeth's because they know what the mental problems are and can articulate them to the doctors. It's very simple. They can also write affidavits and complaints and put it in the correct legal terms and get it right. It's as simple as that."

Of course, no one can predict whether a mentally disturbed person directed to the White House might end up trying to assassinate the president. In at least one case, the practice resulted in an attempted attack on the president. "We did that with one guy [recommended he go to the White House], and the Secret Service shot the guy," Xander said. "He jumped over the fence at the White House with a gun."

"We used to joke, if we wrote a book about Capitol Hill, nobody would believe it," Redden said.

If the Capitol Police can be irresponsible, they also tend to be incompetent. To be sure, compared with the days when Capitol Police were issued no bullets, the force has become more professional. Ever since bombs exploded in the Capitol on March 1, 1971, and again on November 7, 1983, the Capitol Police have been stepping up security. By blocking off streets and erecting barriers, the Capitol Police have made the Capitol a less tempting target for terrorists. With a world-class bomb squad and thirty dogs cross-trained for crowd control and bomb detection, the Capitol Police are prepared for most threats.

The Capitol Police are good at handling demonstrations. "When the farmers came [to demonstrate], we had people in the farmers' group," Carson said. "We know what they were going to do. Capitol Police officers pose as farmers. We have blacks, whites, females. We go into meetings to find out what is going on. . . . We participate in whatever they say. We become part of the group."

The Capitol Police are also patient with protesters like Stacy Abney, who has lived for eighteen years under the main steps on the east side of the Capitol Building. Now eighty-six, Abney claims the Veterans Administration has cheated him of disability benefits, even though he has refused to cash the benefit checks he has received. By his own account, Abney has been arrested fifty-seven times.[47]

Occasionally, the Capitol Police perform heroic acts, as when Capitol Police officer Joel C. Hobbs rushed into a burning apartment building to rescue a woman at 116 North Carolina Avenue SE in April 1996.

But compared with other federal or local law enforcement agencies, the Capitol Police are a disaster. Unlike FBI agents, for example, who are constantly criticized by members of Congress for real or imagined abuses, Capitol Police officers tend to be inarticulate and confused about their law enforcement responsibilities. Asked what a Capitol Police procedure called "unarresting" means, almost every officer interviewed gave a different answer. The procedure allows the Capitol Police to pretend that an arrest never took place. The procedure differs from the practice prior to July 1976 of releasing members because they were legitimately thought to have immunity. Unarresting has no basis in law.

While most officers said they had used the procedure, some said it was illegal, while others said it was not. Some said it was used when the facts did not support an arrest, while others said it was used to nullify and cover up arrests of powerful staffers or members.

In explaining why the force seems so uninformed, one officer said merely asking questions usually results in punishment. "It was probably one of the worst-managed places I had ever seen," said David L. Coon, a former Capitol Police officer.[48] "You had to find out anything on your own. A lot of that was by design. When you went to roll call and you asked a good question, you were usually castigated for asking it."

Dekelbaum, the former Capitol Police officer who is now a Metropolitan Police detective in Washington, said another factor is plain stupidity. He recalled an incident where the Capitol Police caught a visitor to the Capitol with a gun, in violation of the D.C. gun permit law. The man threw the weapon into a reflecting pool at the east front of the Capitol.

"They had a sergeant up there who was so stupid that he said we should put the gun in a bag and fill the bag up with water [as evidence] to show it was recovered from the pool," Dekelbaum said. "He was incredible. They argued about it but never did it."[49]

Some officers are so dense that when the author called their listed home telephone number, they asked, "How did you get my number?"

In one role-playing training session in 1984, Sgt. John Gott accidentally shot and killed another officer, Sgt. Christopher M. Eney.[50] "We were using guns that were not loaded," Gott said. "Chris Eney was the bad guy. Eney wanted to do it again." By then, Gott had loaded his gun, but he forgot to empty it again. "He made a furtive movement, and I pulled the trigger. I had forgotten that I had reloaded."[51]

In its training, the FBI has long used red-handled weapons that are plugged so they cannot fire. But the Capitol Police insisted on using functioning weapons. Nor did the Capitol Police take any action against Gott. "There was no discipline," Gott said. "It's the worst thing in the world that can happen to an officer. What are you going to do to him? There's enough internal suffering. There's so much grief and sorrow."

In contrast, when two FBI agents accidentally shot to death fellow FBI agent Robin Ahrens in Phoenix on October 5, 1985, the FBI fired one of the agents, and the other agent resigned.[52]

Other Capitol Police officers are cowardly. Because several workers have lost their lives while working on the Rotunda, the cavernous area under the 8.9-million-pound dome of the Capitol is said to be haunted. One officer actually shot at a statue he thought was a ghost in Statuary Hall next to the Rotunda. Incredibly, some officers have tried to be reassigned because of their fear.

"The dome is made of sheets of metal," Lacoss said. "In the sunlight, they expand. At night, they contract. When they move, they make these weird, screeching sounds."

"One of the officers hid behind a statue and made noises as if he was the statue," said Raymond Carson, the former Capitol Police lieutenant. "This officer who was afraid to go through there pulled out his gun and started shooting."

The Capitol Police won a national award in 1988 for having the best uniforms among government security forces. Spiffy as their uniforms may be, the effects of being corrupted by Congress can usually be seen in the faces and posture of Capitol Police officers. They tend to slouch and to walk timorously. Their expressions are lifeless.

The Capitol Police have immediate jurisdiction over an area that extends seven blocks from the Capitol, yet the force has about as many officers as the police departments of Newark, New Jersey, or Kansas City, Missouri. In addition, Metropolitan Police from Washington respond to reports of crimes in the same area. Because the Capitol Police perform guard functions as well as policing, it is difficult to equate the force with municipal police departments. But clearly the Capitol Police are overstaffed. The General Accounting Office, Congress's audit arm, has said civilian guards could perform many Capitol Police functions, saving $21,000 per officer per year initially and $10,000 a year over time. GAO also has said that Congress could save money by consolidating the separate Library Police, which guards the Library of Congress, with the Capitol Police.

The Library of Congress, housed since 1897 primarily in a building across the street from the Capitol on First Street SE, is a repository for 108 million items and has a budget of $497 million per year. Because of outrageously lax security, at least three hundred thousand volumes are missing. Deborah Maceda, a Library Police detective, has charged that library officials demoted and tried to fire her when she uncovered the theft and mutilation of $1.8 million in rare books.[53]

In its first attempt to audit the library's operations, the General Accounting Office, the audit arm of Congress, found financial accounting and reporting so "poor" that it could not conduct an audit. Moreover, the library's records were so chaotic that GAO could not accurately determine how many books the library had or whether the library was paying twice for the same goods.

While the library has taken often amateurish steps toward improving security, Congress has ignored such obvious potential savings as combining the Library of Congress Police with the Capitol Police.

"A lot of [Capitol Police] posts were created because a senator or congressman said, 'I want a post here,'" former officer Dekelbaum said. "They're conveniences for them. A lot were started years ago, and nobody had the balls to say it's a waste of manpower."

For example, Trollinger said, when Senator Byrd of West Virginia was a Senate leader, he demanded a post outside his door. "A post was created for Byrd, but it wasn't a bad idea," Trollinger said. "That corner is very busy." But a current high-ranking Capitol Police official said the officer stationed outside

Byrd's door was purely for prestige. "There was no valid reason. . . . We were never allowed to take these people who were window dressing when we needed them."

Coons kept a diary of activities he observed over a three-year period. The diary, which begins on December 10, 1980, records coming across men and women copulating between the bushes and the west front of the Capitol or his being told by superiors to ignore thefts from congressional construction sites. The terraced grounds surrounding the Capitol, designed by Frederick Law Olmsted, cover 58.8 acres.

Back in 1868, Mark Twain observed that the Capitol Police "have grown fat and comfortable dozing in chairs and scratching their backs against marble pillars."[54] Many of Coons's diary entries show not much has changed. "After all this training, it was back to the detail where we would learn to sleep on post with our eyes closed and our ears open ready to spring into action at the sound of the sergeant," Coons wrote one night.[55] "Slept most of the night in my car out on Capitol Drive Southeast."

One night, Coons was patrolling the Capitol Plaza at the west front. "Four or five girls were out on the plaza posing for pictures, which consisted of pulling up their dresses and sitting on the steps with their legs raised high in the air and spread apart," Coons wrote. "Seems they had been partying."

"Caught two love birds making love under the big elm tree by the House crosswalk," he wrote on another warm evening. "He was on the bottom, and she was on top with her jeans pulled down around her ankles. I told them I could name 100 better places to do it than here. At that point, they agreed. She rolled off, and before I knew it, they were gone."

Capitol Police got in the act as well. The Capitol Police hired the first female officers in September 1974. One female Capitol Police officer loved to be assigned to guard the House Select Committee on Intelligence hearing room on the fourth floor or attic of the Capitol, because she could have sex with other officers without fear of being disturbed. The committee office, along with one for the Senate Select Committee on Intelligence in the Hart Senate Office Building, is among the many secrets of the Capitol. Both offices are electronically shielded to prevent bugging and are guarded twenty-four hours a day by Capitol Police officers.

The House room is located off its own corridor inside the Capitol dome. The only way to reach it is to take an elevator from the crypt on the first floor of the Capitol below the Rotunda, where the bodies of John F. Kennedy, Lyndon Baines Johnson, Abraham Lincoln, Dwight D. Eisenhower, J. Edgar Hoover, and many others have lain in state. In front of the elevator door, a sign warns that "authorized personnel only" are allowed to take the elevator. A red velvet rope further restricts access. On the fourth floor, a Capitol Police officer guards the passageway, so that no one can approach the committee offices without permission.

The female officer who delighted in being assigned to this post was a brown-eyed, perky brunette who wore a uniform tightly tailored to show off her well-proportioned body. "She had a foul mouth and was very attractive—stacked. She knew it and flaunted it," said Edward P. Percival, who was on the same detail with her.

According to another officer who often visited her at her post, because the area was so remote, "her screaming climaxes could not be heard outside the fourth floor." Neither the ghosts and the spirits that are said to roam the Rotunda at night nor the Capitol Police sergeants who check up on officers deterred the twenty-six-year-old woman. If a sergeant were to board the elevator at night, the officer would hear the elevator coming. She would then quickly dress, adjust her makeup, and put on her gun belt.

"She was small and a fox," said the officer who helped her pass the time. "She was devoted to your pleasure."

Capitol Police sergeant John A. Gott said a female Capitol Police officer engaged in a "gang bang" in the Fraternal Order of Police Lodge in Washington. "The numbers [of male officers] were twelve to fifteen. It was a train, all dudes and a chick."[56]

"At training there were threesomes . . . ," Thomas F. Nairn, a former officer, said. "It was one girl and two guys."

* * *

Unbeknownst to most visitors and Hillites, in a basement office of the Russell Senate Office Building, nearly a dozen Capitol Police technicians watch on video monitors practically everything that goes on in the corridors through more than one hundred cameras. When movement occurs, the scene appears on one of the monitors. The system also records the scene on videotape. If not needed to document a crime, videotapes are erased every six months. The same command center monitors conventional security systems in offices, credit unions, and the steam tunnels that connect congressional buildings.

"There are cameras that pick up an awful lot," said Arthur S. Koeller, a former Capitol Police officer. "I saw a girl going down an escalator. She was adjusting her panty hose and lifting her dress up so you could see her panties."[57]

Others have seen staffers making out, scratching themselves, or picking their noses.

"We had cameras that responded to infrared energy so you could see in the dark," Trollinger said. "In the summer, you could see through a woman's blouse because the body radiated infrared energy. People [officers] would say, 'Look at this lady here.'"[58]

Thinking he would demonstrate how poor security is in the Capitol, a Washington reporter hung candy canes all over the walls of the building and wrote about it the next day. But the Capitol Police had captured him on videotape. Since the cameras are triggered by any movement, a police monitor watched him playing his prank and alerted an officer in the area. The officer followed him, taking down the candy canes, according to Trollinger.

Ever mindful of their perquisites, members of Congress usually refuse to go through metal detectors or have their bags x-rayed. So that Capitol Police will know who is a member, members are supposed to wear security pins, but many do not. Instead, they insist that Capitol Police recognize them without identification and wave them through security points without checking their bags. Because of that, Capitol Police devote hours to studying photographs of new members so they will recognize them on sight. Identifying nearly a hundred new members is virtually impossible. Yet when members are asked for identification, they become incensed. As a result, "If they say, 'I am a member,' and they keep walking, an officer may let them go," said a high-ranking Capitol Police official. "You compromise security by allowing such a cavalier system."

"You are expected to recognize every member," said Percival, who retired from the Capitol Police in October 1995. "When you have four hundred and thirty-five members [on the House side], how can you possibly recognize them all? They have little pins, but they don't wear them. . . . You don't let a bum in. If they say they are a member, you better wave them through."[59]

"You would not recognize a member and you would ask for identification, and they would holler, 'Don't you know me?'" said Meldon R. Jackson, a former officer. "Every two years, Congress changes, and it takes a while to recognize the new members. I took their word if they said they were members. That's not good for security."

In another example of congressional arrogance, Schaap recalled that Lawrence J. Smith, a Democratic congressman from Florida, had just bought a red Corvette. "He parked his car on a corner," Schaap said. "His back end was just even with the crosswalk. I said, 'Congressman, I wouldn't park your car right there.' He said, 'Why not?' He thought I was giving him hell for parking too close to the crosswalk. I said, 'Well, another congressman parks his car right there in front of you, and he parks by the braille method.' Right then, this other congressman came whipping around the corner. He had a three-month-old Toyota that looked like it had been rolled down a hill. This guy just abused the car. He pulls up and—bang—goes right into the Corvette. He ran into his bumper and they got into an argument."[60]

"Mary Rose Oakar was in the Rayburn Building one day standing in the middle of the hall," Schaap said. "I came by and tried to move her out of the way. She said, 'Do you realize who I am?' Before I could answer, she said, 'I'm Mary Rose Oakar,'" who was then a Democratic congresswoman from Ohio. "I said, 'Well, there's this guy with a cart behind you.' He hit her right in the ass with a cart.'"

Rep. Daniel J. Flood, a Pennsylvania Democrat, insisted that the Capitol Police walk his dog at night, sometimes with Flood's wife.

"I personally escorted her walking the dog," Sgt. John Gott said. "I was told sometimes she wouldn't come out, so officers walked the dog alone. It was a little white poodle."

"He really loved that dog," said Ernest Riddle, who also escorted the dog. "She would hang on to me while the dog went another way. I always felt if she fell, I would hold on to the dog because the dog was more important to the congressman."

"These freshmen would come in, and they were the nicest people," Talmadge Reed said. "It was their first time in Washington, and they were awed by everything. After about three months, they became real bastards, most of them."

Even the practice of giving constituents flags that had supposedly flown over the east and west fronts of the Capitol in years past was a sham. "They took the boxes of flags to the Capitol, took them out of the boxes, shook them, and put them back," Reed said. "Then they certified that they flew over the Capitol."

Symbolically, the cornerstone of the Capitol, dedicated by George Washington himself during an elaborate Masonic ceremony on September 18, 1793, to this day cannot be located. The only written description of where it was buried—an article in the *Alexandria Gazette*—said it was in the "southeast corner." Whether that refers to the southeast corner of the entire Capitol or of the Senate wing is unclear.

Working on the Hill was "an awakening," Terry Coons said. "I talked to my family back in Missouri, and they were appalled at what went on. It's not broadcast, not reported. The people in Missouri can't believe it's happening. It's unreal."

* * * * * * * * *

3

* * * * * * * * *

Virgin Village

In the 1980s, young female pages appointed by Congress put on a nightly show by undressing at their windows. Formerly the Young Women's Christian Home, the four-story brick building where most of the girls lived became known as Virgin Village. At the beginning of their shifts, Capitol Police officers would make it a practice to "stake out" the building at 235 Second Street NE.

"It was nicknamed Virgin Village because female pages undressed there without putting down their blinds," Terry Coons, the former Capitol Police officer, said. "It was a gathering place for officers for the first hour." The girls would "get undressed and get in their pajamas."

"They left their blinds open, and undressed," said Wayne Beckett, another former Capitol Police officer. "The officers watched. They were teases. They knew what they were doing. We would shine flashlights at them, and they would leave the blinds open. . . . They totally undressed and pranced around. Some were real pretty."[61]

Congressional pages are teenagers chosen through patronage to act as messengers. Without the assent of their colleagues, individual members can do little. The one area where they have complete autonomy is in the administration of Congress itself. Delegating to professional managers the task of hiring messengers would undoubtedly be more cost-efficient. But choosing pages from their own hometowns gives members of Congress a sense of power and an opportunity to pay off political debts.

The pages are just one of dozens of congressional perquisites ranging from junkets to cut-rate haircuts, custom-made furniture, and subsidized dining facilities. According to the National Taxpayers Union, Congress pays itself pensions that are two to three times more generous than in the private sector and 50 percent more generous than in the rest of the federal government. Members receive full pensions at age sixty after only ten years of service, compared with twenty years for federal workers covered by the Civil Service Retirement System. Their pensions are also substantially more generous than the other major retirement system covering federal workers.[60]

Besides health insurance, members receive free medical care at work from the Office of the Attending Physician. They may use free health clubs in the Rayburn House Office Building and the Russell Senate Office Building. The Library of Congress gives them surplus books. Members and their families park free at restricted lots immediately adjacent to the entrances of airline terminals at Washington National and Dulles International Airports. The spaces—which also are used by diplomats and Supreme Court Justices—cost taxpayers more than $1 million a year in lost parking revenue at National Airport alone.

The earliest historical mention of congressional "runners" was in 1827, when the House employed three of them. The term *pages* first appeared in the *Congressional Globe*, the predecessor of the *Congressional Record*, in 1839. As used then, the term referred to a youth employed as a personal attendant to a person of high rank. No page could be taller than the shortest member.

Dressed in dark blue suits and black ties, male and female pages are assigned to either the House or Senate and work for the members in their respective chambers. They deliver material to members on the floor and to their offices, answer telephones in the Republican and Democratic cloakrooms, and bring members water and food. The House has an electronic light system to summon a page, while senators clap, wave, or snap their fingers when they want a page.

The pages work for a summer, a semester, or an entire year. Even though they receive schooling of only three hours and fifteen minutes a day, Congress claims the pages get the equivalent of a normal education. The Middle States Association of Colleges and Schools accredits the page schools.

Before 1983, House and Senate pages were taught in a single Capitol Page School at the Library of Congress across the street from the west front of the Capitol. Today they are taught in separate House and Senate schools. In 1965, Sen. Jacob K. Javits, the New York Republican, appointed the first black page. In December 1970, he appointed the first female page.

In the past, Congress appointed fourteen- and fifteen-year-olds and let them run loose in Washington without any supervision. So long as their needs were taken care of, members apparently did not care if minors entrusted to them became corrupted.

Joel C. Raupe, a former congressional page from North Carolina, recalled that at sixteen, he learned to smoke marijuana from other pages. At seventeen, he had his first sexual experience with a female page.

"There was a lot of drug use," Raupe said. "Marijuana, LSD, cocaine. We took our government paychecks and bought drugs."[63]

Meanwhile, "a lot of secretaries were enticing a lot of the good-looking pages and teaching them the facts of life really early, up in the attics and places like that," said Roy L. Elson, the former Senate administrative assistant to Sen. Carl T. Hayden, who headed the Senate Rules and Administration Committee and later the Senate Appropriations Committee for a total of twenty years.

"The girls [pages] would try to make themselves look older," said former Capitol Police officer Ernest M. Riddle. Riddle said he saw a man kissing a young page goodnight outside a page dorm. He asked him for his identification and reminded the man that the girl was thirteen or fourteen years old. The man told Riddle, "I was in one of the bars on Pennsylvania Avenue, and she said she was a secretary and this was her office."

Riddle said female pages wore "wet T-shirts in the fountains. They went skinny-dipping."

"In the fountains on the House side, you'd catch the pages, females and males, swimming bare-ass," said former officer George L. Holmes.

"The pages were wild, but they hushed it up," former officer Wayne Beckett said. "They were f------ everybody they could."

When Steven R. (Rick) Valentine became a House page in 1970, he was amazed that fourteen- and fifteen-year-old pages had no dormitory and basically no supervision. "As long as you showed up for work and dressed well, you were basically on your own," he said. "It was crazy to have kids of that age turned loose on a city like Washington."

In the summer of 1972, Valentine returned as a page in the Senate. This time, he learned from two other male pages that Rep. Gerry E. Studds, the Massachusetts Democrat, had made passes at them. "He would take them out for drinks at night," Valentine said. "They didn't know what was going on. They thought, 'Isn't it great that a Democratic congressman thinks I'm interesting to talk to and wants to take me out for drinks?' " Once he got them out for drinks, Studds made "unmistakably aggressive sexual moves on them."[64]

The two pages did not succumb, but a third did. Since Valentine had been sponsored by Sen. Warren G. Magnuson, the state of Washington Democrat, he complained to one of Magnuson's aides. "He didn't seem outraged, and it didn't seem he was going to do anything," Valentine said.

Just before Valentine left the page program in 1974, an attractive female Senate employee who was about thirty propositioned him. "She said, 'Have you ever slept with a Jewish girl?' I just said no. I knew what she meant."[65]

In 1978, Valentine wrote *Each Time a Man,* a book about his

Quaker roots. The book mentioned some of Valentine's experiences as a page. Without naming him, it referred to some of the incidents involving Studds. In 1982, two pages serving in the House made public allegations about the prevalence of sex and drugs in the page program. The news media picked up on some of the assertions in Valentine's book. The House appointed Joseph A. Califano Jr. to investigate, and he called Valentine to testify in executive session.

The two pages whose allegations led to the investigation ultimately recanted, saying they had made up or exaggerated the charges. Califano found that "most of the allegations" of misconduct were unfounded. But based on the Califano investigation, the House in 1983 censured Studds, along with Rep. Daniel B. Crane, an Illinois Republican, who admitted he had had sex with a seventeen-year-old female page. Despite the incident, Studds, who declared himself homosexual, kept winning reelection. Crane lost his next reelection bid.[66]

"They both should have been expelled," said Valentine, who became a Republican and is now general counsel to Sen. Robert C. Smith, a Republican from New Hampshire. "A member of Congress trying to have an affair with a teenage page who is an employee—what could be worse? If that doesn't merit exclusion, what does?"

As a director of the National Institute of Mental Health, Dr. Bertram S. Brown became an expert on Hill psychology. Then and since, Dr. Brown has referred many members of Congress to psychiatrists. "The staff people would bring up the problems and present them as that of some friend," Dr. Brown said. "It was quite clear that if the problems came out, it might be harmful to their reelection. It was my job to get the person into the right hands."

Dr. Brown came to recognize what he called the "congressional psychological syndrome." According to Dr. Brown, "Members are corrupted by power, but this is followed by a letdown when they realize how powerless they really are as individuals." As a result, members focus on obtaining the perquisites of office.[67]

"They are in two worlds, and there is a stress to living in two worlds," Dr. Brown said. "There is the public exposure because people are visiting them and looking at them as important men carrying out the nation's business. Yet even to get typewriting paper or parking, they have to fight with the power structure. So they have these wild swings. They lead an extremely hypocritical life."

The stress means members of Congress are prone to "depression and anxiety and drug misuse, which is fairly common. A significant number have been alcoholics," Dr. Brown said. Moreover, "whenever you have a campaign situation or a situation with a lot of high tension and a lot of power, power is the great aphrodisiac. Sex is one of the great tension relievers."

Recalling her days as the wife of a congressman, Rita Jenrette said women made passes at John Jenrette in front of her. "The power of the office is very alluring," she said. "It was like being married to a rock star. Women saw me there and still approached him and would hand him the keys to their hotel rooms and their addresses and phone numbers. I was a young model for Clairol. That didn't deter women as old as my mother from pursuing him."

For some members of Congress, pages became a vehicle toward relieving their tension. In the past, marauding congressmen targeted both male and female pages. A Florida congressman "was fooling around with a female page," said Andrew Kruk, a former Capitol Police officer. "She told me he was making passes at her. I told her to walk in the other direction when you see him. I said, 'I can't do anything about it.' She was sixteen or seventeen, a beautiful girl, really built, a brunette. I couldn't go up against him. He'd kick my ass out."[68]

After the 1983 scandal, Congress required pages to be at least juniors in high school. Moreover, pages now live in dormitories patrolled by proctors. The House's seventy pages live in the Thomas P. O'Neill House Office Building at C Street and New Jersey Avenue SE. The Senate's thirty pages live and are taught in a remodeled funeral home at Fourth Street and Massachusetts Avenue NE.

*   *   *

Some members of Congress appoint children of friends or political supporters as pages, while others select from nominations made by schools. After Jimmy Carter left the presidency, his daughter, Amy, was a Senate page. Steven H. Taubenberger, a Capitol Police officer, was assigned to maintain liaison with her Secret Service detail.

"I went everywhere with her," he said. While Amy worked hard, "she was bratty. She was a little user of friends," he said. "She would suck them for whatever they were worth to get into a little group. Once she was there, she would forget all about the person who had gotten her there."[69]

Moreover, Amy "loved Coca-Cola to the point where she drank twenty or more in a working day, at least," Taubenberger said. "If she couldn't have a Coke, she would have a fit. . . . She was used to having her way."

Rosalynn Carter said Taubenberger "certainly has a bad memory or just wants his name in your book. He obviously has Amy confused with someone else, because this is totally out of character for her."[70]

Pages receive the minimum wage, from which they pay room and board, but their schooling and upkeep are not fully covered by their contributions. Congress purchased the building for the Senate page dorm and remodeled it for $8 million, or $264,200 per student. The median cost of constructing a dorm is $22,600 per student.[71] Thus the Daniel Webster Page Dorm, as it is called, has the distinction of being the most expensive dormitory in the nation.

Pages universally love the experience, which often inspires them to enter politics. Indeed, several members are former pages, including Sen. Christopher J. Dodd, the Connecticut Democrat, and Rep. John D. Dingell, the Michigan Democrat.

"It's a blast," Amanda Wheeler, a blond, blue-eyed seventeen-year-old page from Ohio, said. "It's an opportunity to meet a lot of important people and learn how the government works. . . . The best part is living with other pages. One of my roommates is from Alaska, one is from Wisconsin, and one is from Idaho."[72]

After she left the program in September 1996, Wheeler said,

"The supervision is strict. You had to be in at ten and midnight on weekends. . . . We had guards in front of our dorms and had to have IDs to get into our dorm."

Yet the problems continue.

"The page supervisors are having a lot more problems with traditional teenage problems. It's sex, pot, whatever," said a high-ranking Capitol Police official. "That is kept very hush-hush because it would be very embarrassing to the members and to the children. They are considered juveniles, and their records have to be guarded. But most of it is not even getting to the Capitol Police except anecdotally—things that should be reported."

As in the past, Congress tries to cover up the pages' transgressions. In 1993, a page painted "KKK" on the door of another page. "We found out about it several days after it happened," a high-ranking Capitol Police official said. "They [the page supervisors] didn't want adverse publicity. It was painted over so no one could see it."

Nonetheless, by interviewing pages, the Capitol Police established that a page sponsored by former representative Dan Rostenkowski, the Illinois Democrat, had painted it. "We had a responsibility to notify the prosecutors because it was a hate crime," the high-ranking Capitol Police officer said. "But the political powers [in Congress] didn't want us doing that because they were afraid we might want to push for prosecution. They didn't want that to happen."

Because of congressional pressure, the Capitol Police were not allowed to present the case directly to prosecutors. Instead, it went through political operatives. Ultimately, prosecutors declined to prosecute. The page was allowed to quietly leave the program, and there was never any publicity about the incident.

Then on November 29, 1995, a swastika was painted on the door of a Jewish page the morning after he and several other pages became embroiled in an argument. This time, the word got out. *Roll Call*, which covers Capitol Hill, ran a story about the incident on December 7. But the page supervisors did not allow the Capitol Police to freely interview those who might have had knowledge of the incident. "It's so the parents won't be upset and upset the congressmen," a high-ranking Capitol Police officer said. "When we can't interview the kids, our hands are tied." The culprit was never caught.

"We've exhausted all reasonable investigative leads in the case," *Roll Call* quoted Capitol Police spokesman Daniel R. Nichols as saying.

★ ★ ★ ★ ★ ★ ★ ★ ★ ★

4

★ ★ ★ ★ ★ ★ ★ ★ ★ ★

The Favormeister

In 1978, a congressman from South Carolina ordered a $10,000 diamond ring for his wife and had it sent to his congressional office. It never got to him.

Checking House postal records, Richard F. Xander, a Metropolitan Police sergeant who was detailed to the Capitol Police, learned that the package with the return address of the jeweler had been x-rayed in the House Post Office, which was run by House employees. The package had then disappeared, presumably stolen.

Unlike most Capitol Police officers, Xander was a real policeman. He decided to ask for an FBI background check on the seventy House postal employees who could have filched the ring. Robert V. Rota, who had been the House postmaster since 1972, was aghast. No one had done this before. When Xander persisted, Rota agreed to give him the information he needed. But Rota made Xander promise not to reveal that he had gotten the list.

"It was amazing what came back" from the FBI check, Xander

said. "Congress had put these people in these positions. Auto theft, drug problems. The best one there was theft from U.S. mails. This person had been hired by Congress for that job. They had never done FBI checks."[73]

In all, twenty of the seventy employees handling congressional mail—nearly a third—had criminal records. "We became aware that we had a whole bunch of thieves carrying mail around," Xander said.

In the case of the missing ring, the thief was never caught, but Rota's cooperation in trying to find the thief got him in trouble with members.

"They stepped all over Rota because he had cooperated with the police and had given out the names of the employees without going through the post office committee," Xander said. "This had never been allowed because some of these members had said, 'I got Bob Jones his job here because his mother worked for me in the home office. Sure he's been arrested a couple of times for robbery.'"

Thus it was no surprise when, in May 1991, an embezzlement was discovered in the 161-employee House Post Office. For years, House Post Office employees had used the till at the House Post Office as, in effect, personal credit lines. Since the U.S. Postal Service always announced audits in advance, employees had time to replace the funds they had "borrowed" from their cash drawers. An investigation by the House administration committee later reported that financial controls at the House Post Office were "nearly nonexistent."

This time when the auditors came by, Edward Pogue, a House stamp counter clerk, could not come up with the funds to replace the money he had taken. When he did not report to work, his supervisor checked his drawer. Missing was $6,000. The supervisor called the Capitol Police. As it turned out, Pogue had flown to Puerto Rico.[74]

"When he ran out of money, he called his father, who agreed to send him a plane ticket back," a Capitol Police officer who investigated the incident said. When he returned, "We met him at the airport. We interviewed him for many hours. He said, 'You're right. I did borrow against my drawer, and everybody does it. When audit time comes, we lend money among each other to make it seem that our drawers are balanced. So the drawer is never made up.'"

For once, the Capitol Police were aggressive. On May 29, 1991, they conducted their own audit and documented the missing cash. The Capitol Police wanted to continue the investigation by interviewing employees. But after initially agreeing, Rota withdrew his permission, insisting that employees should be represented by lawyers provided by the House.

"The House side provides counsel when employees are accused of stealing government property from their employer," a high-ranking Capitol Police official said. "They want their lawyer to sit there." In reality, the official said, "It's so the political bosses know what is going on." In contrast, the Senate does not represent accused employees. "If someone did wrong, they did wrong. Let them suffer the consequences," the official said.

When the Capitol Police persisted, Steven R. Ross, the House counsel, demanded a meeting with Frank A. Kerrigan, then the chief of the Capitol Police.

Since James M. Powell retired as chief in June 1984, the Capitol Police had been headed by chiefs who tried to maintain independence. As an assistant chief of the Metropolitan Police department, Powell had been detailed as acting chief of the Capitol Police for twenty-one years. In February 1980, under new legislation, he was officially appointed chief.

Powell was a good ol' boy who must have known that to keep his job, he had to bow to members' wishes. Raymond L. Carson, the former Capitol Police lieutenant, recalled that when the Capitol Police arrested a judge from Louisiana for bringing a handgun into an office building, a senator intervened. Carson was ordered to "unarrest" him.[75]

When the then wife of Sen. Howard H. Baker Jr. complained that the congressional license tags on her car had been stolen, Carson said Powell ordered him to remove the tags from a Capitol Police Bronco and put them on her car. "I told him we can't do that," Carson said. "He said, 'Just go ahead and don't worry about it.'" Carson complied.[76]

In October 1984, James J. Carvino, a former New York City police official, was appointed chief. Carvino intended to professionalize the department. He would not stand for any cover-ups.

Almost as soon as Carvino took over, a senator called him to complain. "It had been snowing out," Carvino recalled. "The snow was fourteen inches high." The senator said that his chauffeured car could not get through a Capitol driveway.[77] He insisted that an officer stationed at the driveway should have been equipped with a snow shovel and should have shoveled out the driveway.

Carvino came to consider the incident symbolic of what he faced. The chief was "absolutely shocked" at how Congress and the Capitol Police operated.

Carvino found that Capitol Police officers became soft-headed because they often guarded the same post for their entire careers. But that was how they wanted it, and when Carvino tried to rotate assignments, he ran into stiff opposition from members, who rallied to the officers' side.

Carvino laid down policies against unarresting people and making accommodations for members. They were largely ignored.

Officers were "always sucking up," Carvino said. "It was crazy. That place was very hard to professionalize."

Carvino was successful at introducing basic tools that had been standard in other police departments for years. He required psychological tests as well as tests that measure cognitive ability. He introduced psychological testing of applicants. He also introduced the use of polygraph machines during investigations.

But Carvino's days were numbered. When he made a small misstep, Congress pounced. One day, Carvino asked the Capitol Police to prepare a videotape to commemorate the retirement of Loretta Wahlen, his former secretary in Racine, Wisconsin, where he had been chief. The secretary had helped Carvino in his new job, but Carvino had shown poor judgment by using police resources for the video. But what really sealed Carvino's fate was a more important issue that was never publicized—a proposal of Jack Russ's, the House sergeant at arms, that would essentially have returned the department to the patronage system by giving the House leadership a say in promotions and merit raises.

In the Byzantine world of Congress, the Capitol Police chief reports to a Capitol Police Board. Formed in 1873, the board consists of the sergeants at arms of the House and Senate and the Architect of the Capitol. Russ wanted the sergeants at arms, who were political appointees in charge of maintaining security and enforcing decorum, to decide on promotions and merit pay for half the force.

Besides running much of the House infrastructure, the House sergeant at arms or his assistant has the duty of placing the ceremonial mace at the right of the Speaker's chair each day when the House is called to order. The Speaker presides over the House, while the mace is a traditional symbol of legislative authority. Borrowed from the British House of Commons, it goes back to republican Rome, where the fasces—an ax bound in a bundle of rods—symbolized the power of the magistrates. When the British burned the Capitol in 1814, the House's first mace, dating from 1789, was destroyed. The one used today is a replica. A fancy club, it is forty-six inches long and consists of a bundle of thirteen ebony rods bound in silver and topped by a silver globe with a silver eagle standing on it. When the House is in session, it rests on a tall pedestal at one side of the Speaker's desk. On order of the Speaker, if the sergeant at arms "presents" the mace to a member who is unruly, he is supposed to desist. If he persists, he can be expelled. The procedure has actually been used several times, but not in recent years.

Russ, who made $115,092 a year, had risen through the patronage ranks of Congress. He had started out on the payroll of his congressman, William M. Colmer, a Mississippi Democrat. Soon, he became a House doorman, head page, and deputy doorkeeper. Doorkeepers bring official messages and introduce official guests and members attending joint sessions. In January 1983, Russ became sergeant at arms.

Russ grew up chewing the fat with his father's friends at a gas station his father owned in Mississippi. "I could schmooze with the best of them," he would say. As sergeant at arms, he was the

47

second-ranking House employee. Like the mayor of a small city, he did favors for members and ingratiated himself with everyone. Russ was proud of his nickname: the Favormeister. He thought being sergeant at arms was the best job imaginable and hoped to retain his position until retirement.

Russ boasted that he knew every member from the back of his or her head. He could reel off the names of all the members' spouses. He had security pins made so that spouses of members could avoid security checks, just like the members. Russ would offer members rides home at night in police cruisers, give tours of the Capitol to the parents of members, and make sure members' tickets got fixed. When a deputy Capitol Police chief objected to the practice because tickets were being fixed when they did not meet the exemptions, Russ took over the task himself. In February 1989, Russ sent forty Capitol Police officers to protect members at a legislative retreat in White Sulphur Springs, West Virginia, and two hundred officers to protect members at a bicentennial meeting of Congress in Philadelphia in 1987. Russ also arranged to have the Capitol Police photo laboratory develop members' vacation film for free.[78]

If Russ operated like a ward heeler, he made no apologies. "You have to understand," he would say. "The police officers are the legislative branch's police office. It's like a small town." Members were "always right," he would say. "I always took the member's side. If a member were drunk, I just got him home [rather than arresting him for drunk driving]."

Slight and wiry, Russ was perpetually tanned and took pride in his physical condition. On the side, he raised horses on his farm. He wore a nine-millimeter pistol on his belt and drove Capitol Police cruisers. As a prank, Russ ordered the Capitol Police to arrest Robert V. Fischer, one of his aides, at Fischer's bachelor party at the Frontier Restaurant on Capitol Hill.[79] Fischer became so distraught that he kicked in the side of the Capitol Police car that took him to jail. After Fischer languished in jail for nearly two hours, the Capitol Police released him. No charges were brought against Russ or the police, who could have been criminally prosecuted for false arrest.

When Russ demanded that he have a say in merit raises and promotions, Carvino refused to go along. "They wanted me to appoint fifty percent of the people and give them between seven and fifteen percent merit pay," Carvino recalled. "They would appoint the other fifty percent and give them merit pay. I knew what would happen to that department if I went along with it. It was another form of patronage as far as I was concerned."

Citing the use of police resources to prepare the videotape for his former secretary, and two other minor complaints, the Capitol Police Board forced him out in June 1987.

"I resigned under pressure," Carvino said. "I was very disappointed and very disillusioned. Some of the members were real jerks. They come up as young congressmen and think the world is going to roll over for them. I told my people it didn't matter to me personally [if he was forced out because he refused to accommodate members], and ultimately that's why I'm not there."

Two months later, Frank Kerrigan replaced Carvino. A Capitol Police inspector, Kerrigan was the son of a police officer and had been with the force since 1966. But Kerrigan did not think like most Capitol Police officers. When Kerrigan heard that the House hierarchy did not want the Capitol Police to continue its investigation into the House Post Office, he decided to tape-record the meeting requested by Steve Ross, the House counsel. During the June 19, 1991, meeting, the tape recorder was placed under the coffee table in the chief's office at Capitol Police headquarters at 119 D Street NE. As the tape came to an end, the recorder clicked. To divert attention, Kerrigan commented on how noisy the clock was.

"Ross said the Capitol Police should not investigate," Kerrigan said. "I tape-recorded the meeting because I wanted to make sure I wasn't blamed for stopping an investigation. I had already told the U.S. Attorney."[80]

Ross claimed he wanted U.S. Postal Service inspectors to investigate, but Kerrigan was convinced that Ross meant he wanted an investigation by Postal Service auditors, who usually announced they were coming before they did an audit. Kerrigan believed Postal Service auditors had never found wrongdoing at the House Post Office. "They didn't really want somebody to investigate what went on," Kerrigan said.[81]

Ross told the *Washington Post* later he didn't think the Capitol Police, as a part of the legislative branch, should conduct an investigation for the U.S. Attorney. He also said he had delayed the Capitol Police investigation because he wanted lawyers from his office to represent the House Post Office employees being questioned.[82]

In a portion of the taped meeting broadcast on CNN, Ross said that if the Capitol Police were to become agents of the executive branch with no congressional oversight, "then my recommendation to the House leadership would be that, fine, you know, take them off the House payroll."[83]

Yet the Postal Service is part of the executive branch. "What he said didn't make any sense to me at all," Kerrigan said. During the meeting, Ross "seemed to make threats," the former chief said. Ross noted that Capitol Police officials "want pay raises for the department" and have "legislation pending for increased jurisdiction," Kerrigan said. "Kerrigan's impression was you're not going to get it if you pursue this."[84]

Kerrigan had planned to retire soon anyway, but the experience confirmed his decision. He left the Capitol Police in July 1991. By then, the FBI, at the request of U.S. Attorney Jay B. Stephens, was investigating the House Post Office. Tipped by the information Pogue had given the Capitol Police, the bureau established that for decades, Rota, as House postmaster, had been allowing members to obtain extra funds by exchanging stamps that the post office had issued to them for cash.

To send mail within the United States, members use their frank, which is their signatures preprinted on envelopes. The franking privilege goes back to 1775, when the Continental Congress approved it. Each member has an annual allocation for franked mail, and Congress reimburses the U.S. Postal Service for the cost. But foreign countries do not recognize the frank, so for overseas postage, members had to use standard postage stamps that the House Post Office issued. In addition, they used stamps for air mail and special delivery services.

Ironically, using the frank actually slows mail. Postal employees know that because franked mail is not canceled with a date, the U.S. Postal Service will not count the mail in evaluating delivery promptness. As a rule, they therefore put aside the franked mail until postmarked mail is sorted. For that reason, mail from Capitol Hill offices usually takes several days longer to reach its destination than stamped mail.

From 1962 to 1964, before he became a Capitol Police officer, Talmadge Reed worked as a clerk in the House Post Office. "I remember members of Congress and their staffs bringing in sheets of stamps," he said. "Members would come in and buy large quantities of stamps, perhaps five hundred dollars' worth, charge it to their office account, and then take them back to the office," Reed said. "A few days later, they would say, 'We've decided not to use these. Why don't you give me the cash, and you can sell them back to the public?'"

Reed said the practice was just considered another "perquisite." In fact, it was a laundering operation that allowed members to steal from the U.S. Treasury. When the FBI began investigating nearly three decades later, the practice had become even more common.

The investigation resulted in the indictment of House Ways and Means Committee chairman Dan Rostenkowski, the Illinois Democrat. Rostenkowski was charged with converting $23,100 in postage stamps to cash for his personal use. In addition, he was alleged to have authorized $500,000 in salaries for fourteen "ghost" employees who did little or no official work and to have spent $40,000 in official funds for House stationery-store purchases for personal or political use.[85] Rostenkowski pleaded guilty and was sentenced to eighteen months in prison.[86]

For years, a dining area near the front of the Morton's of Chicago steak house in Washington's Georgetown section was dubbed Rosty's Rotunda. It even had a brass plaque to that effect. As soon as Rostenkowski pleaded guilty, the plaque came down.

Rota, meanwhile, pleaded guilty to embezzlement.[87] He admitted he had provided three members, including Rostenkowski, with a total of more than $30,000 in federal funds over more than a decade by allowing them to convert stamps and stamp vouchers to cash. In addition, three House Post Office employees pleaded guilty to stealing more than $35,000 in cash and stamps.

In a report, the House administration committee concluded that Ross did not "interfere with or obstruct" the investigation.[88] Instead, the committee faulted the Capitol Police for not "keeping the proper authorities within Congress informed."

Kerrigan said the committee took his deposition by phone, and he could tell from the questions that the committee was going to side with the House counsel.

For more than one hundred years, the House Bank had quietly cashed the members' paychecks—tinted a distinctive pale orange—out of a little first-floor Capitol office. The bank neither paid nor charged interest. It made no loans. Other than members' salaries, it took no deposits. Yet to House members, it was another way to chisel money from the federal government. As in the case of the House Post Office, Congress had been covering up the practice for decades.

As far back as 1949, the General Accounting Office had mentioned in footnotes to audits of the office of the House sergeant at arms that large sums at the House Bank were "due from members." According to John Cronin Jr., the GAO auditor who did some of the reports, the footnotes meant that the House bank was covering checks that members had written on their overdrawn accounts. Meanwhile, the members got to use the money interest-free. In effect, the members had sanctioned their own misconduct. It seemed to be the perfect scam. While the GAO reports were made public, and the footnotes spelled out what was happening, no one read the footnotes. If they did, they did not know what they meant.

"I wanted to make an issue of it and criticize it, but GAO was conservative," Cronin said, noting that the GAO worked for Congress. "My bosses said, 'Come on.'"[89]

Then in December 1989, the GAO gave House Speaker Thomas S. Foley, the state of Washington Democrat, a letter warning that six hundred bad checks totaling more than $462,000 had been written on the House Bank in the previous nine months. Beyond admonishing Russ, whose own bad checks GAO had cited, Foley took little action. A fitness buff who had an impressive command of Shakespeare, Foley knew how to work Washington and enjoyed good press. But he was a passive man who displayed little leadership. On the other hand, his wife, Heather, who was his unpaid chief of staff, was a feared power in the House, yet she appeared unwilling to confront her husband about matters he should have been attending to.

One Capitol Police official will never forget how Heather Foley asked the Capitol Police to stop her husband's Capitol Police driver from getting so much overtime pay. When Foley was majority leader—the party's floor leader—the driver collected $52,000 in total pay in one year.

"The problem was this guy [Foley's driver] was making too much money," the official said. "She wanted to know what we were going to do to stop it and how we could put a can on it. She was going to develop legislation to limit how much drivers can earn. . . . My view was, why don't you just tell your husband to get rid of him? I couldn't figure out that relationship, why she had no control over him, yet she was his chief of staff."

As a result of Heather Foley's efforts, Congress passed legislation to reduce overtime for Capitol Police drivers. It established a higher base pay for drivers for the congressional leadership and limited their overtime to 25 percent of their base pay.

"Heather was the whip of the House," Henry F. Arrett, a former House doorman, said. "She controlled just about everything."[90]

In February 1990, the GAO made public its report on the House Bank. This time, instead of referring in footnotes to sums "due from members," the GAO made it clear that members were kiting checks. A spate of news stories followed. In September 1991, another GAO audit said members had written a total of 8,331 bad checks in the fiscal year that ended June 30, 1990.

At first, members stonewalled. "None of your damn business.

None of your damn business," Rep. Dan Rostenkowski said when asked if he had bounced any checks at the House Bank. But Republicans made the bank an issue, demanding that the names of the chief perpetrators be released. Because the scandal involved bounced checks, it became known as Rubbergate.

Until then, "you had no right to ask questions about the House Bank or Post Office," said Rep. Scott L. Klug, a Wisconsin Republican who was one of the "Gang of Seven" who demanded changes. "There was a code of silence: I won't squeal on you; you won't squeal on me."[91]

Foley promised to stop the practice of bouncing checks but did not want details to come out, Klug said. "We said, 'What GAO audit? How many checks were involved? Who was bouncing them? Refer them to the ethics committee.'"

In retrospect, Foley should have disbanded the bank immediately, said Werner Brandt, who was executive assistant to Foley and was later appointed by Foley as sergeant at arms. "Trying to reform it was a waste of time."[92]

As manager of the bank, it was Jack Russ, the sergeant at arms, who allowed the overdrafts to take place. Russ himself wrote $56,300 in bad checks on the House Bank. Meanwhile, Russ ran a company that sold wooden boxes for preserving ceremonial flags. He had the House Stationery Room buy his boxes for sale to members.

On March 1, 1992, in the middle of the investigation, Russ reported that two men and a woman had accosted him while he was walking his Australian shepherd in Garfield Park just after 10 P.M. at First and F Streets SE, five blocks south of the Capitol. Russ said one of the men shot him. But the gun had apparently been inserted in his mouth. The small-caliber bullet pierced his left cheek. The Capitol Police believe he shot himself, either accidentally or purposely.

"We were not able to substantiate his claims," a high-ranking Capitol Police official said. "A lot of the pieces don't fit. . . . Why would someone shoot him through the cheek? It wasn't a consistent trail [of blood]. . . . There should have been splatters of blood where he said he was shot. He was not able to account for a weapon of the same caliber that the police had issued to him. . . . The theory was he did it to get sympathy or intended to kill himself and chickened out at the last minute."

"Most of the police believe Russ tried to commit suicide and chickened out," Dave Curry, the Capitol Police captain, said. Eleven days after the shooting, Russ resigned.

The subsequent investigation by the ethics committee found that 269 current and 56 former members of the House had been allowed to routinely overdraw their accounts without paying interest or penalties. Among the then current members, the biggest abusers were Stephen J. Solarz, a New York Democrat, who had written $594,646 in bad or overdraft checks and was overdrawn for thirty months; Carl C. Perkins, a Kentucky Democrat, who had written $565,651 in bad checks and was overdrawn for fourteen months; Harold E. Ford, a Tennessee Democrat, who had overdrawn his account by a total of $552,447 and was overdrawn for thirty-one months, and Robert J. Mrazek, a New York Democrat, who had written $351,609 in bad checks until was overdrawn for twenty-three months.⁴⁰

Charles Hatcher, a Georgia Democrat, had written 819 bad checks and had been overdrawn a total of thirty-five months. Ronald D. Coleman, a Texas Democrat, had written 673 bad checks and had been overdrawn a total of twenty-three months.

Among the abusers from the Republican side was Newt Gingrich, the minority whip, who had written twenty-two bad checks with a face value totaling $26,891.

Anyone who has paid a $20 fee because his check has bounced by as little as $5, or who has paid interest to cover overdrafts, can appreciate how flagrantly members misused government funds by writing bad checks of as much as $60,625 each. Twenty-four members alone accounted for $899,000 in overdrafts. The scandal and its initial cover-up was but another example of how members of Congress expect everyone but themselves to play by the rules.

As a result of the Justice Department investigation into the House Bank, Russ pleaded guilty to three felonies, including embezzling $75,300 from the federal government by writing seventeen bad checks cashed at the House Bank. He was sentenced to two years in prison.[94] Two former members were also sentenced.

"The credo of the House Bank was to serve the House of Representatives and never embarrass a member," Malcolm R. Wilkey, a former federal appeals court judge who was appointed by the Justice Department to investigate the House Bank, said. "This credo, which underlay the bank's policies, indeed its very existence, ultimately led to its downfall."

★ ★ ★ ★ ★ ★ ★ ★ ★ ★

5

★ ★ ★ ★ ★ ★ ★ ★ ★ ★

Civility

As a doorman in 1974, David S. Kiernan's job was to seat visitors in the galleries overlooking the floor of the House. Kiernan was asked on occasion to act as matchmaker.

"As a doorman, you have a certain amount of control," said Kiernan, who earlier was a Capitol Police officer. "If you work in the public galleries, you could direct attractive women to certain areas. Occasionally, you'd get a request from a member to isolate extremely attractive women from their districts so members would have more access to them."[95] Kiernan would then ask the women what they were doing in town. Kiernan would pass along the information, and the member would use it to strike up a conversation with them. A member from the Midwest would use the line "I'm really single, not like some of the others."

"Sometimes the women blew the guys off. Other times, the members would lead them away," Kiernan said.

More recently, Rep. Bob Stump, an Arizona Republican, made it a practice of making obscene noises on the floor while other congressmen were speaking, said Charles L. Hoag, who was a doorman for thirteen years and continues to work for Congress as a security aide.

Stump "used to sit in the back with Larry J. Hopkins [a Republican from Kentucky], and they used to make funny jokes and comments about people during their one-minute speeches and also do weird sounds like somebody farting all the time," said Hoag.[96]

Hopkins denied that they made jokes. "I don't tell jokes about other people," he said. "As far as farting on the floor, I confess. I'm sure there isn't a congressman who hasn't farted on the floor."[97]

Stump said Hopkins made the farting noises with a device available from joke stores.

"As far as ridiculing people, that did not happen," Stump said. "It was all good fun. It was just jokes," he said. "I guess the laughing was because of that noise sometimes."

Many Hill staffers and members claim that in the old days, Congress was a cleaner place, where "giants" such as Senators Richard B. Russell Jr. and Everett M. Dirksen gave mellifluous speeches and civility reigned in the chambers.

"The greatest senator I've ever known was Dick Russell," said J. Stanley Kimmitt, a former secretary of the Senate. Like the clerk of the House, the secretary of the Senate processes legislation and administers operations.[98] Russell "was not selfish, he was never on the take, he was frugal with government funds in his office. There was something about him that, if you walked in the room, you had the feeling of being in the presence of a significant person," Kimmitt said.

In those days, "you could get into a big legislative fight, but then you would meet at the Carroll Arms Hotel and discuss how you beat them or they beat you," Roy L. Elson, administrative assistant to Sen. Carl T. Hayden, said. "There was trust. Now members lie to each other. They'll renege on commitments. The way I learned politics was the only thing you had was your word. I see so much gamesmanship and lack of trust and nastiness that was not there."

"I had just as many close, personal friends on the Democratic side as on the Republican side," said Sen. Thad Cochran, a Mississippi Republican who was first elected to the House in 1973. "I wasn't sanctioned or looked at with suspicion by my colleagues for having friendships on the other side. Now you are viewed with suspicion for having friendships on the other side. Certainly that is true if you join with the other side in offering legislation and amendments."[99]

"The House manual leans heavily on the need for civility," said Donnald K. Anderson, who spent thirty-five years working for Congress as a page, elevator operator, and eventually clerk of the House. "One should never question another's motives. There had to be an underlying assumption that public men and women, whatever their opinions, are honorable people and are not motivated by unethical and dishonest reasons. Now motives are questioned on a daily basis. It goes on all the time."

In September 1995, for example, Democratic members of the House Ways and Means Committee three times likened their Republican counterparts to "Nazis" and "fascists." In May 1995, Rep. Randy (Duke) Cunningham, a California Republican, referred to members who support "homos in the military," then told Rep. Bernie Sanders, an independent from Vermont, to "sit down, you socialist."

"Parliamentary question, Mr. Chairman," Rep. Pat Schroeder, a Colorado Democrat, retorted. "Do we have to call the gentleman a gentleman when he is not?"

During President Clinton's State of the Union address to a joint session of Congress on January 23, 1996, press secretaries to Republican congressmen laughed, jeered, and threw wads of paper at the screen as they watched Clinton on a television monitor in the Capitol.

The Constitution's framers set up the Senate as a check on the House, to be a more dignified, more deliberative body where debate could go on almost endlessly, and members—elected for six years instead of two—could take the long view.

Thomas Jefferson, who had been in France during the Constitutional Convention, is said to have asked George Washington why he had agreed to a second chamber. "Why," asked Washington, "did you pour that coffee into your saucer?"

"To cool it," Jefferson responded.

"Even so," Washington said, "we pour legislation into the senatorial saucer to cool it."

A creature of habit and tradition, the Senate kept its old-fashioned desks and spittoons, while the House got rid of theirs. In the Senate, a clerk still reads the roll of its members when a vote is taken, and senators have fifteen minutes to indicate their preference. In the House, members vote by inserting their personal plastic voting cards into a machine and then punching a button that records a yes or no vote or that simply records them as being present.

"The House tends to be rather provincial, occasionally brash, high-spirited," Anderson said. "It's a larger body. It's made up of people who represent small geopolitical entities, so they tend to be provincial in the way they react to issues. The senators, who are elected from larger areas, tend to look much more broadly at issues."

"The Senate is much more congenial, with less go-for-the-throat rhetoric," said Sen. Ben Nighthorse Campbell, a Colorado Republican who previously served in the House. "They give you more time to speak. In the House, everything is screened by the Rules Committee. Whether you can offer an amendment depends on whether you can get your rule."

While both the House and Senate are governed by rules that dictate their procedures, the House, because it has so many more members than the Senate, has tight rules that determine how each bill is to be debated. These rules, set by the House Rules Committee, include whether an amendment may be offered and, if so, under what circumstances. Because the rule imposed on a bill may be critical to its survival, debate on these issues within the Rules Committee can be fierce.

In contrast, in the Senate, "everybody has the right to reserve time on the floor to offer anything he wants," Campbell said. "On the House side, you're limited in the amount of time you can speak. Here you're not, which may be good or may be bad."[100]

Yet many perceive that the Senate has changed as much as the House.

In years past, "there was a respect for process," said a Senate clerk who has sat near the Senate rostrum every day for several decades. "People wanted the system to work. It's a whole different mind-set now. . . . There are other things that are more important now. Perception is everything. Reality is nothing. So many here now don't care whether they pass anything. They just want to be perceived as being on the right side. They just want to get reelected, and everything will be fine."

"Each senator comes up with his own policy," said Sen. Judd Gregg, a New Hampshire Republican who previously served in the House. "The sense of teamwork that is essential to functioning in the House doesn't exist here, or is minimal at best. It's very difficult to maintain a coordinated effort. Senators actively try to shut people out of issues. Each man is an island here. It's frustrating, coming from a coordinated, agenda-driven place to a place that is not agenda driven but is driven by the egos of the parties involved."[101]

The introduction of television to the House chamber in 1979 and the Senate chamber in 1986 has had a major impact. "I think TV is the biggest evil that has come to the House," said Anderson. "Speaker O'Neill predicted what would happen. . . . We now have four hundred and thirty-five potential stars of daytime television who are acutely aware that there are cameras in the chamber. They use them to get messages out. They plan for sound bites, things that can be quickly snatched by the evening news. It's created a nastiness and a level of personal attack that was unheard of—or rare—in earlier times." The vituperative attacks—together with the relentless need to garner more campaign contributions—figured in the retirements of fourteen senators and thirty-five representatives from the 104th Congress in January 1997.

In particular, the House's practice of allowing members to make one-minute televised speeches about anything they feel like before floor action begins contributes to a feeling that members are only interested in promoting themselves.

"I think TV has ruined the legislative process as we know it," William F. Hildenbrand, a former secretary of the Senate, said.[102] "There is no reason why a member should be able to come over at eight P.M. because it's a good time in his state for watching TV and get the floor and ask unanimous consent that he be allowed to speak out of order to make a speech for political reasons. Sen. Arlen Specter, when he was running for president, would come over at five-thirty every night and make a speech. All that does is extend the days the Senate is in session."

"A huge percentage of time is spent on how to use the political process to create a vote that will embarrass the other side or create an argument or debate," said former representative Eric D. Fingerhut, an Ohio Democrat. "Imagine going to work where, instead of everyone working together for the common good, you basically have people working to make each other look as bad and stupid as possible."[103]

"They talk more," the Senate clerk said. "They bring more staff with them, too. They used to come by themselves. They didn't come unless they had business. They didn't come to make speeches. They tended to know more about what the bills were about. They offered few amendments."

In those days, the clerk said, the leaders controlled the Senate. "They didn't bring up a bill unless they knew they could pass it. The train ran on time. Everyone had a shot at a bill, but they did it differently. They used to fight it out behind closed doors. Now they do it publicly." Moreover, members "had more time. I'm sure they didn't have the need to raise money the way they do now." Today, the members "have too much to do, and too little time to do it. It makes for pretty poor business."

Yet the facts belie the claim that Congress was once a tranquil bastion of civility, where everything ran smoothly and members behaved honorably. In 1985, House majority leader Jim Wright, a former Golden Gloves boxer, stepped down from the rostrum and threatened to punch Republican representatives Dan Lungren of California and Robert S. Walker of Pennsylvania in the mouth.

In earlier days, when Daniel Webster, John C. Calhoun, and Henry Clay walked the corridors of the Capitol, whips, canes, and pistols were often brandished on the floor of the House and Senate. Back in 1888, for example, Sen. Daniel W. Voorhees, in an argument with Sen. John J. Ingalls of Missouri about rich men's practice of buying substitutes from prisons to serve for them during the Civil War, jumped to his feet and shouted, "Liar! Scoundrel! You are the dirty dog!" And when Charles Sumner, an abolitionist senator from Massachusetts, gave a speech in May 1856 denouncing pro-slavery forces, Preston Smith Brooks, a congressman from South Carolina, knocked him senseless with a cane. Sumner was not able to resume his Senate duties for three years. Censured, Brooks resigned his seat but was reelected.

In the 1850s, a pistol concealed in a House member's desk accidentally discharged. Instantly, there were "fully thirty or forty pistols in the air," recalled Rep. William S. Holman. In 1808, Rep. George Washington Campbell of Tennessee accused Rep. Barent Gardenier of New York of "falsehood" and "baseness." Before long, they were dueling it out in a grove of trees in Bladensburg, Maryland. Gardenier was wounded, while Campbell was unharmed.

From the days when Congress first convened in Federal Hall in New York in 1789, members have taken graft, accepted illegal contributions, and comported themselves in less than savory ways on the floor of the House and Senate.

"In the old days, senators would stand up and say, 'Let the record show I'm not sitting in my seat,'" recalled Walter Trohan, who covered the Senate before World War II for the *Chicago Tribune*. "A senator would come in drunk and fall asleep in his seat."

An arrogant drunk, Sen. John G. Tower took advantage of his position to grope women who were in no position to complain.[104] In 1977, for example, as chairman of the Senate Armed Services Committee, an intoxicated Tower toured Bergstrom Air Force Base in Austin, Texas. At a hangar, Tower, who was then married, approached a female mechanic working on an airplane. "When the senator approached, the young female mechanic stood at attention, and then Senator Tower placed his hand on her shoulder and moved his hand down the female mechanic's back until his hand reached her hips . . . ," Bob Jackson, an Air Force public information officer who witnessed the incident, told the FBI during a background investigation for

Tower's nomination by President George Bush to be secretary of defense.

The following year, Tower again visited the base and again was drunk, stumbling and having difficulty opening doors. This time, Jackson escorted Tower to the chief maintenance officer's office. Tower greeted a secretary in the office by placing his hand on the secretary's shoulder. Then his hand "slid down the secretary's chest and rested for a brief period on one of the secretary's breasts," Jackson told the FBI.[105]

At the Monocle, a Capitol Hill restaurant frequented by senators; at the bar of the Jefferson Hotel in Washington; and at restaurants and nightclubs in Dallas and Houston, Tower often became roaring drunk and began groping his female companions or the female patrons. After his alcoholic binges, he could not remember what he had done, according to what aides and friends told the FBI. The FBI obtained Tower's bills from Marty's, a Dallas liquor store. They averaged $123 a month, mostly for wine and champagne.

Like Tower, former representative Robert N. C. Nix Sr., a Democrat from Pennsylvania, "tipped the bottle pretty good," recalled Melvin F. Parker, another former Capitol Police officer. "He was in the hallway, and the vice president [Spiro Agnew] was coming up. We were trying to get him up from the floor. I said, 'Get up, I'm trying to help you.' He said, 'You can't help me, but I can help you.'"[106]

"Members would walk in [drunk] and go to a staff person or even a page and ask them how to vote on a bill," Lee Schmalbach, who was a clerk in the House doorkeeper's office from 1974 to 1995, said.[107] "They had no idea what was going on. . . . The page would know what the bill was generally about." Usually, members asked the advice of pages of their own party. "I've seen it happen quite a few times," Schmalbach said.

In December 1932, a twenty-five-year-old department store clerk entered the House gallery waving a loaded pistol. Dangling one foot over the railing, he demanded the right to speak. A mad scramble for the cloakrooms ensued. Melvin J. Maas, a member from Minnesota who was a psychologist, quietly talked the man into surrendering his weapon. Asked by a reporter later whether he had had experience handling deranged people, Maas replied, "Why not? I've had six years in Congress."

Nor has hot air been confined to the modern Congress. The word *bunk* was coined because a North Carolina congressman in 1829 told his colleagues they needn't listen to his speeches. They were only for the folks in Buncombe County, his district.

Like the doormen, clerks, sergeants at arms, parliamentarians, and Capitol Police, the official reporters who produce transcripts of floor debates and committee hearings get an uncensored look at members.

"Dirksen used a spittoon and would lean over and miss and it would go all over me," Robert G. Cantor, a former official reporter, said.[108] "He didn't even say 'I'm sorry' or apologize. He chewed tobacco. You never knew when you would get it on you."

Based on eighteen years of sitting in on members' speeches and testimony, Cantor said, "They're almost all a bunch of prevaricators and will do anything to get where they want to go, based on my knowledge of what they say in closed hearings."

While congressional arrogance is perennial, occasionally members treat the little people with compassion. One of Steven R. (Rick) Valentine's first duties when he became a page was to put through a call to Sen. Robert J. Dole.

"I was new and forgot which line it was on," Valentine said. "I put him in a booth with a blinking light. He said, 'Hello, hello,' and no one was there. After the third try, I got it right. One of the people who worked there started screaming at me for screwing up. He was just really furious. Dole came out and put his arm around me and said, 'Don't be so hard on him. He's new, right?' Then he walked me out to the floor."

But by and large, the members "do what they want, when they want, and how they want," Henry F. Arrett, a former House doorman, said. "They don't care about you and me. All they care about is getting their retirement. They are a bunch of selfish people."

Even television doesn't show what really goes on in floor debates. The basic C-SPAN channel presents House debates to

63 million homes, while C-SPAN 2 covers the Senate, reaching 39 million homes. But as Brian Lamb, C-SPAN's founder chairman, has said, viewers are deceived into thinking that what they are seeing is brought to them by independent television crews.[109] In fact, Congress controls what is shown on C-SPAN.

Senate rules require cameras to remain fixed on whoever has the floor. Initially, the House had similar rules. When Newt Gingrich and Rep. Robert S. Walker, a Pennsylvania Republican, claimed that Tip O'Neill was soft on communism because of his criticism of the Vietnam War, O'Neill retaliated by ordering the cameras to pan the chamber as the other two were speaking to show that no one was listening. This led to a change in rules that allowed panning of the chamber. Still, the cameras do not show members chatting among themselves while speeches drone on, nor do they show "frivolous or extraneous" conduct, such as nose-picking. Both houses insist that their employees operate the cameras.

"If the people who elect members of Congress sat in the gallery for one day and watched their members in action or in inaction, they never would elect them," said Richard Xander, the Metropolitan Police officer who was detailed to the Capitol Police. "Time is wasted, some members never come to the floor. A good portion of them don't do anything. They talk to empty chambers and a couple of doorkeepers and Capitol policemen."

Nor does Congress make it easy for Americans to understand what is happening. The legislative rules are complex, and few members are versed in all of them. According to the Senate clerk, "Only one senator knew all the rules, Sen. Robert C. Byrd," the West Virginia Democrat. Others who came close were Senators Robert J. Dole, Ted Stevens, and Wendell H. Ford.

Instead of using their real names, members persist in calling themselves "distinguished gentleman" or "honorable friend" from this state or that. Unless a member is well-known, it is impossible for visitors watching from the galleries to know who is speaking.

"You have people who have only basic knowledge of congressional functions," said Scot M. Faulkner, the former chief administrative officer of the House. "They have no idea what is going on."

Meanwhile, the Capitol has few signs to point visitors in the right direction.

"The number of times I am stopped and asked where basic things are tells me there could be more signs," Faulkner said.

If members control the television cameras, they also control the *Congressional Record*. Ostensibly a transcript of floor proceedings, the *Record* is actually edited by members so they can put their own spin on events. In one example reported by *Washingtonian* magazine, during a House debate on a Republican-sponsored bill to repeal the assault weapons bill, Rep. Patrick J. Kennedy, the Rhode Island Democrat, told Republicans, "Shame on you. . . . Play with the evil, die with the devil." Turning to one of the bill's cosponsors, Gerald B. H. Solomon, a New York Republican, Kennedy said, "You'll never know, Mr. Chairman, what it's like, because you don't have anyone in your family who was killed."

Solomon responded with anger, telling Kennedy that his own wife lived alone five days a week in a rural area of upstate New York. "She has a right to defend herself when I'm not there, son, and don't you ever forget it. Don't you ever forget it." Solomon then threatened to throttle Kennedy outside the chamber.

Kennedy had the record changed to show he was addressing the presiding officer, not Solomon. Solomon deleted his reference to Kennedy as "son" and expunged his threat. And, in true congressional doublespeak, both members added a number of references to each other as "gentleman."[110]

Members also include in the *Record* statements that they never gave on the floor. House members include these statements—often sappy tributes to constituents—under "extensions of remarks." Senators call the bogus material "additional statements." Taxpayers wind up paying for the extra verbiage, such as "Tribute to Dodge County High School Indians," "Tribute to Philip Huss," and "A Tribute to the Orkland Corporation." Each day, 13,000 to 14,000 copies of the

Record are printed, requiring 700,000 to 800,000 pounds of newsprint a month. The publication goes to members and staff, libraries, lobbyists, and newspapers.

Just watching members gabbing with each other before and after votes can be unnerving. Off camera, some look dissipated, shifty, even disreputable. Seeing them in this unguarded state also gives the lie to the claim that Congress has become an unfriendly place. Off camera, members joke and smugly slap each other on the back as if they were at a country club reception. In a sense they are, as members of the most exclusive club in the United States.

"The rise of partisanship is a caricature that I think largely arises from watching CNN's *Crossfire* and Sunday-morning shows," Rep. Scott L. Klug, a Wisconsin Republican, said.[111] "Before I met with you today, I met with Democratic staffers to try to figure out if there is a way to craft a compromise on FDA [Food and Drug Administration] reform." Klug cited the bipartisan congressional baseball team and the Amendments, a rock group. Until the defeat of Rep. Martin R. Hoke, an Ohio Republican, the rock group consisted of Klug, Hoke, and Rep. Collin C. Peterson, a Minnesota Democrat. In contrast, the Singing Senators, who sing everything from "This Is My Country" to "Elvira," consist of Senators Trent Lott of Mississippi, James M. Jeffords of Vermont, Larry E. Craig of Idaho, and John Ashcroft of Missouri—all Republicans. "There are a number of Democrats here that I consider among my closest friends," Klug said.

"I flip on C-SPAN a lot," said former Rep. Romano L. Mazzoli, a Kentucky Democrat who served in the House from 1970 through 1994. "It often looks repetitive and pointless and empty and petty. . . . I take issue with people who look backwards and say, 'In my day, it wasn't like that.' Things were not so wonderful and civil when I was there."

To be sure, there is a congressional ebb and flow. When one party has been in power for a long time and then loses its majority, as the Democrats did to the Republicans in 1994 after controlling Congress for forty years, it is likely to feel abused.

Thus, over time, there are incremental, cyclical changes in the way Congress operates.

"It's a messy process, like making sausages," said Rep. Lee H. Hamilton, an Indiana Democrat. "One of the things television has done is expose the messiness of the process to an unusual degree. So one thing you hear is, 'Why can't you stop bickering all the time? Why can't you agree? Why is there so much partisanship?' Maybe it's exacerbated now, but the political process is a messy process. It's confrontational, adversarial. A lot of people get uneasy about that. It's always been there, but it is getting more exposed."

In fact, by the end of 1996, Rep. Collin Peterson, the lone Democrat in the rock group the Amendments, had dropped out.

"They wanted me to play at a Republican dinner," Peterson said. "I can't see playing with them if they're raising millions for the Republican Party."

6

No Tips

Pierre-Charles L'Enfant designed Washington so that its broad avenues radiate from the Capitol. Northwest, northeast, southwest, southeast—the city's quadrants—fan out from the Capitol Rotunda. Thus, in the design of the nation's capital city, the Capitol—not the White House—is the cardinal national structure.

Characteristically, the Capitol has only fronts—no back doors. Tour groups mount the broad staircase at the center of the east front and enter through the most famous of the Capitol's three sets of formal bronze doors, the Columbus doors. Depicting scenes from the life of the explorer, the Columbus doors weigh ten tons and are reminiscent of the Gates of Paradise, the renowned east doors of Florence's Baptistery of San Giovanni, which depict stories from the Old Testament.

The Senate corridors were fashioned by Constantino Brumidi, an Italian painter, to resemble a nineteenth-century Italian church interior. But his frescoes reflect the New World with the native fauna—squirrels, mice, bluebirds, mockingbirds, eagles, foxes, and copperhead snakes. Morning glories twist their vines around the edges of the walls and encircle vases of roses and cornucopias of apples, pears, and grapes. Patriotic shields in red, white, and blue appear intermittently in the frescoes and, like heraldic shields, imply a sort of Old World heritage.

Up near the ceiling, semicircular areas are painted with the images of such dignitaries as Benjamin Franklin and Robert Fulton. These frescoes Brumidi and his assistants painted, but Brumidi was forward-thinking and allowed his frescoes and the nation room to grow. He left blank some framed lunettes for later generations to fill in with their current history: recent additions are the 1969 moon landing and the 1986 *Challenger* disaster.

The corridors of the House side are more proletarian. Instead of being lined with colorful Minton tiles from Minton, England, the House floor is made of stark blocks of polished sandstone. The differences emphasize the dichotomy of the Capitol and by extension the new nation that built it, in contrasting the elegant European influence with the rough-hewn pioneering spirit of America.

Nearly every chief of state, prime minister, movie star, or pop singer has made a pilgrimage to the Capitol. Something is always going on—demonstrations, film shoots, press conferences. Here, parts of Frank Capra's classic 1939 movie *Mr. Smith Goes to Washington* were shot, as well as Otto Preminger's 1962 film *Advise and Consent*.

Tourists are eager yet restrained, worshipful and intense, as if this were their one chance to approach the seat of power. Now and then they are rewarded with a well-known member who hurries past. The member—whose arrival is heralded in the subway station by three buzzing rings—looks around him like a hungry bird to see if he has been recognized, or whether there is someone in the vicinity he needs to glad-hand. Seeing neither, he continues on his way, with perhaps a disappointed shrug, into his individual subway car. With a nod to the driver he climbs in, and his aide follows.

In the Capitol, Members and Staff Only signs and Senators

Only elevators mark the difference between royalty and commoner. Everywhere there are bright crimson Moroccan leather, red velvet drapes with silk tassels, gilt chandeliers, and gilt mirrors. Thus, in this palace of splendor, it is easy for members to decide that they are princes sent to Washington to be served, rather than the other way around. And if that is so, aren't they entitled to perquisites not available to ordinary mortals?

In that respect, not much has changed. In 1859, Congress ordered marble bathtubs from Genoa so members could bathe.

"In the nineteenth century, when members lived in boardinghouses, they did not have plumbing," Donald A. Ritchie, associate historian of the Senate, explained.[112] "So when they extended the building in the 1850s, they built a room for tubs and masseuses. They would get manicured and then do battle. They would pamper themselves." Today, two of the historic tubs remain in the basement of the Capitol, their fixtures rusting.

For years, Congress appropriated funds for the Congressional Cemetery at 1801 E Street SE so that members could be buried there free of charge. One hundred thirteen members were buried there; fourteen were later buried in their home states. Besides members, former FBI director J. Edgar Hoover, suffragette Adelaide Johnson, and composer John Philip Sousa are buried there. The cemetery is no longer connected with Congress.

For decades, Congress also provided members and staff with free haircuts in more than half a dozen barbershops scattered through the Capitol and congressional office buildings. In the 1970s and 1980s, Congress started charging, but at subsidized rates. Men's haircuts were priced at $3.50, then $5, when most barbershops on Capitol Hill charged $10.

The Republicans privatized the House barbershops. Now there is only one barbershop for men in the Rayburn House Office Building and a beauty salon for women in the Cannon House Office Building. Men's haircuts are $10, which is still below the going rate in Washington. Women's haircuts, at $28, are also a good deal. The Senate, which has a barbershop in the Russell Senate Office Building, charges just $9.

No Tips

The barbers get to know members as the voters never do. Eugene J. Kuser, a House barber for thirty years, most recently supervised the House barbershops. He recalled that members of Congress constantly complained that the barbershops were not bringing in enough money. Yet those same congressmen made appointments for haircuts and expected the barbers to keep their chairs free until they showed up—sometimes two hours late. One such congressman was Leon E. Panetta, the California Democrat who became Bill Clinton's chief of staff. Panetta was chairman of the House administration subcommittee that ran the barbershops.

"Just after Panetta made chairman of the subcommittee, his first question was, 'Is there any way you guys can make more money?'" Kuser said. "I said, 'I'm glad you brought that up. This is your fourth attempt at getting a haircut. The first three times you never showed up at all; I kept your chair open for a half an hour.' He said, 'How often does that happen?' I said, 'It happens a lot.'"[113]

For all his nice-guy demeanor, House Speaker Thomas P. (Tip) O'Neill was one of the worst offenders. "A lot of barbers wanted to cut Speaker O'Neill's hair so they could say they cut the Speaker's hair," Kuser said. "On the other hand, they didn't want to because we worked on commission. He would call up and say he wanted a haircut. He might be there in half an hour or two hours later. You had to hold that chair, and you weren't making any money. If the guy finally took another member, he [O'Neill] would show up and growl, 'I thought that chair was supposed to be open for me.'"

With members and staff, it was monkey see, monkey do. Before Jim Wright had ethics problems related to financial arrangements for his 117-page book, everyone wanted to mimic his trademark bushy eyebrows. Members and staff "wanted the same thing: 'Don't touch the eyebrows,'" Kuser said. "But when he had his problems, they wanted the eyebrows cut."

Even though the price of a haircut was ridiculously low, some members tried to get the House administration committee to waive payment altogether. Most members "did not tip," Kuser said. "Most of them felt you were there to be there."

"One of the barbers years ago decided to do hairpieces," Kuser said. Congressman Claude D. Pepper, the Florida Democrat, bought one but refused to pay the barber. "Pepper expected the public to pick up the tab. The guy finally got his money, but where it came from, I don't know."

After thirty years of cutting members' hair, Kuser has little respect for them. He came to realize that their word means nothing, and that they will always blame someone else for their failings.

"Even if they come in very nice, once they are there awhile, the system gets to them," Kuser said. "You can tell they are changing by the way they make demands. They are trained to work the crowds, in effect. It's a strange place to work. They don't understand that the people who work there are people.

"I think we're in big trouble," Kuser said. "We're being sold out. They have failed us miserably. They are there for themselves and are so wrapped up in being reelected. If they can make a deal for themselves, that's it."

Like the barbershops, congressional dining rooms and cafeterias have long been subsidized by taxpayers, additional perquisites for the denizens of the Hill. Recently, the House turned its catering operations over to a joint venture with the Marriott Corporation. But the Senate continues to have the Architect of the Capitol run its facilities. The House began making a profit of $180,000 a year, but the Senate dining rooms lose as much as $780,000 a year.[114]

Besides the cafeterias open to the public and staff, the House and Senate each operate members-only dining rooms in the Capitol. The Senate has one where members can take guests, and another "inner sanctum" dining room with crystal chandeliers for members only. Here, members generally eat in two separate areas, one for Republicans and one for Democrats.

Robert Parker, who was a maître d' in the Senate dining rooms until 1974, used to serve members in their hideaway offices. At times, he or his staff would walk in on a member having sex. Parker began as a messenger for Lyndon Johnson. In that capacity, he said his duties included driving Texas oilmen and other contributors to see call girls paid for by Johnson.

"I would drive LBJ's friend to the hotel, usually to a side entrance," he said. Eventually, a Johnson aide got Parker a credit card in his own name, and Parker used the card to pay for the call girls' hotel rooms. "At the end of the month, I'd hand in the credit card statement, and LBJ's office would pay the bill," Parker said.[115]

Since 1985, Kenneth Derreck Cohen has been serving senators in both dining rooms. Like Parker, Cohen serves members in their hideaway offices when they want to kick back. He has delivered bottles of liquor to such senators as Christopher J. Dodd, the Connecticut Democrat, and Ted Kennedy.

"Dodd had a pretty young lady guest," Cohen said. "I brought glasses for two."[116]

Both the Senate and House serve bean soup every day. On their menus, both sides proudly attribute the standing item of soup to various former members—Fred T. Dubois of Idaho or Knute Nelson of Minnesota in the Senate, or Joseph G. Cannon of Illinois in the House.

Each house uses a slightly different recipe and refers to its version as Senate Bean Soup or House Bean Soup. The Senate version is far better, but over the years, it has undergone change. For some years, the Senate left out ham hocks, which are called for in the original recipe.*

When John L. Hitzel, who took over the Senate dining services in 1984, discovered that the chefs were not using ham hocks in the Senate bean soup, but rather a soup base, "we went back to the ham hocks, and there was a real difference," Hitzel said.

Sen. Arlen Specter, the Pennsylvania Republican, orders the bean soup "about every day," Cohen said. It is also "the usual" for Conrad Burns, a Montana Republican, and Frank H. Murkowski, an Alaska Republican.

---

* The recipe for Senate Bean Soup appears as an appendix to this book.

While most senators order sandwiches on rye or whole wheat, Sen. Wendell H. Ford, the Kentucky Democrat, likes "open-faced bacon and grilled cheese" sandwiches on white bread. A number of senators usually help themselves to the $12.50 buffet. They include Ted Kennedy; Pete V. Domenici, the Republican from New Mexico; Barbara A. Mikulski, a Maryland Democrat; Lauch Faircloth, a North Carolina Republican; and Ted Stevens, an Alaska Republican.

Ben Nighthorse Campbell, the Colorado Republican, is "a heavy eater," Cohen said. "He goes to the buffet, cleans his plate, and gets a dessert. He fills the plate up. He puts butter on his crackers." On the other hand, Daniel R. Coats, the Indiana Republican, eats very little. John Glenn, the Ohio Democrat, "has a bowl of soup. That's it." Similarly, Fred Thompson, the Tennessee Republican, "likes large bowls of bean soup. That's all." Charles E. Grassley, an Iowa Republican, usually has a club sandwich, while Daniel K. Inouye, the Hawaii Democrat, asks for a "grilled burger and scrambled eggs."

Some members never glance at the menu. Herb Kohl, a Democrat from Wisconsin who is a multimillionaire, has a standing order: a peanut butter sandwich on white bread. Instead of eating with his colleagues, he usually scarfs his sandwich down in a public dining room adjacent to the clubby "inner sanctum."

Always on hand is chicken noodle soup, because John W. Warner, the Virginia Republican, likes it. Because he is a member of the Senate Rules and Administration Committee, which administers the dining rooms, the dining room goes out of its way to please him.

Some members are less particular about what they eat. Some say because of his alcohol consumption, Daniel Patrick Moynihan, the New York Democrat, is often difficult to understand.

"I've seen him incoherent for lunch, for dinner," Cohen said. "He drinks wine when he comes in, maybe two glasses of red. He is so intelligent that even when he's stoned, whatever comes out of his mouth is still right on the money." Yet Cohen said, "He can't dial a phone number. I bring cordless phones to the table. He can't say what he wants to eat. He doesn't finish his food," which is usually a hamburger or hot dog. "He hardly touches it, just drinks the wine."[117]

When Moynihan has been drinking, Cohen said, "he slurs. You can't understand what he wants. It's not every day, but the majority. The other senators treat him as if it's a normal occurrence. They have conversations with him."

"I've seen him [Moynihan] come out of the Monocle [Restaurant] and not be able to walk in a straight line," said Jeffrey T. Robinson, a former Capitol Police officer. "This might be after a late session around ten-thirty P.M."[118]

"Sometimes when he is alleged to be drinking, he makes some of his more cogent statements," Sen. Orrin G. Hatch, a Utah Republican, said of Moynihan.[119]

In fact, some claim Moynihan's speech is always slurred, and no one knows if the mumbling is related to his drinking. Nor can anyone cite instances of drinking affecting his work. Intoxicated or not, he remains an effective and respected senator.

John Kerry, the Massachusetts Democrat, recently married Teresa Heinz, who inherited the $760 million H. J. Heinz food company fortune. In a debate with Massachusetts governor William Weld, Kerry talked about his experiences "sitting in somebody's kitchen" and hearing of the problems of the poor. What he learned was that "people are poor because the deck is really stacked against them. Because people like the governor fight even raising the minimum wage."[120]

But Cohen said Kerry's compassion ends in the television studio. He is "real cheap. He tips, but it is ten percent and below." Cohen said a number of other senators either do not tip or tip very little. They include Daniel R. Coats, an Indiana Republican; Thad Cochran, a Mississippi Republican; John B. Breaux, a Louisiana Democrat; Conrad Burns, a Montana Republican; and Trent Lott, the Mississippi Republican who is Senate majority leader. "They might go out without signing their check or they might sign the check with no tip," Cohen said. (They are billed anyway.)[121]

In fact, a report released by the House in 1991 showed that members owed $300,000 in bills to the House dining room.[122]

"You have a few that give you a good tip no matter what they have," Cohen said. "They come in for lunch and give you two dollars. For dinner, they give you two dollars. They might order a sandwich." Among the good tippers, according to Cohen, are Ted Kennedy; Robert F. Bennett, a Utah Republican; Patrick J. Leahy, a Vermont Democrat; Connie Mack, a Florida Republican; and John D. Rockefeller IV, a West Virginia Democrat.

As Speaker of the House, Newt Gingrich was occasionally invited to the Senate's "inner sanctum." According to Cohen, Gingrich ignored the help, never saying "please" or "thank you." But in Congress, that is not unusual. "Supposedly, they are into their conversation," Cohen said. "A lot of them don't say thank you." In fact, Cohen said, "Most of them don't."

★ ★ ★ ★ ★ ★ ★ ★ ★ ★

7

★ ★ ★ ★ ★ ★ ★ ★ ★

Mr. Burns

When what was then known as the Congress House was being designed, there were only thirty senators and sixty-nine representatives. They had no personal staffs, and their desks in the House and Senate chambers were their offices.[123]

Today, including the five nonvoting delegates from American Samoa, the District of Columbia, Guam, the Virgin Islands, and Puerto Rico, Congress has 540 members. Three Senate office buildings, three House office buildings, and innumerable annexes have sprouted on either side of the Capitol, housing for members and their staffs.

Since 1929, the number of House members has been fixed at 435. The number of senators has remained at 100 since Hawaii became a state in 1959. Yet congressional staff has grown briskly. Since 1960, the number of employees in the legislative branch has grown by 50 percent, compared with a decrease of 20 percent for the rest of the government.[124] Moreover, while total legislative branch employment has increased sharply, members' personal and committee staffs have increased the most—165 percent for the Senate and 170 percent for the House. Thus, while the rest of the government shrank, members almost tripled their own staffs. Personal and committee staffs number 17,566 employees—32 per member—of the total legislative branch complement of 33,396.

In fact, Congress has more staff than any other national legislature. The Canadian parliament, with just over 400 members, employs a staff of 3,500.[125]

To be sure, Congress attracts some of the most qualified, hardworking people in the country. Besides drafting legislation, developing hearings, following up on constituent problems, and writing speeches, the staff acts as a filter, separating the trivial from the important. But the burgeoning staff means each member has his or her own bureaucracy to administer. In fact, in a survey taken in 1992 by the Joint Committee on the Organization of Congress, almost half of the members responding said they believe Congress is overstaffed.

"I think the biggest problem we have is too much staff," Rep. Collin C. Peterson, a Minnesota Democrat, said. "There are too many subcommittees. Nobody really knows what is going on. Every member has a staffer involved in every legislative issue. You can't get in the committee rooms because there are so many staffers."[126]

"We are more dependent on staff than we used to be. That is not good," said Rep. Lee H. Hamilton, an Indiana Democrat. "It makes consensus-building more difficult. You have to keep in mind that the role of the Congress is to build a consensus behind an approach or a solution to a problem."

Like many other members interviewed, Peterson said his own state legislature, where he began as a state senator, operated far more efficiently than Congress.

"We relied on each other [for information]," he said. "It's going to be impossible to say to members, 'Get rid of your staff.' I don't have an AA [administrative assistant]. Most of the time I don't have a press secretary. I make my own calls. If I don't have enough time for an issue, I don't take it on."

Yet Peterson has not turned down staff allocations. Instead, he has assigned two of his eighteen staffers to promote the economy in his district.

If members of Congress are princes, their staffs are their court, defining how important they are. Members rail against waste in the executive branch, but when it comes to their own staffs, they are self-indulgent. Often, the biggest critics of congressional staff are the worst abusers. As vice president, Dan Quayle was also president of the Senate. Quayle railed against the "unbelievable" expansion of the congressional payroll, yet he had forty aides in his Hill entourage, compared with thirty for George Bush when he was president of the Senate and twenty-seven for Walter Mondale when he had that role.[127]

Since 1980, Bill Tate has been administrative assistant to Rep. Jim Leach, an Iowa Republican. Tate, who wears a bow tie under his beard, attended elementary school, junior high, and high school with Leach. He calls himself Leach's "headwaiter or butler." Besides running the staff, Tate advises Leach on as many as twenty-five votes a week, decides who gets to see the congressman, administers his annual budget of $865,804, and oversees responses to the thirteen hundred letters Leach receives every month. House members are allowed to spend an average of about $900,000 a year on salaries, postage, equipment, travel, and district-office rent. This does not include allowances for franked mail. Each senator is allowed to spend an average of $2 million on franked mail, depending on the population of his or her state and other factors.

In filtering information, "you have to learn to be selective in your choices of sources," Tate said.[128] "You have to be more aware of your own biases in making that selection so you are not getting only one side. That is very hard. If you agree with one position, you have to seek out the opposition and consciously seek to get the other side. Sometimes, I'll ask people who come in, 'Why is there so much opposition to what you are saying?' If they are smart, they'll give a true answer and say, 'You ought to talk to so and so.' If they don't, we can ask the Congressional Research Service and other sources."

Tate is careful about forming friendships, mindful that many in Washington seek access to his boss, the chairman of the House Banking and Financial Services Committee.

"There is no truer saying than if you want a friend in Washington, get a dog," Tate said. "A friend is a person for whom nothing you could do would really alienate him. All relationships in Washington are power relationships. Very seldom do you see genuine friendships."

Because Congress is televised and more open than it was in the 1960s, responses to speeches come in quicker. "Now they are on record, as opposed to taking voice votes," Tate said. "Now it is extraordinary when committee hearings are closed. When Jim appears on the floor, we'll get calls from all over the country." Responses come in even quicker because most members now have electronic mail.

"No one will argue that that kind of openness is bad, but it is a complicating factor," Tate said. "If you are going to make a difficult vote, it might be for what you believe is the public good, yet your opponent is going to target it if it is in opposition to your constituency's interests."

Like most Hill employees, Tate has seen his share of nuts. He has refined the art of keeping people at bay. As he puts it, "I can be energy absorbing by being quiet. You can stop aggressive, belligerent people by letting them run out. My job is to impose order on these four rooms.

"A young man neatly dressed came in," Tate said. "He wanted to talk about agriculture and was from Iowa. He said he had a way to generate electricity with feeding troughs that go out like spokes. The animals would generate electricity. A colleague called me on an intercom and said, 'I see what is going on. Why don't you tell him you have a meeting?'"

When Tate told the man he had to attend a meeting, the visitor responded, "I'll walk along with you." So Tate walked out the door, not knowing what he would do. He walked to the Congressional Research Service reading room, which keeps its door closed. Tate told the visitor he could not go in with him. When the receptionist asked if she could help him, Tate said, "You can just let me stand here for five minutes."

* * *

Committee staff that specialize in different agencies assist personal staff in advising members. For seventeen years, Robert Gellman was counsel and staff director on a House subcommittee that had jurisdiction over the Freedom of Information Act and the Privacy Act. Because these issues have little impact on business or labor, the chairmen of the subcommittee left Gellman alone to develop laws he thought were in the public interest.

"The acts apply to federal agencies," Gellman said. "We weren't regulating the private sector. So interest was limited."[129]

Gellman fended off Reagan administration efforts to gut the Freedom of Information Act. He also helped draft measures that reduced the fees charged for FOIA responses from government agencies.

When members become involved, they often act for strictly political reasons. Knowing a bill will never pass, they introduce it anyway so they can claim to constituents that they favored the measure. Or, knowing the Senate has blocked a bill, the House will pass it knowing it will never be adopted. For similar reasons, according to Gellman, Congress established a drug czar, knowing the person who occupied the post would always fail.

"What we did with express intent was to set up a process where the drug czar would have lots of responsibility but no clout," Gellman said. Members could then rail at the drug czar for failing to solve the drug problem. "We set it up so it wouldn't work."

Committee staffs obtain additional help from House and Senate offices of legislative counsel, which provide advice on the technicalities of drafting legislation, and from the Congressional Research Service. The House legislative counsel has thirty-five attorneys, while the Senate side has twenty-five. Both offices have a strictly nonpartisan tradition, and many of their attorneys have held their positions for decades. Presented with a legislative result members want to achieve, the attorneys often come up with new approaches that committee staff may not have considered.

"The office could be misused," said a House legislative

counsel attorney who, characteristically, asked not to be quoted. "An unscrupulous counsel could push one way or the other. We might suggest options. Our office is largely invisible to people. That is our preference."

The Congressional Research Service provides members with analyses, summarizes legislation, and conducts special studies. Established in 1914 within the Library of Congress, the CRS has a staff of seven hundred.

CRS staffers tack inane requests from members on their office walls.

"We got bizarre requests all the time," said Daniel P. Beard, a former CRS staffer.[130] "One was from a congressman who wanted his bow tie tied. There was someone in the reference room who knew how to tie a bow tie, so he went over and showed him."

As part of its legislative function, Congress conducts investigations and hearings before proposing solutions. It also conducts oversight hearings to determine if the executive branch is carrying out lawfully, effectively, and efficiently the laws Congress has passed. Finally, the Senate alone is charged with ratifying treaties, accepting or rejecting federal judges, cabinet officers, and other high-level officials.

In years past, Congress undertook hard-hitting investigations such as those headed by Sen. John L. McLellan into labor racketeering, by Sen. Estes Kefauver into organized crime, and by Sen. Philip A. Hart into violations of antitrust laws. More recently, Rep. John D. Dingell, the Michigan Democrat, undertook investigations into oil companies and defense contractors.

Hearings are part show business. Usually, key findings are leaked to the press before hearings to attract more coverage. If members can grab headlines to illustrate findings, they have a greater chance of passing legislation to correct abuses.

"You have to use dramatic examples that mom and pop will understand," Dingell's former chief investigator, Peter D. H. Stockton, said. "You have to take a case study. You can't look at a program or policy. No one will understand it. You have to generalize from the particular."

To illustrate the general problem of Defense Department

waste, Stockton highlighted expenses General Dynamics Corp. had billed to taxpayers as part of defense contracts.

"Dingell was brilliant," Stockton said. During a hearing, Dingell asked an executive of the defense contractor, "Who is this Fursten at Silver Maple Farm?" General Dynamics had billed the government $300 to board a dog named Fursten, owned by an executive.[131]

While Dingell often exhibited "political courage," he had his limits, Stockton said. Being from Michigan, Dingell would not take on the auto industry. One day, Dingell asked Stockton to write a memo demonstrating that the auto manufacturers could not comply with a deadline to develop catalytic converters.

"The car manufacturers said they can't make catalytic converters because we are running out of rhodium [which is used in them]," Stockton said. But Stockton consulted the Central Intelligence Agency, which said rhodium is in abundant supply. In a memo to Dingell, Stockton relayed the information.

"Oh, my God, he went berserk," Stockton said. "He said, 'That is not the answer I want.' So he never asked me to do anything else like that again."

While the Senate Governmental Affairs' permanent investigations subcommittee has done useful work, it fails to measure up to the groundbreaking, eye-opening investigations of the past. The subcommittee has roughly twenty-five staff members, compared with two hundred in the 1960s. Between 1957 and 1959, the Senate Select Committee on Improper Activities in the Labor or Management Field heard 1,726 witnesses whose testimony filled 46,150 pages. Staff members submitted 128,204 documents to the committee, conducted 253 field investigations, and served more than 8,000 subpoenas. Now members are reluctant to take on powerful interests that may be big contributors to their campaigns. As a result, "there are no more in-depth investigations on the Hill," Stockton said.

"You have hearings that are an absolute joke," a former Senate Judiciary Committee staffer said. "It will be two or three members. A couple of senators will make an appearance, ask a few questions, and then leave. The idea that they can devote any real attention to more than a handful of issues is complete folly.

It's alarming to see them voting on issues they know nothing about."

The former staffer said, "Congress runs on an issue cycle that lasts about a week. One week you are working on proliferation, the next week you are getting an appropriation for some company in your member's home state. It's totally political. It is so mind-numbingly difficult to get real legislation passed. There is always some other issue that pops up."

The fact that the National Reconnaissance Office, which builds and operates the nation's spy satellites, could get away with accumulating $4 billion in unspent funds—more than the combined budgets of the FBI and State Department—demonstrates how lax congressional oversight can be. Another example was the misleading way the Central Intelligence Agency responded to inquiries from the House and Senate intelligence committees about the loss of human spies in the Soviet Union while CIA officer Aldrich H. Ames was compromising them. The committees undertook no independent investigation to find out the truth.[132]

When legislation is passed, it is no longer crafted as expertly as it once was. Sloppy drafting leads to endless litigation in the courts.

"The number of errors has increased," said U.S. district court judge Charles R. Richey, who, as a federal judge in Washington for the past twenty-six years, has interpreted bills passed by Congress so he can make rulings. "The staff writes the bills and the members spend so much of their time raising money, they don't know what they're doing."[133]

Richey said the errors are especially egregious when Congress pulls late-night sessions, as it does with increasing regularity. Moreover, "the legislative history doesn't mean as much as it did fifty years ago, making it more difficult to interpret what Congress's intent was in passing the laws," Richey said.

"The turnover rate is very high now," said Joseph R. Crapa, staff director for Rep. David R. Obey, a Wisconsin Democrat. "An average legislative aide is in the job two years. Decisions are being made by people who don't know the system or what has gone before. It takes three to five years to train a decent legislative person, especially if that person has to deal with appropriations. You can't be certified as an LA [legislative assistant]. You have to learn by experience." Moreover, Crapa said, unlike in earlier times, "the Republican and Democratic staffs don't know each other and don't trust each other. When you have to deal with complicated legislative issues, you need to know whom you are talking to and if you can trust that person. Is that person speaking for the member? Does he have the member's attention? Does he have the judgment to make the right decision?"

"Most of the staff don't know what they are doing," Representative Peterson said. "They're twenty-one years old. They don't have anything to do, so they generate more paper and letters. You have to hire people just to read them."

Because Congressional Research Service staffers work with all members of Congress, they have a unique perspective. CRS staffers may work for weeks with one member on a particular project, sitting in on meetings with them and their staff. They quickly learn which members are class acts and which ones are boors.

In the view of a CRS staffer, one of the meanest members is Sen. Arlen Specter, a Pennsylvania Republican. The staffer said Specter's staff refers to him as "Mr. Burns," the nasty, petulant, demanding boss in the television show *The Simpsons*. Like a "child," the staffer said, Specter "yells at people. He is incredibly short-tempered. He is impulsive and has mood shifts." If a staffer's work doesn't please him, Specter has been known to fire him on the spot. He'll say, "Get out. Grab your things and get out of here," according to the CRS staffer. "No chance to explain. He cuts you off. Doesn't want to hear explanations."

Recalling Specter's reaction to a floor statement a staffer had put together, another Specter aide said Specter told the man it was "incomprehensible, inane, and illegible."

While Specter is a "very intelligent, articulate individual," he could be "mean and nasty," confirmed Scott M. Waitlevertch, a former legislative assistant.[134] If a staffer arrived at 12:55 for an event scheduled for 1 P.M., and Specter happened to have arrived five minutes earlier, Specter "expected you to be there when he walked in," Waitlevertch said. "There were times when he could upset female staffers to the point of tears."

"He had his temper," said Douglas B. Loon, Specter's former legislative director.[135] "But once you figured out how to deal with that, you got along very well. He would come down on people, but he also had periods of reconciliation or apology. He would not come right out and apologize, but he had his own way of doing it."

"If he is left waiting for thirty seconds, it provokes a tantrum," a former Specter staffer said. "He will raise his voice and say, 'This is unacceptable.' He will be angry about the fact a staff member doesn't know where the men's room is. If he is away from the Senate, before he goes on to give a speech, he has to go to the men's room. If he is kept at the curb because the car is thirty seconds late, it will provoke a tantrum."

"He dealt with his own frustration at other people's incompetence by cross-examining people," said Neal Manne, a former administrative assistant to Specter.[136] A former prosecutor, Specter "would ask people very specific questions. When they gave excuses for not knowing the answers, he would wear his DA's hat and cross-examine them and show the inadequacy of their response, which is extremely painful to people who realize they haven't done a good job."

Manne told Specter there were more productive ways to motivate staff, by "encouraging them to do better rather than by destroying their confidence or making them so angry they leave. He responded well. He thought if I could do it, that would be wonderful."

Why staffers put up with the abuse provides insight into the psychology of working for members of Congress. Some staffers grow to accept Specter's outbursts as the price they pay for working in the Senate. Sylvia Nolde, Specter's scheduler for fourteen years, said Specter was as demanding on himself as he was on his staff. "He was like the taskmaster professor," Nolde said.[137] "You had a chance to take an easy professor and get an A or you had a chance to really learn from someone who expected a lot from you, and get maybe a B."

Others who have left Specter's staff think that his aides have a masochistic streak for staying on. Some said their own fathers treated them in a nasty way, so the abuse created a sort of perverse kinship with their boss. Even if the apology is veiled, they placed great significance on the fact that Specter later apologizes. In a childish way, this suggests the aides are important.

"In some cases, the congressperson becomes an extension of the staff's ambition," said Dr. Bertram S. Brown, the psychiatrist who became an expert on the psychology of Congress. "Some study how to replace their boss. Quite a few staff become congressmen. The personal staff's careers become intimately linked with the congressman."[138]

Beyond personal ambition, staff tolerate abuse from a member because "sometimes they can't get another prestigious job, or the member apologizes, or taking the abuse makes them feel closer to the member and hence more powerful," Dr. Brown said. "They may expect to be rewarded later, or they may have low self-esteem in the first place."

Specter's petulance is not just directed at his staff. In late 1995, Specter became enraged when the FBI did not immediately follow his wishes by interviewing House members about a leak revealing levels of funding being discussed in Congress for the Central Intelligence Agency's covert action in Iran. Going back to the CIA's sponsorship of the 1953 coup against Prime Minister Mohammed Mossadegh, that the CIA had been engaging in such covert action had been widely known and reported. Indeed, six months before the congressional dispute, the *New York Times* ran a story saying the CIA had asked Congress for $19 million for covert action to destabilize Iraq and to curb Iran's expansionist ambitions. The story said $4 million was to be spent on spreading propaganda against the Islamic government in Iran, about the same amount as in the previous year.[139]

Thus, when a story appeared in the October 26, 1995, issue of Congressional Quarterly's *Congressional Monitor*, it revealed nothing new about the CIA's operations in Iran.[140] The story said House Speaker Newt Gingrich was pushing for a provision in the fiscal 1996 intelligence authorization bill to provide more funding for covert action in Iran, assuming President Clinton issued an intelligence finding authorizing such operations. A subsequent story in the *Wall Street Journal* said Gingrich wanted to provide $18 million for the operations. Specter, as chairman of the Senate Select Committee on Intelligence, wanted to retain the current level of funding.

After the *Congressional Monitor* article appeared, one of the four reporters who wrote it was chatting with a security officer of the Senate committee. The reporter mentioned that the information had come from a House member who sat on both the House Select Committee on Intelligence and the House Appropriations' national security subcommittee.

After the Senate staffer reported the conversation to Specter, Specter asked the Justice Department to launch an FBI investigation into the leak of classified information and to interview the House members. His letter, cosigned by Sen. Bob Kerrey of Nebraska, the ranking Democrat on the committee, was dated November 2, 1995. When the FBI took no action, Specter became more determined.

According to Jamie S. Gorelick, then the deputy attorney general, the reason for the delay in interviewing House members was that Specter's letter had initially been overlooked. She said that because Specter's committee staff informed the Justice Department that Specter's letter requesting an investigation could only be seen by Atty. Gen. Janet Reno herself, the letter "avoided our log-in and tracking system." The letter "went to the attorney general, but she did not know there was no other action copy tasked to someone else to respond. That was a glitch in our system. So the letter got lost essentially for a month. It was retrieved at the beginning of December after a call from committee staff asking the status of it."[141]

Meanwhile, the CIA had asked for a leak investigation. On December 22, Gorelick informed Specter that an investigation had been started, but that was not good enough. As if the FBI had nothing else to do but obey Specter's commands, Specter called a special, closed hearing purely to badger the Justice Department about why agents had not immediately been dispatched to interview members of the House. After that, the FBI interviewed the three House members who fell within the *Congressional Monitor* reporter's description: Representatives C. W. Bill Young, a Florida Republican; Jerry Lewis, a California Republican; and Norm Dicks, a Washington Democrat. The FBI also tried to interview the reporter but was rebuffed. The fact that a leak investigation had been launched remained a secret.[142]

The three congressmen flatly denied being the source of the leak. The FBI probe never determined who had provided the information. Leak investigations rarely produce results and are considered by most FBI and Justice Department officials to be a waste of time that drains resources from more serious matters. Moreover, requests for leak investigations are often politically motivated. When he was director of central intelligence, William J. Casey would demand leak investigations when stories portrayed him or the agency in a bad light. Meanwhile, Casey himself was leaking classified information to journalists such as Bob Woodward.

Since Specter had become embroiled in a dispute with Gingrich over funding levels in Iran, some thought his insistence on FBI interviews of House members was a way of exacting retribution from those who disagreed with him. What is clear is that Specter used the heavy club of a hearing to try to enforce his will.

"They [Specter's committee] wanted more aggressive action sooner, and I think they were unhappy with the delay we had in responding to the letter, which was a result of a flaw in our logging system," Gorelick said. "We wrote them a letter saying we were going to do it. They viewed this as quite serious and were concerned about it."

Specter had no comment.[143]

Like Specter, Sen. Dianne Feinstein, a California Democrat, yells and is "real tough. You see a lot of turnover [on her staff]," a CRS staffer said. "She has a horrible temper. I've seen her really be very sharp with her staff, hard, not listening. Not able to know when people have done their work and are trying to communicate something valuable." In her first six months in office, Feinstein lost fourteen aides, including eleven who quit.[144]

A CRS staffer described Sen. Robert C. Byrd, the Democrat from West Virginia, as a "tyrant," and Mitch McConnell, the Kentucky Republican, as "mean." Sen. Alfonse M. D'Amato, the New York Republican, "blows up and says outrageous, mean things," the staffer said, and Sen. Ted Stevens, the Alaska Republican, is also out of control.

Melvin F. Parker, a former Capitol Police officer, said he was assigned to the House side of the Capitol when Stevens walked in. "I asked him to show identification," Parker said. "He flung his card at me."[145]

Another congressional staffer who has worked with Stevens said that like many members, Stevens bristles if a staffer says hello to him.

"If he wants to acknowledge you, he will," the staffer said. "He is a little king. . . . The Hill is the last plantation. You have a lot of egos to deal with."

"This is a situation where these guys pretty much have absolute power, absolute control," a CRS staffer said. "If no one calls them to account for their behavior, they just sort of think it's normal. They don't see how they are perceived. They live in this atmosphere where that may be the norm or not unusual."

Like many other members, Stevens expects his staff to perform personal errands, such as walking his dog. Two former aides to Rep. Bart Gordon, a Tennessee Democrat, have said he regularly used staffers to perform household chores and to write his checks for personal expenses. His administrative assistant, Eric Altshule, said staffers sometimes care for the congressman's house, but "it's not part of anybody's job."[146]

In the 104th Congress, which ended in January 1997, Specter was chairman of the Senate Select Committee on Intelligence and of the Senate Judiciary's subcommittee on terrorism, technology, and government information. A CRS staffer said that Specter used interns on the staff of the subcommittee to answer constituent mail.

"They have an office with interns just answering constituent mail," the congressional staffer said.

In contrast, Sen. San Nunn, a Georgia Democrat, was known as a "stand-up guy." Sen. Richard G. Lugar, the Indiana Republican, has the same reputation. Others who have a reputation for treating staff well are Senators Max Baucus, the Montana Democrat; Barbara Boxer, the California Democrat; Dale Bumpers, the Arkansas Democrat; and Orrin G. Hatch, the Utah Republican, a CRS staffer said.

Sen. Olympia J. Snowe, a Maine Republican, "asks good questions," a CRS staffer said. "She has a good grasp of lots of issues." Similarly, Sen. Pete V. Domenici, a Republican from New Mexico, is "a cool guy, the salt of the earth," the CRS staffer said.

When he was a lobbyist for the Interior Department, Talmadge Reed recalled that Domenici resisted pressure from constituents to overturn an Interior Department decision to close an office of the Geological Survey in Artesia, New Mexico. Costing $2,500,000 a year to maintain, the office had outlived its usefulness. The mayor of the town "raised hell," Reed said. At a meeting, "the senator looked at the mayor and said, 'I have to agree with the Geological Survey.' Which is one of the few times I've seen members come down in favor of the government in front of us. I've seen them many times later have a staffer say, 'He had to put on a show.' I always admired Pete Domenici for having done that."

Of all the legislators, few get higher marks than Sen. Ted Kennedy for having a crack staff and being well prepared, thorough, and effective. Since his recent marriage to attorney Victoria Anne Reggie, Kennedy has curtailed his drinking and gets nothing but praise from both sides of the aisle.

"I've never seen him say, 'To hell with you all, I'm not going to move from my position,'" former senator Alan Simpson, a Wyoming Democrat, said. "Because if you do that, you're not a legislator. You either have to learn to take a crumb when you can't get a loaf, or you have to learn to cry yourself to sleep at night."

Other members have proved heroic. Sen. Bill Frist, a Tennessee Republican who is a surgeon, revived a man who had gone into cardiac arrest in the Dirksen Senate Office Building. On another occasion, the doctor saved the life of an eighty-four-year-old woman who had choked on her food at a California beach club.

When Sen. Ben Nighthorse Campbell, a Colorado Republican who is a former police officer and Olympic judo team member, saw a man purposely push Sen. Strom Thurmond in the Senate subway station, he went into action.

A Capitol Police officer had tried to subdue the man who attacked Thurmond, but the man fought back. Campbell removed the officer's radio to call for assistance. Campbell then subdued and handcuffed the suspect.[147]

Thurmond did not seem to notice what had happened.

"Everything you hear about Thurmond is true," a CRS staffer said, referring to the ninety-four-year-old senator, the oldest senator in American history. "He has long left this planet. He reads big-print script and even then struggles. As chairman of committees, he is supposed to be running a hearing. If he doesn't follow exactly what is written for him, he can't find his way back."[148]

In April 1996, Thurmond, while riding coach class, reportedly shoved a USAir flight attendant who would not let him hang his coat in the first-class compartment.[149] Chris Kelley Cimko, Thurmond's spokesperson, said Thurmond always hangs his coat in the first-class section and had never been told he could not. The attendant spoke in a "very discourteous tone," Cimko said.

Of all the members, perhaps none is as dense as Sonny Bono, the former straight man to Cher. A Republican from Palm Springs, California, Bono went to work driving a meat company truck after high school. He never voted until he was fifty-three. But he composed the immortal "I Got You Babe," from which he still receives royalties, helping to give him a net worth of $2 million.

Before entering Congress, Bono served as mayor of Palm

Springs. Marilyn Baker, who ran his mayoral campaign, later told the *Los Angeles Times* that she had to present Bono with a script so he could conduct official business. "For call to order, I wrote, 'Sit,'" she said. "For salute the flag, I wrote, 'Stand up, face flag, mouth words.' For roll call, I wrote, 'When you hear your name, say yes.'"[150] She served on his staff for three months before quitting in disgust.

When her former husband was elected to Congress in November 1994, Cher said, "I have no belief in the system. So Sonny's perfectly at home there."[151]

Soon, her meaning became clear. During a Judiciary Committee hearing, Bono complained that the members were becoming needlessly bogged down in "technical" matters and legalese— which is, after all, what laws are. "You break down words to the nth degree, and sometimes I find it rather disgusting," Bono intoned. "We have a very simple and concise bill here," he said on another occasion, "and I think it would be to everyone's pleasure if we would just pass this thing." Rep. Charles E. Schumer, a New York Democrat, shot back, "We're making laws here, not sausages." Perhaps it was a reference to Bono's days as the owner of an Italian restaurant.

Faye Fiore, who covers the California congressional delegation for the *Los Angeles Times*, asked Bono how he planned to cut the deficit and still cut taxes.

"Cut government. Just get rid of it," Bono remarked. "Some departments are running at two billion dollars a year, you start chopping departments like that and—"[152]

"What departments are those?" Fiore asked.

"HRD."

"HRD? What's that?"

"Health and Human, uh, Health and Human . . ." Bono peeked outside his office and asked his staff for help. "What is, uh, Health and Human what?"

"Services!" a voice yelled back.

"Services," Bono echoed.

"HHS!" the voice added.

"HHS!" Bono repeated. "I was right about the department but wrong about the letters."

A glance at the Washington telephone directory gives some idea of the scope of services Bono suggested should be eliminated. Among other agencies, Health and Human Services encompasses the Social Security Administration, the National Institutes of Health, the Public Health Service, the Food and Drug Administration, the Centers for Disease Control and Prevention, and the Office of the Surgeon General. Thus HHS sends out Social Security checks, runs Medicare and Medicaid, administers research grants to find cures for cancer and AIDS, and prevents companies from selling drugs that are unsafe or ineffective.

Bono rarely speaks in Congress, but when he does, he sounds like a third grader trying to make sense out of the world. His theme is that everything is really simple, as in the case of the government shutdown over the issue of a balanced budget. "Now, how complicated is this issue?" he asked one day. "Let me tell my colleagues how complicated this issue is. Why did all this start? It started because we had a position that we should balance the budget. Now, we could lie to the American people and tell them not to worry about it, that they will keep getting their money and should not worry about it; they will get it forever. But, see, it runs out in fourteen years. Everybody admits that. So that is like saying, well, yeah, everything is going to crash, but we should not worry about it."[153]

Rep. Bruce F. Vento, a Minnesota Democrat, reminded Bono that the problem was government employees were not getting their money then because the Republican-controlled Congress was not passing appropriations bills. "It is our responsibility, in terms of acting on this, to make certain that these bills, not for fourteen years but for this year, in 1996, are enacted," Vento said.

In another of his rare statements, Bono congratulated his colleagues for "sticking to their guns" on the budget issue. "Everything is rhetoric," he added inexplicably.

Even voting seems too hard for Bono, who—like many other members—regularly takes to the floor to explain he was "unavoidably detained" and therefore could not vote. Pointlessly, he then states how he would have voted had he cast a vote.

The *Progressive* magazine named Bono one of the "10 Dimmest Bulbs in Congress," and *Washingtonian* magazine, in its catalog of the best and worst members, listed him charitably as "no rocket scientist." The *Washington Post* called him the "idiot savant from way beyond the Beltway."[154] Just what talents Bono had as an idiot savant, the *Post* did not say.

If nothing else, Bono has become a favorite subject of late-night shows. David Letterman noted during the government shutdown of 1996, "They sent all nonessential government employees home. Sonny Bono showed up anyway."

But Bono's constituents love him. In the last election, he got 57 percent of the votes cast. He may be a dolt, but Bono is almost as well known as Elvis Presley. In Congress, celebrity is all.

Follow the Money

In the 1960s and 1970s, it was not unusual for Capitol Police officers who were assigned to examine packages to find wads of cash intended for members of Congress. "We had two gentlemen who came through the southwest door of the Dirksen Building," said Jimmy Young, a former Capitol Police officer. "They had a briefcase. So I asked them to open it. They said, 'We'll open it, but can we do it in private?' There was a table in the corner, and I told them to open it there. It [the briefcase] was full of money."[155]

Young estimated it to be several hundred thousand dollars. "I asked, 'Where the hell are you going with that?' One of them said, 'Well, let's just say it's campaign funds.'"

Young waved them through. "If you investigated, you'd stand a chance of losing your job," said Wayne Beckett, who was in charge of inspecting Capitol Police x-ray machines and said he was told of similar incidents by other officers.

Members often retired as multimillionaires on their government salaries.

"Without naming the senator, one practice was to sell him one hundred head of cattle for, say, one hundred dollars a head," said J. Stanley Kimmitt, the former secretary of the Senate.[156] "Then about three months later, buy them back at fifteen hundred dollars a head. It was a nice way to increase a senator's capital."

Still another way to influence members was to give them inside tips. "A lot of them [members] got tips on stocks and made extra money that way, from inside information from Wall Street or companies that were going to issue new stock," Roy L. Elson, a former administrative assistant to Sen. Carl Hayden, the Arizona Democrat, said. "They would tell them in order to get access or as a trade for support on legislation."[157]

In his book, Robert G. (Bobby) Baker, a former page who became secretary to Senate majority leader Lyndon B. Johnson, described how, on behalf of Texas interests, he personally delivered $25,000 in cash to an aide to Sen. Estes Kefauver to influence Kefauver's findings on an antitrust issue.[158] Baker himself was convicted of pocketing contributions from savings and loan executives meant to influence key members of Congress debating a bill to increase taxes on the S&L industry.[159]

"I have personally taken sealed envelopes full of significant cash and delivered them to a senator who was in a campaign," Kimmitt said.

Lobbyists often supplied members with women. "There was a cathouse right across from the New Senate Office Building where the Hart Building is," Elson said. "They were mainly housewives who were making a little extra money. Some members went across to it [courtesy of lobbyists]."

In her effort to promote agricultural interests, Paula Parkinson, a well-endowed blond lobbyist, said she had sex with eight members of Congress. The story broke after she took a Florida golf trip in 1980 with three members, Republicans Tom Evans of Delaware, Tom Railsback of Illinois, and Dan Quayle of Indiana. Evans, who was married, said he had been dating Parkinson for several months and shared a room with her in the cottage they all shared on the golf outing. Quayle announced that he had roomed with lobbyist William Hecht. "I guess you want to make something homosexual out of it," Quayle remarked to reporters.[160]

All three members later voted against a crop insurance bill that Parkinson opposed. She went on to pose nude for *Playboy*, revealing that she had had sex with three congressmen in their offices. "The whole thing was knowing that someone could burst in at any moment," she explained. Her estranged husband apologized for creating a "sexual Frankenstein."

But when it comes to influencing members, money is more reliable than sex. In theory, payments from corporations to members had long been illegal. Special interests—known as factions when the government was being formed—have always tried to influence legislation. In the early days, they tended to be disorganized. Yet scandals such as the Crédit Mobilier affair of 1872, when Rep. Oakes Ames distributed railroad stocks to members in return for their support of railroad legislation, focused attention on the need for reform.

In 1907, Congress passed the first federal campaign finance law. Called the Tillman Act, it banned corporations or national banks from making a "money contribution in connection with any election" of candidates for federal office. With that law, and another in 1943 that extended the ban to labor unions, Congress established the principle that organizations with large aggregations of wealth should not be allowed to unduly influence elections. Otherwise, the principle that every citizen should have one vote would be undermined. If those who controlled corporations could pump cash into an election, they would have undue influence on the political process.

"Who are to be the electors of the federal representatives?" asked James Madison, a key drafter of the Constitution, in *The Federalist Papers*. "Not the rich, more than the poor. . . ."

But in passing the 1907 law, Congress also established a tradition of creating enough cavernous loopholes so that no legislation would unduly prevent members from getting money if they wanted it. Thus, the 1907 act proved to be irrelevant when it turned out that corporations could still contribute to candidates between elections.

In 1923, hearings began into what became known as the

Teapot Dome scandal. An official of the company that had leased a naval oil reserve in Wyoming called Teapot Dome had bribed the official in charge of leasing and had contributed generously to the Republican Party so it could pay off its 1920 campaign debt. Because the contribution had been made in a nonelection year, it did not fall under the 1907 law. The public outcry over the scandal led Congress to pass the 1925 Corrupt Practices Act. The new law incorporated the previous ban on corporate contributions and applied the ban to any federal campaign. The law also set limits on the amount a candidate could spend, and it required reporting of campaign finances. But it included the usual array of loopholes. Reporting requirements were vague. Candidates could evade the spending limitations by funneling the contributions they received through separate, outside committees—now known as political action committees (PACs)—which did not have to report expenditures.[161]

Often, candidates reported that they had received nothing and spent nothing on their campaigns. That was obviously untrue, but Congress had made sure no one would suffer any consequences for violating the law. Characteristically, the law included no provision for enforcement; no one was ever prosecuted under the act. In any case, J. Edgar Hoover, the longtime director of the FBI, was averse to investigating politicians.

Enforced or not, the Tillman Act served as the basic campaign finance law until 1971, when Congress again came up with legislation that gave the appearance of reform while allowing members to receive even more money for their campaigns than before. Combined with amendments in 1974, 1976, and 1979, the Federal Election Campaign Act tightened reporting requirements and set new limits on contributions. Much of the legislation was passed in response to disclosures during the Watergate scandal that at least twenty-one corporations had illegally contributed $968,000 in corporate funds to 1972 presidential campaigns, most of it to Richard M. Nixon's reelection effort.[162] Just how much money corporations contributed to other candidates in this way is difficult to pinpoint. Estimates begin at 10 percent of total campaign funds.[163]

As in the past, the new laws created so many new loopholes

that the legislation made a mockery of reform and fueled an explosive infusion of cash into election campaigns. When they passed the laws, members had only a glimmer of understanding of what they were doing. Few comprehended the meaning of the most important provision, which allowed contributions from political committees formed by government contractors. Previously, if a company or union had a government contract, it could not form a PAC. In enumerating the act's thirty-one provisions, *Congressional Quarterly Almanac* listed the change, which was pushed by business and labor, third to last. Yet the provision created a monster. From supplying the government with pens and missiles to organizing employees, nearly all major companies and labor unions have contracts with the government. Most PACs are formed by business or labor, although some are created by ideological or professional groups. Thus the change permitted the explosive growth of political action committees as a mechanism for funding campaigns.[164]

A 1975 advisory opinion by the newly established Federal Election Commission further fueled the growth of PACs. Requested by Sun Oil Company, the ruling established that PACs could solicit money from employees of the companies that set them up, not just from their stockholders.

In 1974, there were 608 PACs. By 1994, there were 3,954. They included 1,660 corporate PACs, 333 labor PACs, and 1,169 trade association or other special interest PACs. In 1994, an astounding $724 million was poured into House and Senate races. More than a third of this came from PACs. Since 1990, PACs have given $427 million to these candidates.

"I'm not sure any of us knew what PACs meant," said former representative Romano L. Mazzoli, a Kentucky Democrat who voted for the measure. "It sounded wonderful—a lot of little people coming together so their money means something. In practice, it became distorted."[165]

Under the bizarre system that Congress created, corporations, labor unions, and other special interests still could not contribute directly to candidates. Instead, they could organize PACs, provide offices for them, underwrite fund-raising efforts among their own employees or members, and pay salaries and other costs of PAC administrators, who decide which candidates should receive the money. While corporate employees or union members contributed from their salaries, they often felt coerced to contribute.

"One of the least understood aspects of PACs is they are voluntary in quotes. There is collegial coercion to contribute," said Jim Leach, an Iowa Republican who refuses PAC money.

The effect was the same as if the money had come from corporate or union treasuries. Just like PACs, companies and unions are composed of people. Contributions made by a company ultimately come out of the pockets of stockholders or—indirectly—from corporate employees. Contributions by unions come from union members. But while Congress outlawed contributions by companies or unions to candidates, it allowed PACs to stand in for the companies and unions. Under the "reform," special interests could still accumulate large sums of money, and they could still direct where the money went. Only now, under the guise of reform, it was legal.

While Congress placed limits on the amounts PAC's could contribute, the limits gave PACs far more muscle than individuals had. While individuals can give up to $1,000 per candidate per election, a PAC can give $5,000. Thus, for a primary and a general election, PACs can contribute up to $10,000, compared with $2,000 for individuals. An aggregation of PACs with similar interests—in one industry, for example—can quickly come up with hundreds of thousands of dollars per candidate.

Yet this was just the start of the loopholes. If companies, labor unions, or wealthy individuals contributed directly to political parties for get-out-the-vote efforts, all restrictions were waived. In some cases, these so-called soft-money donations from corporations and wealthy individuals are as large as $1 million each. In October 1994, Amway Corporation alone gave $2.5 million in soft money to the Republican National Committee. In 1996, the major national parties received more than $200 million in soft money alone for congressional and presidential races.

While soft money is not supposed to be used to help individual candidates, and the donors are not supposed to be able to specify which candidates should receive the money, these prohibitions are routinely evaded. In his diary, former senator Bob Packwood referred to a discussion he had had with Sen. Phil Gramm, who was head of the Republican Senatorial Committee, the party's fund-raising arm for senatorial candidates. According to Packwood, Gramm was talking about funneling $100,000 in soft money from the party into Packwood's campaign.

"What was said in that room would be enough to convict us all of something," Packwood wrote on March 6, 1992. Referring to himself in the third person, he went on: "Now, of course, you know there can't be any legal connection between this money and Senator Packwood, but we know that it will be used for his benefit. . . . I think it's a felony, I'm not sure. This is an area of law I don't want to know." When he surrendered the diary to the ethics committee, Packwood altered this portion. He later claimed the entry was inaccurate. Gramm said he had done nothing improper.[166]

Senate Democrats have gone even further, instructing donors to credit soft-money contributions secretly to individual candidates. The practice, known as tallying, is an obvious violation of the spirit of campaign finance laws.[167]

Even if the rules are not evaded, by defraying overhead expenses, soft money magnifies the impact of regular contributions to candidates. If R. J. Reynolds Tobacco Co. pays for the photocopying machine and the telephone bill, a candidate can use all of his contributions for advertising.

Yet soft money is now used so freely that, under the guise of educating voters on the issues, it pays for ads that promote candidates. For example, the parties may use soft money to pay for ads by a senator saying his opponent is soft on crime. So long as they don't explicitly instruct voters to vote for a candidate, such ads are claimed by the parties to comply with the law. In a letter to the Justice Department, Common Cause challenged that interpretation and called for the appointment of an independent counsel to investigate what Common Cause president Ann McBride called "massive violations" of the campaign finance laws by both the major 1996 presidential candidates. Responding to that complaint and others, Atty. Gen. Janet Reno formed a task force to investigate campaign finance law violations. Regardless of the outcome, the soft money loophole alone guts legislation going back to 1907 to ban corporate contributions to campaigns.

In the Alice-in-Wonderland atmosphere Congress created, lobbyists may contribute their time to political campaigns. Individual lobbyists can "bundle" checks from individuals with similar interests and give them to a candidate in a single envelope—thus evading the contribution limits. In this way, MBNA America Bank gave $143,339 to Sen. William V. Roth, a Delaware Republican, while Amway Corporation and its distributors gave $133,870 to Rep. Sue Myrick, a North Carolina Republican. Or lobbyists can accomplish the same thing by holding fund-raisers where hundreds of people give $1,000 each. Cassidy and Associates, a major Washington lobbying firm, holds dozens of such fund-raisers a year in its boardroom, ingratiating its lobbyists with members.

Rep. Bud Shuster, a Pennsylvania Republican, shamelessly goes even further. According to press reports, he is said to on occasion lodge with Ann Eppard, a lobbyist who was previously his congressional aide and now makes hundreds of thousands of dollars representing clients before the House Transportation and Infrastructure Committee, which he chairs. While Eppard is no longer on Shuster's congressional payroll, she continues on Shuster's campaign payroll as his top political aide. Shuster insisted he doesn't "live" with Eppard and that he and his wife, Pat, "have a small place here in town."[168]

Members can even create their own leadership PACs, soliciting money directly from special interests and using it for any purpose they choose. In theory, leadership PACs give their money to other members of Congress to help promote good candidates. In fact, the money buys their support and votes. By doling out hundreds of thousands of dollars a year from special interests like tobacco companies and casinos, members of Congress get to be speaker, majority or minority leader, or party whip.

"When the leadership gives to candidates, especially freshmen, and later on the leader puts pressure on a member to vote his way, the member may vote in the interests of that leader and not in the interest of a constituent," said Rep. Nancy Johnson, a Connecticut Republican who heads the House ethics committee.

Yet buying votes is only part of the story. Very little of the total money received by leadership PACs actually winds up being given to other members. A study by Public Citizen, a consumer advocacy group, found that of $111 million contributed to leadership PACs from 1984 to 1994, only about 15 percent went to other candidates. The rest, as Joan Claybrook, president of Public Citizen, has pointed out, was used for members' personal expenses like meals and car rentals or for other costs of running for office. Newt Gingrich spent less than one percent of the $6.1 million his leadership PAC received on contributions to other candidates. Bob Dole spent 11 percent, Ted Kennedy spent 10 percent, and Rep. Edward J. Markey, a Massachusetts Democrat, spent three percent.

In concept, leadership PACs are grand slush funds of the type created by Richard Nixon when he ran for vice president in 1952. After the *New York Post* revealed Nixon had secretly accepted $18,000 from private contributors to defray his personal expenses, he addressed the issue in what became his "Checkers" speech. Because of its seamy appearance, Dwight Eisenhower almost dumped Nixon as his running mate. Yet the only difference between the Nixon slush fund and leadership PACs is that Congress has legally sanctioned leadership PACs and, like other PACs, required them to file public reports on receipts and expenditures. In legalizing what was once recognized as an abuse, Congress demonstrated to what lengths it will go to protect its own.

Unlike money contributed to leadership PACs, political contributions given to candidates during campaigns may not be used for personal expenses. But in the unreal world of campaign finance, the line between the two is almost nonexistent. A *Los Angeles Times* study found that in the 1990 election, more than half the $466 million that candidates spent was "virtually

Follow the Money

unrelated to contacting voters." Candidates often used campaign money for leasing or buying cars used for personal business.

Illegal as that may be, Congress has made sure few violators will ever be called to task. The Federal Election Commission, which is supposed to enforce election laws, is so understaffed that it can only audit a dozen campaigns per election. The commission could not possibly sort out which expenses are legitimately related to campaigns. Moreover, Congress gave the agency no power to levy fines. The FEC must negotiate penalties with those who violate election laws or hope the Justice Department prosecutes the offenders. Because the FEC has six commissioners split evenly between Republicans and Democrats, controversial cases before the commission go unresolved. If it would be difficult to imagine a more useless agency, that is because Congress wanted it that way.

Members can also set up for themselves state PACs that do not have to abide by the federal limitations and do not have to report to the Federal Election Commission. States generally have less stringent reporting requirements and contribution limits. While foreign governments and corporations are barred from contributing, they can easily hide the source of the funds by funneling them through foreigners living in the United States or legally funnel the money to campaigns through their American subsidiaries. In this way, Democratic operative John Huang raised more than $1 million from Lippo Group, an Indonesian conglomerate, and other Asian sources.[169] Finally, candidates can orchestrate so-called "independent expenditures" to buy campaign advertising, totally evading the legal limits on contributions. In the 1996 election, Sen. Alfonse D'Amato, a New York Republican, urged Republican senatorial candidates across the country to hire his political consultant, Arthur Finkelstein. He then funneled millions of dollars in contributions from PACs and individuals through the consultant so that Finkelstein could coordinate how the money was spent for television ads. The effect was the same as if the money had been funneled through one committee, which would have been illegal because

107

the contributions would not have been made independently. Using such stratagems, Senate Republican candidates received $7 million in 1996 alone.[170] The Democratic Party used a similar ruse to evade the law by laundering money through state parties before handing it to the DNC's media production company, Squier Knapp Ochs.[171]

In his diary, Packwood referred to this subterfuge and the way he made sure neither the contributions nor the expenditures were tied to him. "Apparently the Auto Dealers are willing to do some spending against [Les AuCoin, his opponent]. Of course, we can't know anything about it. . . . We've got to destroy any evidence we've ever had . . . so that we have no connection with any independent expenditure."[172]

If such transparent evasions sound more like the way organized crime launders drug money than the way a free country maintains democracy, it is because that is the way Congress wants it. As a result, powerful interest groups fund elections just as they did when the Capitol Police routinely found suitcases full of cash coming into congressional offices. By all accounts, the amount of corporate and special interest money now supporting candidates far exceeds the sums parceled out in the old days. An entire industry with its own jargon—*maxing out, salting, sewer money*—has been founded on guiding the money flow from special interests to candidates. In turn, groups such as Common Cause and the Center for Responsive Politics have been founded to chart the money and the many spigots candidates use to receive it.

While some of the contributions have to be disclosed, they are so pervasive and so widely accepted that it is impossible for a voter to make any decisions based on the data. Newspapers run dizzying lists of PAC contributions, and public interest groups list contributions to members on the Internet.* But the sad fact

---

* Listings of contributions to members of Congress can be found on the Internet through Project Vote Smart at http://www.vote-smart.org/congress/; through FECINFO at http://www.tray.com; through the Center for Responsive Politics' Follow the Money at http://www.crp.org; and through Common Cause's website at http://www.commoncause.org.

is that most citizens do not know who represents them in Congress. Asked in a survey taken by the *Washington Post*, the Kaiser Family Foundation, and Harvard University, only 24 percent knew who their congressman and senator were. Only 53 percent knew who the Speaker of the House was. To suggest that the public should study lists of contributions, remember which candidates got substantial sums from hundreds of special interest groups, match the information with the thousands of bills and resolutions members vote on, and then draw some conclusion from it all is unrealistic. Short of genuine reform, the only alternative available to the public is to vote for those candidates who refuse to accept PAC money. Because there are so few of them, most voters are left with no choice but to vote for candidates who take PAC money.

Only three senators—Edward M. Kennedy and John Kerry, both Democrats from Massachusetts, and Herb Kohl, a Wisconsin Democrat—take no PAC money, according to the Center for Responsive Politics. Eighteen House members—only four percent—do not take PAC money. They are Bill Archer, a Texas Republican; Jay Dickey, an Arkansas Republican; Wayne T. Gilchrest, a Maryland Republican; Bill Goodling, a Pennsylvania Republican; James C. Greenwood, a Pennsylvania Republican; Peter Hoekstra, a Michigan Republican; Steve Horn, a California Republican; John Hostettler, an Indiana Republican; Bob Inglis, a South Carolina Republican; Jim Leach, an Iowa Republican; Edward J. Markey, a Massachusetts Democrat; Martin T. Meehan, a Massachusetts Democrat; Rob Portman, an Ohio Republican; Glenn Poshard, an Illinois Democrat; Ralph Regula, an Ohio Republican; Mark Sanford, a South Carolina Republican; Nick Smith, a Michigan Republican; and Zach Wamp, a Tennessee Republican.

Many of these members could afford to refuse PAC money because they are independently wealthy. Senator Kohl financed his 1988 election with $7.5 million of his own money. In fact, 30 percent of U.S. senators are millionaires, as are more than fifty representatives. Among the wealthiest are John Kerry, with $760 million; Kohl, with $250 million; Jay Rockefeller, a West Virginia Democrat, with $200 million; Dianne Feinstein, a

California Democrat, with $50 million; and Frank Lautenberg, a New Jersey Democrat, with $40 million. The wealthiest House member, Rodney Frelinghuysen, a New Jersey Republican, has $30 million.

Some candidates who say they turn aside PAC contributions wind up secretly taking them. Three days after Mark R. Warner, who ran for the Senate in Virginia largely on his own money, vowed to refuse PAC money, his fund-raisers sent out a letter explaining how PACs could contribute to him anyway. The letter suggested donating the money to a Democratic Party organization and "tallying" it to his campaign. Warner, who contributed nearly all of the funds for his campaign from his own telecommunications fortune, said he knew nothing about the letter.[173]

Rep. Edward J. Markey, a Massachusetts Democrat, and Sen. John Kerry both claim they refuse PAC money, but both receive major contributions that are bundled by businesses. Markey, in particular, gets contributions from the telecommunications and finance industries, whose legislation he oversees.[174]

Even the porous laws that Congress has passed are too restrictive for some members. Each year, the Federal Election Commission initiates more than three hundred enforcement actions over campaign law violations, most by candidates for Congress.[175]

"It could probably be shown by facts and figures that there is no distinctly native American criminal class except Congress," Mark Twain said. Echoing the sentiment, humorist Will Rogers noted, "Congress is the best money can buy."

In the past ten years, more than sixty members have been prosecuted and convicted or have become the subject of congressional ethics committee investigations for illegal or improper conduct. From House Speaker Jim Wright of Texas to Rep. Mario Biaggi of New York, from House majority whip Tony Coelho of California to Rep. Bill Chappell of Florida, members of Congress have entangled themselves in an endless web of improper or illegal deals, most of them having to do with money.

When the FBI set up its ABSCAM "sting" in 1980, the Bureau captured on videotape the greed of seven members of Congress eager to trade the power of their office for money. One of them, Sen. Harrison A. Williams Jr., a New Jersey Democrat, assured an FBI agent posing as an Arab businessman he would help him secure a government contract and a resident visa in exchange for stock in a Virginia titanium mine. On the tape, Williams boasted of the influence he would bring to bear on behalf of the bogus sheikh.[176]

"[I am] in a position to go to, ah, well, you know, right to the top on this one," Williams said. The senator pledged to do "everything in my power" to advance the sheikh's cause.

While accepting a bribe of $50,000, Rep. Michael J. "Ozzie" Myers, a Pennsylvania Democrat, boasted, "Bullshit walks, money talks." Rep. John W. Jenrette Jr., a South Carolina Democrat, was videotaped telling the FBI agent, "I've got larceny in my blood." And Rep. Richard Kelly, a Florida Republican, asked, "Does it show?" as he stuffed $25,000 in cash into his suit, coat, and pants pockets.[177]

Williams and six congressmen—including Myers, Jenrette, and Kelly—were convicted of bribery and other crimes in the scandal. Significantly, of all the members offered the bait, only one—Sen. Larry Pressler, a South Dakota Republican—did not bite. "Wait a minute," Pressler said. "What you are suggesting may be illegal."

To be sure, members routinely deny that money influences them, as though PACs give money for altruistic reasons. Indeed, a mythology has been created by members who assert that in Congress, unlike in the rest of the world, money has no impact.

According to this line, PACs are not evil but rather strengthen democracy by encouraging little people to contribute small amounts. Members have to finance their increasingly expensive campaigns in some way, and voters at least know in the case of PACs where the money is coming from. The money may buy access to members, but no one is going to be bought off by PAC contributions.

"I can't think of any issue when I had a PAC that wanted me to vote for an issue and that entered into the picture," said Sen.

John B. Breaux, a Louisiana Democrat who is one of the top recipients of PAC money.[178]

Do members consider whether they will lose PAC contributions they are already receiving if they vote against PAC interests?

"It has never occurred to me that if I vote against a PAC, it will not give me money," said former representative Robert S. Walker, a Pennsylvania Republican.[179] "I'm not sure I could give you a list of the PACs which have contributed to me."

"I presume most of them want good government and are motivated by the highest ideals of American democracy," said Sen. Thad Cochran, a Mississippi Republican whose own leadership PAC has handed out $203,481 to other Republican senators. "They would like to see someone who is well qualified elected to serve, whether on the local level, state government, or in Washington."[180]

"Most PACs are made up of literally hundreds of people," Sen. Orrin G. Hatch, a Utah Republican, said. "They contribute to a PAC to contribute to people who support their point of view."[181]

To be sure, artful lobbyists, even without PACs behind them, can have an impact. Nearly thirteen thousand people lobby Congress, an average of twenty-four for each voting member. "You study every congressman and senator," said Charles (Chuck) Lipsen, a longtime Washington lobbyist.[182] "You review what he came from, his life. You know more about him than he knows about himself. You talk about things that he is interested in."

In his diary, Senator Packwood repeatedly admitted favoring lobbyists who had helped him, making the lobbyists rich. Packwood fostered an impression that if they wanted access to Packwood or his staff, it would be helpful to hire Packwood's friend, Ronald Crawford, a lobbyist for Shell Oil Company.

When Crawford urgently needed Packwood's help in 1989, Packwood wrote, "Ron, I still hate the oil companies, but I'll do you a favor." The Senate Finance Committee, on which Packwood was the senior Republican, then passed a special tax bill Shell had sought. The bill became law.[183]

In turn, when Packwood wanted companies to hire his estranged wife, Crawford agreed to "put up $5,500 a year" toward her salary, Packwood wrote.

Besides such favors and contributions, lobbyists use an array of other emoluments to ingratiate themselves with members. During 1992 and 1993, more than eighty-five members of Congress participated in 181 trips sponsored by the health care industry, including trips to Puerto Rico, Paris, and Montego Bay. New congressional rules have banned such trips, along with meals, but Congress made sure the rules could be evaded. If trips are to attend meetings or speeches or to gather facts in connection with their law-making duties, members can take all the free trips they want. Thus, twenty-four members traveled to Boca Raton, Florida, and Hot Springs, Virginia, at the expense of the Securities Industry Association. In one year, Rep. Patricia Schroeder, a Colorado Democrat, alone accepted trips worth $48,259.

Moreover, under the new rules, members can still accept "finger food," so Washington caterers imaginatively began serving everything from smoked salmon wrapped in dill profiterole, seared Asian tuna rolls, and house-cured prosciutto duck breast to entire meals of shrimp, steak, and grilled vegetables on huge skewers.

Since Congress makes the rules, Congress can approve waivers of the rules. So the House and Senate ethics committees routinely grant exceptions to the rules so members can take lavish congressional trips paid for by private interests. In 1996, for example, two senators, 18 House members, and 124 staffers took $500,000 in trips financed by Taiwanese business and government organizations.[184]

The biggest loophole in the new rules allowed special interests to take members to restaurants so long as they called the meals fund-raisers and gave them contributions. "I had lunch with a member and asked how the gift ban is," former representative Peter H. Kostmayer, a Pennsylvania Democrat, said. Referring to a private club for members, lobbyists, and staff at C and Third Streets NE, Kostmayer quoted the member as saying, "We just go to the 116 Club." Said Kostmayer, "A lobbyist presents him with a campaign check. He has lunch with the lobbyist, who gives him a five-hundred-dollar contribution. How stupid. That makes people more cynical."

The rules not only allow members to indulge themselves in all the luxurious vacations the special interests want to give them, they also permit lobbyists to mingle with the lawmakers while they enjoy themselves. Thus lobbyists who wanted a duck-hunting weekend with Representative John D. Dingell of Michigan, the ranking Democrat on the House Commerce Committee, gave $5,000 to the Democratic Congressional Campaign Committee and got to spend as much time with him as they wanted. Lobbyists who wanted to attend the Super Bowl with powerful Republican Representatives John Linder of Georgia and Bill Paxon of New York could contribute $6,000 and get their wish. A $3,000 donation bought a week of skiing in Aspen with eight Democratic members of Congress. And a $3,000 donation bought a ski trip in Vail with Representative Michael G. Oxley of Ohio and a handful of other House members who will be shaping legislation changing the utilities industry, according to the *New York Times.*

"With the tighter ethics rules and gift ban in the House, it doesn't take long for people to figure out that you can't buy a congressman lunch or a drink, but you can give him five thousand dollars from your PAC," said Steven F. Stockmeyer, executive vice president of the National Association of Business Political Action Committees.

Thus, in the name of banning lunches, Congress created a bonanza for PACs, the source of the real money. The new rules are "going to place much more emphasis on the fund-raising and PAC process," said Wright H. Andrews, president of the American League of Lobbyists.

In the first half of 1995 alone, companies, trade groups, unions, and other special interests spent at least $400 million to lobby the federal government, most of it aimed at Congress. The number of registered lobbyists was twelve thousand. But without PACs behind them, lobbyists would have little to offer except their own personal contributions. Still, in some cases, these contributions are considerable. In one year alone, C.

Boyden Gray, a lawyer who is a lobbyist, gave $142,910 to Republicans, while Lawrence F. O'Brien III, another lawyer-lobbyist, gave $77,500 to Democrats. Even the amounts most lobbyists give are trivial compared with the gusher of money PACs deliver.

It is axiomatic that money buys influence. For that reason, the executive branch bars employees from receiving from outside sources anything but a lunch or dinner valued at up to $20, aggregating no more than $50 a year. Judges may not receive money from parties who appear before them. Thomas Jefferson urged that "where the private interests of a member are concerned in a bill or question, he is to withdraw." Yet even when they have large stock interests in companies affected by their votes, members rarely recuse themselves. Instead, when it comes to their personal or campaign finances, members of Congress pretend that they are uniquely immune from the laws of human nature.

By definition, a political action committee is a legal entity established by an interest group to raise and spend money in an attempt to influence elections. What do PACs give money for if it is not to influence votes? At the very least, if PACs buy access, as even their defenders acknowledge, it means that members are more likely to vote for PAC interests because they have listened to their pitches.

"It's just implicit around here that when those accountable for large campaign contributions call, you put them through," Rep. Jim Leach said.

If a member "knows you aren't politically active, he may be polite to you, but if you really want to see him perk up and be interested in what you say, let him know you represent a political action committee that is going to be active in the next election," said former representative W. Henson Moore, a Louisiana Republican.

In his diary, Packwood documented that even a $1,000 contribution buys an audience with a member. Referring to a contributor who had met with Packwood, the senator wrote, "He runs a publishing house in Alexandria. He has 220 employees and what they publish are forms to tell Medicare providers how to comply with the law. He gave me $1,000. That's worth 10 minutes."[185]

"People who contribute get the ear of the member and the ear of the staff," said former representative Romano Mazzoli. "Access is power. Access is clout. That's how this thing works."

PACs "buy a willingness to hear their argument," Mel Levine, a former Democratic congressman from California, said. "You are acting in a quasi-judicial capacity. You have the opportunity to weigh both sides, but more often than not, you don't. It influences your willingness to listen. If you disproportionately hear one side, you are more likely to vote that way."

If PACs simply contribute to members who already support their position with the goal of keeping them in office, as defenders also say, then PACs distort the political process by perpetuating in office supporters of PAC positions. Conversely, PACs target members who vote against their positions, further subverting the democratic process. When the late representative Mike Synar, an Oklahoma Democrat, called for a ban on tobacco advertising and a waiting period for prospective gun buyers, both the tobacco PACs and the National Rifle Association's PAC, among others, vowed war on him—and won.

But the impact of PACs is far greater than their defenders admit. The only difference between a bribe and a PAC contribution is that in accepting a bribe, a member of Congress states that he will vote for a position because of the money he expects to receive. That, of course, is not the way it is done. There is no need for members to articulate a quid pro quo. But in accepting money, members usually agree implicitly to vote favorably with the understanding that if they don't, the money may be cut off. The effect is the same as a bribe or an illegal gratuity, which is accepting compensation for representing people before the government. In fact, since members want PACs to continue giving them money, the impact of PAC money can be even greater than when members accept a onetime bribe payment.

"Money makes the world go 'round, and the money keeps rolling in. That's what gets the initiative going in Congress," said Charles F. Gardner, a former lobbyist for Unisys Corporation who was convicted of bribery and tax evasion in connection with Pentagon procurement. "The difference between the charges against me for bribery and what happens between congressmen and PACs is like arguing about how many angels can dance on the head of a pin. . . . No congressman ever said to me, 'I'm voting for this program because you gave me money.' They wouldn't be that stupid."[186]

"There is not a direct exchange. It doesn't work that way," said former representative Kostmayer. "Nobody ever admits it, nobody ever acknowledges it. Everybody does it."

PACs are "implicit contracts," said Representative Leach. "There is an obligation to a giver for a past contribution, but there is also a future commitment by the giver to give more in the future." Leach added, "I don't think members can look you in the eye and say they are not influenced by PACs. I know what people say, and I also know how they vote."[187]

"No person wants to believe he was bought off," said former representative Levine. Yet, "on the tax side, the appropriations side, the subsidy side, and the expenditure side, decisions are clearly weighted and influenced . . . by who has contributed to the candidates."[188]

"We are all human beings," said former representative Anthony C. Beilenson, a California Democrat. In Congress, Beilenson refused PAC money. When he was in the California state legislature, he initially accepted it. "You feel kindly toward people who help us. You feel kindly towards a lobbyist who can get you ten thousand dollars from his clients. It's money you really need."[189] Conversely, because he did not take PAC money, "the one thing I didn't have to think about is what I believe a lot of other members have to think about: How will this vote affect my ability to go back to x, y, and z interests, who have supported me in the past, but this time will they be angry because I cast this vote?"

Ironically, some members who claim PAC contributions do not influence them can see clearly that it influences others. "I am vehemently against leadership PACs," former representative Walker said. "I think if you are going to choose leaders, it should be done on the basis of the qualifications of the members, rather than by who can raise the most money and get an advantage in the race."

In the same way, while members deny that domestic money influences them, they are quick to criticize Bill Clinton for taking foreign money because of the influence they know it buys. Meanwhile, members quietly take foreign money themselves. House minority leader Richard A. Gephardt's leadership PAC received $13,000 from individuals associated with Lippo Group and its subsidiaries.

To be sure, in deciding how to vote, members do not always favor their sources of money. Rather, they weigh the impact of losing a source of funds against the issues that their constituents care about. "The only time they will go against a fund-raiser is if the public is aware of the issue and they make a rational decision that they will gain more votes by voting against the lobbyists' interests than by taking their money and buying TV time," said Martin Lobel, a lawyer who is a former aide to Sen. William Proxmire and now represents state governments.[190]

"It's not always a question of what PACs get members to do. It's often a question of what it gets them not to do," said former representative Kostmayer.[191] "It's the amendment not offered, the speech not given, the letter to committee chairman X that is not signed, it's the committee session or markup session not convened. The nots are much more difficult to trace than affirmative actions."

Another effect is an increasing amount of legislation that is never implemented because Congress purposely wrote the laws vaguely. "Because of the power of lobbyists, Congress writes laws in the most general ways," said Judge Charles R. Richey of the U.S. District Court in Washington. "They delegate power to the agencies to come up with rules implementing them. Then the agencies do little or nothing."[192]

In an example cited by Richey, in 1985, Congress passed the Improved Standards for Laboratory Animals Act, which was intended to require research facilities and zoos and circuses to abide by standards to enhance the psychological well-being of animals. Instead of setting the standards, the law required the

Agriculture Department to formulate appropriate regulations. Congress even left to the discretion of the Agriculture Department whether inspections or investigations would be necessary to enforce the law, according to an opinion by Richey in a lawsuit brought by Animal Legal Defense Fund Inc.

The National Association for Biomedical Research, formed by medical-research and pharmaceutical companies to counter arguments of animal rights activists, swamped the department with thousands of complaints.[193] The Agriculture Department took six years to come up with final regulations implementing the law.

Ultimately, the regulations left it to research laboratories to develop a plan for treating animals properly. Thus, Congress made a show of passing a law to protect animals when, in fact, it had done nothing.

"The genesis of it is that Congress is controlled by special interest groups with money," Richey said. "There is no public accountability anymore."

The net effect of the campaign finance system is that it "shifts enormous power to the moneyed interests," Rep. Lee H. Hamilton, an Indiana Democrat, said.[194] "It decreases the power of the ordinary person. There are so many decisions made here by all of us; none of us is free from sin." Even contributions from individuals can be significant. "You have to raise one million dollars for contested House races today, and several million dollars in the Senate. . . . If a person gives you a thousand-dollar check or raises twenty thousand dollars for you, you just can't ignore that. You have to pay attention to it. That doesn't mean you agree with them every time. But you can't afford to anger them too much if you want to seek their financial support. So all kinds of decisions are distorted here because of our dependence on money."

Hamilton, who was cochairman from the House of the Joint Committee on the Organization of Congress, added, "All of us would say we are not affected by it, but as a practical matter, we are affected by it. The agenda is affected by it. What bills come forward and what bills don't come forward. Amendments are affected by it. What bills are permitted, what bills are not permitted. The pervasive influence of money is much more than people think."

Unlike PACs, "individuals give for complex reasons," said Rep. Bob Inglis, a South Carolina Republican who refuses PAC money. "I have people who agree with me on nine out of ten issues or agree with me on one issue but feel strongly about it. PACs are very simpleminded. They have one goal, to have access to decision makers. They focus enormous sums of money on accomplishing a very narrow agenda. Whereas if individuals give to me, they give for all kinds of complex reasons."[195]

On his door, Inglis has this sign: "Notice to all PACs: Remember you didn't give me a dime, and I don't owe you a thing. Bob Inglis."

"It's naive and wrong for anyone to pretend that campaign contributions do not influence votes. They obviously do," said former representative Eric D. Fingerhut, an Ohio Democrat. "In some cases you can argue whether the chicken or egg comes first. You can say that a PAC supports me because I already am for their position. They just want to keep me in this position. In other cases, it's much more obvious. The knowledge which every politician has is that if he votes in a certain direction, there will be large amounts of financial support out there. That is so pervasive that to say it doesn't impact my position is ludicrous."[196]

"You'd be foolish to say it has no impact or doesn't influence you very much," said Rep. Jim Kolbe, an Arizona Republican.[197]

"I was on the Ways and Means Committee for six years," said former senator Wyche Fowler, a Georgia Democrat. "And every single interest that comes to you has a special private interest where they are seeking to get subsidized, through the tax code. . . . I am sure that on many occasions—I'm not proud of it—I made the choice that I needed this big corporate client and therefore I voted for, or sponsored, its provision, even though I did not think that it was in the best interests of the country or the economy."[198]

"I presume a lot of them rationalized it [taking PAC money] by saying it only buys access," said former senator William

Proxmire, the Wisconsin Democrat, whose only campaign expenditure for his last of six elections was $697, much of it for postage to return contributions. "But of course, they know darn well that unless they come through, that source of money will cease. Big contributors wouldn't contribute if it didn't work."[199]

"Members acknowledge the influence of money in all sorts of ways," Hamilton said. "We joke about it a lot on the floor. You vote a certain way, and you'll hear the comment, 'Well, I gotta go pick up my check from such and such an interest group. I made a hell of an argument on this amendment. That ought to be worth five thousand dollars to them.'"

Thus, under the monster that Congress has created, the "one man, one vote" system that the founding fathers envisioned has become a cruel joke. In effect, Congress legalized corruption, sanctioning the aggregations of cash that the 1907 law banning corporate contributions was supposed to have stopped. Instead of representing the people at large, each with his own interests, members wind up representing the special interests that can raise the most money.

"This town is awash with money, and it is reaching dangerous levels," said Richard K. Cook, a former lobbyist with Lockheed Corporation. "When you have some candidates deriving sixty percent of their funds from PACs, it means they are more likely to have an agenda [favoring the PACs]."[200]

Because of the corrosive influence of PACs, the deficit over the years has widened as members pump more and more money into programs advocated by special interests. With the Cold War over, Congress insisted on increasing by $12.9 billion the amount requested by the Defense Department for weapons systems supported by PACs. Spurred on by millions of dollars in PAC contributions, Congress has voted to build even more B-2 Stealth aircraft at a cost of $11 billion, even though their ability to evade radar is in question and the Pentagon does not want more of them. From 1993 through 1995, PACs representing thirty-two B-2 subcontractors gave nearly $8 million to members of Congress, urging their support for the program.

Meanwhile, in recent years, the government has been spending more than $300 billion a year just to fund interest on the national debt. Much of the deficit is attributable to breaks to corporations that cost Americans $51 billion from direct subsidies and $53 billion from tax breaks. In one example of what is known as corporate welfare, Congress has given a subsidy to ethanol producers of $3.6 billion over five years. The break primarily favors Archer Daniels Midland Company, an agricultural processing giant that has 80 percent of the ethanol market. Since the 1970s, Dwayne O. Andreas, chief executive officer of ADM, has given contributions of $4 million to candidates of both political parties.[201] Similarly, since 1979, sugarcane, beet, and corn-sweetener PACs have given $11.9 million to the campaigns of federal candidates. Congress has continued to give a range of benefits to the producers, raising the price of sugar by $1.4 billion a year, according to the General Accounting Office, while lining the pockets of a few sugar producers.[202]

Because each initiative is opposed by some powerful interest, few real reforms ever emerge from Congress. Indeed, when Congress announces a "reform," it usually makes things worse. One such "reform" was the 1974 law that was primarily responsible for allowing PACs to flourish.

According to former representative Timothy J. Penny, a Minnesota Democrat, money from special interests through PAC contributions has created a congressional "culture" that causes lawmakers—Democrat or Republican—to "spend more than the country can afford; abuse power in ways that undermine the national interest; [and] engage in acts of hypocrisy that keep them in office while allowing serious problems to fester."[203]

"You ran for office with a concept of making necessary changes. Forget that concept; you will never get around to it," said Cec Heftel, a former Democratic House member from Hawaii. "To get by, you have to belong to the system. In Congress, the system is based on spending money. . . . From my first days in office, I was astounded at how easily Congress could spend money that didn't exist. And it was being spent on behalf of the special interests which were the source of campaign contributions."

"When you look at the deficit issue, what do the PACs want?" Representative Leach said. "One type wants special interest spending, the other wants special interest tax cuts. When anyone offers an amendment to provide more to a given area, if they get PAC money from that area, it's hard to say anything but yes. PACs bifurcate, and Congress should pay more attention to the whole."

"As secretary of the Department of Health, Education, and Welfare, I saw the PACs' ability to veto legislation on every major issue, from hospital cost containment to restrictions on the tobacco industry," Joseph A. Califano Jr. said. "If it were not for PACs, we would have had health insurance reform."[204] Indeed, opponents of comprehensive health care reform gave more than $25 million in campaign contributions to congressional candidates in 1993 and 1994, when Congress was considering health care reform legislation. In its fight against regulation of tobacco products by the Food and Drug Administration, part of Califano's former department, Philip Morris Inc. alone gave $2.7 million in 1996.

Because of the costs of television advertising, members spend large chunks of their time trying to raise more money, rather than attending to the business of the nation. In the 1996 election, $800 million was spent on congressional races, three times the amount spent just four years earlier. Business outspent labor—which originally started PACs—seven to one.

Besides raising money from special interests, members take money directly from the Treasury to pay for vast amounts of franked mail. While some of it is used for office correspondence, often the mail is "thinly veiled political mail," as Rep. Andy Jacobs, an Indiana Democrat, put it. The franking limits vary by district, but the average is $108,000 a year.

"In the old days, you could get away with spending relatively little money," Beilenson said. "What that meant is there was sort of more generalized propaganda. The Republicans who ran against you would say, 'Vote for so-and-so instead of your Congressman Tony Beilenson, who is too liberal and is for big government and votes for abortion rights.' Or, 'He voted to raise taxes.' Some general stuff. Now with five-hundred-thousand-dollar to eight-hundred-thousand-dollar campaigns, there are TV ads that talk about specific votes. There didn't used to be that. It comes back to money. Elections are much bigger affairs. A lot more information, most of it negative, is sent out. . . . Everybody hates it, but this is what people respond to, apparently. You are wasting your money if you buy nice ads."

"There's a lot more need for campaign money," said Sen. Ben Nighthorse Campbell, a Colorado Republican. "A Senate race is about four point three million dollars. I have to raise two thousand dollars a day, seven days a week, six years straight, to finance it. It's outrageous."[205]

"I used to go to the Democratic National Committee headquarters, and they had carrels or booths there for members to go," said former representative Kostmayer. "You took your campaign credit card [for charging calls], and you stayed there. You went in at two P.M. and got out at six P.M. You made one call after another [asking for money]. You'll see tons of members sitting around there. It dominates your life. They [members] complain, but they have no choice."

"I have seen thirty-five to forty members there," Rep. Martin Meehan, a Democrat from Massachusetts, said. "It's ridiculous that we have to do that."

"When I ran for the Senate, I spent all my time raising money," Levine said. "It drove me absolutely crazy. . . . I spent a very good chunk of a year and a half, the overwhelming majority of my time, running for the Senate."

"There's more of an element of extortion to it [contributions from PACs] than bribery," said Steven F. Stockmeyer of the National Association of Business Political Action Committees. "I really don't think it's either, but if you had to characterize it, there's more of an element of extortion. You go see a member of Congress, and with the smart ones, you get a call a couple of days later. They say, 'Glad you came by the office. Just wanted you to know we have a fund-raiser coming up. I hope to see you there, too.' What's that?"[206]

Some members are even more explicit. Sen. Alfonse M. D'Amato, a New York Republican, and his staff are known for using crude and threatening tactics. Lobbyists say D'Amato staff members solicit contributions while discussing pending legislation the lobbyists are interested in. "Al's guys reach through the phone and say, 'We're helping you, and you have to help us,'" one lobbyist said. When a lobbyist, on behalf of a client, called a D'Amato aide to ask about a pending issue, the aide replied, "Well, we haven't seen a contribution from them." The client then sent a $5,000 check, and the matter got taken care of.[207]

While such tactics could well come under the legal definition of bribery, they only underscore what is wrong with the system Congress created.

As campaign money drives more and more decisions, members have become beholden to PACs rather than to party leaders. This has produced both legislative gridlock and more divisiveness.

"All of us are entrepreneurs," former senator Timothy E. Wirth, a Colorado Democrat, said just before retiring in 1992. "The leadership has no handle on us. They can't really do anything for or to us. . . . The leadership has no power any more."

If the PACs are in charge, members do not want to alienate them. "The PAC community talks with each other," said Rep. Christopher Shays, a Connecticut Republican. "They are like-minded, and if you meet with one, you may get from another. They can get turned off to you. A whole group will say, 'Don't contribute to Shays.' If you turn off a block, you may see fifty thousand dollars disappear from your next campaign and go to your opponent."[208]

Because they like safe bets, PACs tend to favor incumbents, perpetuating in office members who are most likely to continue the present system of financing campaigns. At a June 1996 seminar in Washington given by the National Association of Business Political Action Committees, managers of the major business PACs spent two days listening to political experts expound on which candidates were most likely to win. Since 1985, members of this organization have given current members of Congress more than $100 million.

Overall, Senate incumbents are able to outspend challengers

two to one. In House races, 76 percent of PAC contributions go to incumbents. In Senate races, PACs give five times more money to incumbents than to challengers. In House races, PACs give six times more money to incumbents than to challengers. Members with more seniority are then in a better position to help the PACs with legislation.

"Now members spend half their time raising money," said Roy Elson, the former administrative assistant to Sen. Carl Hayden. "It's disgusting and degrading. . . . Senators are willing to sell out the institution to some of the special interests."

★ ★ ★ ★ ★ ★ ★ ★ ★ ★

9

★ ★ ★ ★ ★ ★ ★ ★ ★ ★

Revolution

Claiming moral superiority, Republicans in 1994 took over control of Congress pledging to reform the process and return government to the people.

"To put it simply, values count, not just in our lives, but in our society," Senate majority leader Robert J. Dole said. House Speaker Newt Gingrich claimed to be an "outsider" who pinned his campaign to "moral values."

But as in the case of most congressional reforms, such pledges were Trojan horses, rolled out to disguise an agenda that made Congress more beholden to the special interests the Republicans had blamed for corrupting it. During their first year in office, the seventy-five House Republican freshmen got more than $24 million in campaign contributions, 40 percent of it from special interest groups. The average freshman member raised $114,334 in PAC contributions, one and a half times the amount raised by the average freshman in 1993. By the 1996 election, political action committees or individuals from outside candidates' states were providing the freshmen with half of their reelection money, compared with a third when they came in promising reform. Contributions from out of state are assumed to be part of special interest efforts to influence members.

To be sure, nothing the Republicans did differed in any material way from what the Democrats had done when they controlled Congress. Americans are still paying for the $480.9 billion savings and loan debacle, which occurred largely because a Democratic-controlled Congress, inundated with $11.6 million in contributions from the industry, freed savings and loan associations from traditional constraints in the 1980s. Four of the five senators who were among the largest recipients—Alan Cranston of California, Dennis DeConcini of Arizona, John Glenn of Ohio, and Donald W. Riegle Jr. of Michigan—were Democrats. The fifth was Republican John McCain of Arizona.

The Keating Five, as they were known, made extraordinary efforts to persuade regulators to help the S&Ls avoid stricter regulation and particularly to help Charles H. Keating Jr., chief executive officer of Lincoln Federal Savings and Loan Association. Keating gave $324,000 in contributions to the Keating Five alone. In 1989, Keating boasted to reporters of the influence his $1.5 million in campaign contributions had bought: "One question among the many raised in recent weeks had to do with whether my financial support in any way influenced several political figures to take up my cause," Keating said. "I want to say in the most forceful way I can, I certainly hope so."

When former representative Tony Coehlo was chairman of the Democratic Congressional Campaign Committee, the Democrats were the first to accept soft money in the 1980s, allowing corporations and labor unions to funnel money directly into campaigns. Coehlo started the Speaker's Club, which offered PACs, for a contribution of $15,000, the chance to become "trusted, informal advisers" to the Democratic members of Congress.[209]

In his groundbreaking book *Honest Graft*, then *Wall Street Journal* reporter Brooks Jackson showed how Coehlo made thinly veiled threats to recalcitrant PACs by suggesting that their "good relationships" with House Democrats might be damaged if they didn't contribute to particular candidates.

What made the Republicans different from the Democrats is that they won election in 1994 on a platform of reform, sanctimoniously impugning the Democrats.

"Ten years ago, they did it [took special interest money] and didn't say they were cleaning it up. Now they say they are, and they aren't," a staffer on the Senate Rules and Administration Committee said.

Soon, the Republican-controlled Congress, with the help of Democrats, was cutting back on government regulation of the industries that gave them the most money. Over a three-year period, the PACs of companies regulated by the Food and Drug Administration invested $881,635 in thirty-three Republican and ten Democratic sponsors of bills to gut the FDA's power to keep unsafe drugs and food off the market. One provision even prohibited the regulatory agency from requiring drug companies to warn patients of possible dangers of prescription drugs.[210]

In the end, the bills failed to become law. But Congress passed a bill to limit stockholders' ability to file lawsuits accusing companies or stockbrokers of fraud. Rep. Thomas Bliley Jr., the Virginia Republican who sponsored the bill, had received $125,000 from securities, banking, and insurance industry PACs. Rep. Jack Fields, a Texas Republican who introduced legislation to provide less information on new stock offerings, had received $220,000 from PACs from those same industries. Clinton vetoed both bills, but Congress overrode his veto of the securities bill, which became law.

Awash in contributions from manufacturers of infant formula, House Republicans stopped requiring competitive bidding to supply infant formula to the Women, Infants, and Children Program, a welfare program. Since competitive bidding had been required, the program had saved $1 billion a year. In the previous five years, nearly $4 billion had been saved. The savings had been plowed back into the program, making more formula available to needy infants. In the three months before the House approved the measure to stop competitive bidding, the three companies that make 90 percent of infant formula— Abbott Laboratories, Bristol-Meyers Squibb Company, and

American Home Products—had boosted their giving to the Republican Party. Ultimately, the bill stalled in the Senate.[211]

In the meantime, Congress vacillated on passing antiterrorism legislation proposed by President Clinton after the Oklahoma City bombing that killed 168 people. A year after the bombing, Congress passed a watered-down version. It did not require companies that make explosives to include in their manufacture taggants, which allow law enforcement to trace the source of the explosives through codes placed in the powder. Swiss police over the years have used taggants successfully to trace the source of explosives in more than five hundred cases of bombings or illegal possession of explosives.

While Congress refused to order such simple remedies to counter real threats, it continued to support special subsidies for industries that contributed to their campaigns. The same day that Rep. Gerald B. H. Solomon, a New York Republican, succeeded in retaining federal subsidies for the dairy industry, the National Milk Producers wrote to dairy industry lobbyists, "To show your appreciation to Mr. Solomon, please join us for a breakfast." The letter added, "PACs throughout the industry are asked to contribute $1,000."[212]

Some members were so well nourished by special interests that they received more than half their money from PACs. They included Rep. Roger Wicker, a Mississippi Republican, who got 84 percent of his money from PACs; Rep. Frank R. Mascara, a Pennsylvania Democrat, who got 65 percent of his money from PACs; and Sonny Bono, the California Republican, who got 63 percent of his money from PACs.

"I see some of my freshman friends getting used to the stink—forgetting what they came here for," said Rep. Linda Smith, a Washington Republican who helped lead an effort to reform the campaign financing system.

As if there were any doubt that special interests own Congress, some Senate Republicans' home pages were linked to the Internet sites of such groups as the National Rifle Association and the Christian Coalition, including to their fund-raising efforts.[213] Besides individual members' home pages, the House, the Senate, and the Architect of the Capitol each have a home page. The Library of Congress provides a range of information about Congress and the status of legislation through the Thomas Legislative Information service.*

Perhaps the ultimate illustration of how completely special interests had taken over Congress was that, before the 1996 election, the Senate delayed its adjournment by two days solely to debate whether the Federal Express Company should be given a special exemption from a 1923 law regulating railway express companies. The effect would be to allow FedEx to resist labor union efforts to organize its employees. Federal Express won its exemption, and the reason was clear: the company runs one of the top five corporate PACs in the nation. During the 1994 election, the FedEx PAC gave $800,000 to 224 House and Senate candidates. In addition, during one six-month period, the company spent $1.2 million on lobbying, hiring nine lobbying firms. Beyond that, FedEx takes advantage of a loophole in the new gift rule that allows the company to fly members around the country on one of its four corporate jets. Members need only reimburse the company for the price of a first-class ticket, when the true value of such trips is equivalent to chartering a private jet.

"I was stunned by the breadth and depth of their clout up here," said Sen. Russell D. Feingold, a Wisconsin Democrat who has battled for campaign finance reform and who opposed the special FedEx exemption. When Feingold tried to round up their support, other members explained that they were backing FedEx because they had flown in a FedEx plane or gotten other favors.[214] Sen. Paul Simon, an Illinois Democrat, said that in a caucus of the Senate's Democrats just before the recess, a senior senator had said he would not oppose the company. "I know who butters my bread," the senator explained to his colleagues.

---

* The House home page is at http://www.house.gov; the Senate home page is at http://www.senate.gov; the Architect of the Capitol's home page is at http://www.aoc.gov. In addition, the Thomas Legislative Information service provides links to the status of congressional legislation, to the *Congressional Record*, and to the Library of Congress on-line catalog. The Thomas home page is at http://www.thomas.loc.gov/.

The exemption won by FedEx is not its first. In the past, Congress has handed FedEx exemptions from trucking regulations and from noise-abatement requirements.

The spectacle of the Senate staying in session to reciprocate favors was grotesque. But nothing symbolized how out of control Congress had gotten more than the fact that House Republican Conference chairman John A. Boehner from Ohio distributed checks from tobacco PACs to members on the floor of the House. After Bob Herbert broke the story in his *New York Times* column, Barry Jackson, Boehner's chief of staff, noted that no tobacco-related legislation was being debated when Boehner distributed the checks in the last week of June 1995.[215]

"It's a common practice," Boehner's chief of staff said. "He [Boehner] knew it was neither illegal nor against the rules of the House."

The incident brought to mind the Crédit Mobilier scandal of 1872. Jackson's comment suggested that Americans are so gullible that they would think that if tobacco legislation was not being debated at the moment the PAC money was passed out, it would have no impact. The Democrats apparently had the same low opinion of American voters. Minority Leader Richard A. Gephardt, a Democrat from Missouri, and Minority Whip David E. Bonior, a Democrat from Michigan, immediately blasted the Republicans for the practice of handing out checks on the floor. They said they would move for a "no-check zone" around the House floor. If Democrats gain control of the House, "my very first act as Speaker will be to ban the outrageous practice of distributing checks on the House floor—so that members of Congress vote their consciences, not their contributions," Gephardt said.

This was the most outrageous statement of all. By suggesting that Americans would buy the notion that if PAC checks were given to members in their offices instead of on the floor of the House, the money would not influence them, Gephardt demonstrated how contemptuous Congress is of the American voter. Moreover, by suggesting that PAC money does buy influence without disclosing how captive he is to PACs, Gephardt was engaging in deceit. In the House, Gephardt has been among the top three recipients of PAC money, with more than $1 million collected from PACs during the 1996 election alone. Gephardt is also a frequent flier on corporate jets. When asked if he had also passed out PAC checks to other members on the House floor, Gephardt refused to discuss it.

"It's a distinction without a difference to say that the checks can be delivered out here on the street or at the Capitol Hill club, but not on the floor," Rep. Bob Inglis, a South Carolina Republican, said. "That feeds the cynical attitude [of voters]."

"The problem is the money, not where it is given," former representative Anthony Beilenson, a California Democrat, said. "If you are allowed to give out special interest checks on the floor of the House, it is odious. But if the checks are passed out outside, it is the same money and has the same corrupting effect."

The hypocrisy did not end there. Like Gephardt, Gingrich seemed to think Americans were so gullible that he could make almost any untrue claim and get away with it. A chameleon who flitted from idea to idea, Gingrich had decided that the way to win in Congress was, in effect, to burn it down. Thus, when he was in the minority, Gingrich attacked Congress, launching an ethics investigation that led to the downfall of House Speaker Jim Wright. He called former Speakers Wright, Tom Foley, and Tip O'Neill a "trio of muggers." House Democratic leaders were "sick." And the House was "institutionally corrupt."

As recently as 1990, Gingrich supported legislation to outlaw PACs. "Congress is increasingly a system of corruption in which money politics is defeating and driving out citizen politics," he said then. In the foreword to a book published in 1988, Gingrich described an "imperial Congress reigned over by an imperial Speaker enacting special interest legislation."[216]

Nothing was beneath the Gingrich operation. When Gingrich was Republican minority whip, an aide called more than a dozen reporters trying to get into print an untrue rumor that former House Speaker Tom Foley was a homosexual who liked young boys. Gingrich later disavowed the aide's actions.[217]

Gingrich orchestrated the Republican takeover of the House on the premise that he and his supporters were paragons of virtue who would restore family values to America. Yet while married to his high school math teacher, Jackie, Gingrich had engaged in extramarital affairs. When Jackie Gingrich lay in a hospital recovering from a third cancer operation, Gingrich appeared at her bedside with a yellow legal pad to discuss the terms of a divorce.[218]

In his book *To Renew America*, Gingrich wrote that "any male who doesn't support his children is a bum." Yet while Gingrich and his wife were separated, Jackie Gingrich filed court papers saying she could not pay the bills she was incurring for herself and their two girls, then seventeen and fourteen. When her utilities were about to be cut off, local church members took up a collection to help out. At the time, Gingrich was paying $700 a month for the support of his family. Meanwhile, Gingrich was spending $400 on his own food and dry cleaning alone.

In response to her claim that he appeared at the hospital with a legal pad, Gingrich said, "It did not happen that way from my side. . . . Every person [in a divorce] has his own unique story of what happened, and it doesn't relate to anyone else's." Asked about his own adultery, Gingrich said, "I'm not saying all my life was lived totally as a saint."

If Gingrich's platform of family values was a joke, so was his claim to be an outsider who would reform the system. Once the Republicans took over the House, Gingrich warned PAC representatives that they had better open their coffers to the Republicans. "For anybody who's not on board now, it's going to be the two coldest years in Washington," Gingrich informed PAC representatives.[219]

Soon, Gingrich and his cohorts—Rep. John Boehner of Ohio, the chairman of the House Republican Conference, House majority whip Tom D. DeLay of Texas, and Majority Leader Richard K. Armey of Texas—were setting up their own leadership PACs. Gingrich's, called the Monday Morning PAC, began by inviting fifteen corporations and trade associations to kick in $5,000 each to attend a dinner with him. Among the first takers was the Independent Insurance Agents of America Inc., which held its own event that raised $50,000 for Gingrich. In his first six months as Speaker, Gingrich raised $869,000, with 42 percent of it from insurance, casino, telecommunications, and medical industry PACs. In 1995, DeLay received at least $175,000 in soft money for his leadership PAC, with most of it coming from tobacco companies. R. J. Reynolds alone contributed $73,000.

In turn, the Republicans let lobbyists "put together talking points for members, run briefings for aides, and help draft House rules that have been crucial to passage of legislation," according to the *National Journal*.[220]

All the while, Gingrich masqueraded as a defender of the ordinary man. While leading an assault on environmental protection laws, Gingrich posed with exotic animals to show that he supported protection of the environment. His House Republican Conference put out a memo to members suggesting that the way to overcome the image of Republicans as anti-environment was to plant trees, adopt a highway, tour a recycling plant, clean up a park, and invite the press. Such media coverage would "help further insulate yourself from attacks of the green extremists," the memo said.

To the extent civility was diminished, Gingrich was largely responsible. Quoting Mao Tse-tung, Gingrich said, "Politics is war without blood."

"It was confrontational politics," said David K. Rehr, a former aide to one of Gingrich's lieutenants who sat in on many of Gingrich's strategy sessions. "He ended comity," said Rehr, now vice president for government affairs of the National Beer Wholesalers Association. "He felt the only way to save the House was to destroy it."[221]

Gingrich essentially ran the House, instructing committee chairs on how to handle legislation. Soon, Democrats were excluded from key conferences. There was nothing new about that, either. When the Democrats were in power, House Judiciary Committee chairman Jack Brooks arrogantly told Rep. Bill McCollum, a Florida Republican, that he was not welcome in negotiations to hammer out a crime bill. Like Gingrich, Speakers Sam Rayburn, Joseph G. Cannon, and Thomas B. Reed were known as czars whose rule was unquestioned.

Given the demonstrable flaws in Gingrich's character and the ruthlessness he had displayed in his personal life, it should have come as no surprise that, if he did not get his way, he was willing to shut down the U.S. government by refusing to compromise with President Clinton and even to threaten to renege on the government's debt obligations.

While Gingrich claimed his aim was to balance the budget, in the end, the Republicans actually increased Defense Department appropriations $11 billion beyond what the Clinton administration had requested. Moreover, the Republicans left virtually untouched the $104 billion in tax breaks and subsidies corporate America receives each year. Instead, the Republicans took aim at the little people with little PAC money to offer—the poor, the elderly, and the disabled who were on Medicare or Medicaid.

Having railed against Wright for improperly raising money through a book deal, Gingrich himself became the center of an ethics investigation. After two years of denying wrongdoing, Gingrich admitted that he had improperly set up some of his political projects as nonprofit organizations and had given untrue information about the projects to the House ethics panel. One of the projects solicited funds to help inner-city poor children but actually funneled almost all of its money to Republican recruiting activities.

Rather than accepting responsibility, Gingrich claimed his only failure was in not consulting a tax attorney. He blamed the inaccurate information on his lawyer. In fact, two lawyers had warned Gingrich six years earlier that using charitable organizations for political activities was wrong.[222]

Republican henchmen rallied around their leader. Forgetting about his steadfast denials of wrongdoing, Rep. John Boehner of Ohio said Gingrich's willingness to acknowledge a mistake was "refreshing." Rep. Dick Armey of Texas attributed the mistakes to the fact that Gingrich was "so busy, occupied with trying to do these policies and public service."

This was an argument for the divine right of kings—that the country's leaders are so important and so busy trying to help the populace that they should be excused for extracting money improperly or for misleading a committee of Congress. America made its break with royalty when it broke away from England, but members of Congress are so infatuated with power that they still don't get it.

When Gingrich was in the minority, he attacked former House Speaker Tom Foley on the floor of the House for having a Capitol Police officer assigned to guard him. Now that he is Speaker, Gingrich has twelve officers assigned to him. In 1981, Congress gave the Capitol Police enforcement powers throughout the country. Often, officers traveled with Gingrich out of town. To be sure, Gingrich generated more threats than Foley did. But Capitol Police say the security force assigned to Gingrich is excessive.

"He [Gingrich] was teaching a class in Georgia and taking all his security with him," said David A. Curry, a former Capitol Police captain who was in charge of the security details for both Speakers. "That's not cheap. Gingrich has more officers protecting him than Foley did. One recently went to six different cities in seven days." For the Republican National Convention, Curry said, the Capitol Police sent thirty officers, all paid overtime, to protect Gingrich and other Republican members.[223]

Finally, with Republicans in power, Gingrich decided that what was needed was not a ban on PACs, as he had earlier proposed, but rather *more* money to finance elections.

If Gingrich was a hypocrite, he was also arrogant. The Speaker was piqued that Clinton had not talked with him enough on a trip taken on *Air Force One* to attend the funeral of Israeli prime minister Yitzhak Rabin. Gingrich said the slight contributed to his intransigence on budget negotiations, leading to the government shutdown.

"It's petty . . . but I think it's human," Gingrich told reporters at a breakfast meeting.

In closing down the government, Gingrich was supported by Bob Dole, the majority leader of the Senate. While he treated the little people with respect, Dole symbolized what was wrong with Congress. During his twenty-seven years in the Senate, Dole had so compromised himself with PAC money and, in return, had engineered so many tax breaks and subsidies for those same interests that he had little integrity left.[224]

Having received $400,000 in tobacco contributions, Dole claimed cigarette smoking is not addictive, then repeatedly waffled on the issue. As far back as 1968, the *Wall Street Journal* had reported scientific evidence to support what every smoker knows: that smoking produces a physical craving for cigarettes reinforced by withdrawal symptoms if smoking is stopped. In other words, it's addictive.[225] Dole's refusal to acknowledge the obvious—even though it gave young smokers an excuse to continue their hazardous habit—could only have been motivated by a desire not to alienate his benefactors, the tobacco companies. Over the years, Dole had helped the tobacco industry in other ways, including the rescue of its subsidy program.

Dole not only supported the interests of the groups who gave him the most money, he also introduced legislation to give special breaks to individual contributors. For example, as wine barons Ernest and Julio Gallo and their wives were giving $97,000 to Dole's Senate reelection campaign and to his Campaign America funding mechanism, Dole, as Senate majority leader, supported a change in the tax laws that became known as the Gallo Amendment. Part of a tax-overhaul bill that was supposed to make federal income taxes "simpler and fairer," it allowed the Gallo family to pass on to their grandchildren some $80 million without incurring a 33 percent estate tax. Few other families stood to gain so much from this change.[226]

Meanwhile, Dole took hundreds of free rides on corporate jets owned by interests he supports. In one two-year period, he flew twenty-six times on aircraft owned by UST Inc., the country's largest smokeless tobacco manufacturer. He then introduced an amendment cutting the tax rate on smokeless products to a fifth of the tax on other tobacco products. This was despite a Department of Health and Human Services report predicting "an impending oral cancer epidemic" because of increased sales of smokeless products such as UST's Skoal.

Dole's public statements consisted of sentence fragments, suggesting an attention span so short that he could not maintain a thought until the end of a sentence. When asked what was the most important quality he would like voters to know about him, Dole replied, "Beats me."

If Dole came across as unfocused and lacking in ideas, it epitomized how vapid members of Congress are. The fact that Dole could come out for a 15 percent tax cut during his presidential bid after participating in shutting down the government to cut the deficit highlighted how shamelessly opportunistic members of Congress can be. Dole claimed the tax cut would stimulate the economy enough to produce greater tax revenues, offsetting the cut. But just a year earlier, Dole had said in a magazine interview, "What I could never understand is why, if you just cut taxes, you'd have this big, big revenue increase. . . . In the 1980s, we said, 'Everything's going to be fine.' Well . . . it wasn't."

In the same vein, during his presidential bid, Dole proposed campaign finance reform. Yet when push came to shove, in the Senate, Dole had filibustered six times against campaign finance reform.

Commentators noted Dole's inability to convey his message and his failure to articulate a vision for the future. As if his campaign existed outside of him, they blamed his advisers or Dole's refusal to accept their advice. No one wanted to say the obvious: that Dole's campaign reflected the man, who had no values beyond expediency.

Nor was Sen. Trent Lott of Mississippi, Dole's successor as majority leader, much better. He had the distinction of having the biggest leadership PAC in the Senate. In 1995 alone, he raised $567,200 for his PAC and spent $297,900 for overhead and contributions to candidates. One of Lott's first acts was to order the hundred-thousand-volume Senate Library, used by members, staff, and members of the press galleries, from the Capitol to the basement of the Russell Senate Office Building so that senators could have even more hideaway offices. Before Lott took over, senators had seventy hideaway offices, while the House leadership had about twenty-five. Lott declared he would build enough hideaways for each of the one hundred senators.

Some other Republican freshmen who claimed moral superiority turned out to exemplify the very evils they railed against.

During his campaign, Jon Christensen, a Nebraska Republican and evangelical Christian, attacked homosexuality and abortion and recommended prayer and belief in creationism. He criticized his opponent for using his position on the House Ways and Means Committee to raise campaign funds. The former Amway salesman said he would never accept trips paid for by lobbyists. And he suggested he and his wife, Meredith, whose family owned one of the largest title insurance companies in the country, represented traditional family values.

At an Omaha Press Club ball, Meredith, wearing a sleeveless, sequined gown, sang a tribute to her husband to the tune of Little Peggy March's 1963 pop hit "I Will Follow Him": "I will follow him right on to Washington; His right hand I will always be; Jon will make everyone see it is his destiny. . . . He'll always have my money, my money, my money; As long I'm his honey, his honey, his honey."

It was all a sham. Twice before Christensen was elected, he and his wife had filed for divorce. Once her husband was in the House, Meredith signed an affidavit as part of a divorce petition: "I regret the fact that during our marriage I have engaged in marital infidelity," she said. Despite counseling, she said, "I was unable to remain faithful."[227]

Even before he was sworn in, Christensen raised so much soft money for the Republican Party that Gingrich named him to the Ways and Means Committee. Being on the powerful tax-writing committee always boosts members' PAC contributions. Soon, he had raised $1.1 million for his next campaign. The amount from PACs—$383,738—was the third-highest amount contributed by PACs to the freshman class. Moreover, as Al Hunt pointed out in the *Wall Street Journal*, Christensen took at least three trips financed by business interests.

Like Christensen, fellow Republican freshman Steve Stockman of Texas was a born-again Christian who ran on a guns-and-God platform. On his résumé, Stockman claimed to be an accountant who had worked for IBM and had graduated from the University of Houston, where he worked as a computer consultant. It turned out Stockman had not graduated from the college, had never worked for IBM, and had never been a consultant for the university. Instead, he had worked as a temp for Manpower Inc. and had been a homeless person in Fort Worth.[228]

In Congress, Stockman tried to repeal the ban on assault weapons. A consultant to Gun Owners of America drafted many of the fifteen bills Stockman introduced.[229] Stockman wrote an article for a gun publication claiming that Atty. Gen. Janet Reno had engaged in "premeditated murder" when she approved an FBI plan to introduce CS gas, which is more effective than tear gas, into the Branch Davidian compound in Waco, Texas. In fact, infrared photography and electronic eavesdropping on their conversations documented that, after the FBI introduced the gas, the Branch Davidians purposely set fire to the compound, burning themselves and their children to death.[230] Stockman lost in the November 1996 election.

During the 104th Congress, which ended in January 1997, the House was in session an unprecedented number of hours. The Senate stayed in session longer than at any time since World War II. But until the last few weeks of the session, what Congress produced was mostly hot air. While congressional rhetoric focused attention on the need to balance the budget, in the end total outlays agreed on actually increased from $1,519 billion in fiscal 1995 to $1,572 billion in fiscal 1996 and $1,635 billion in fiscal 1997. Mandatory increases in spending for programs such as Medicare and Medicaid more than offset tiny decreases in discretionary spending. Only because receipts are expected to increase due largely to an improvement in the economy was the deficit expected to decrease from $164 billion in fiscal 1995 to $146 billion in fiscal 1996, and $140 billion in fiscal 1997—all minuscule reductions. When congressmen boast of budget cuts, they usually mean reductions from expected increases—not real reductions.[231]

"The whole thing [budget struggle] turns out to have been a giant scam from day one," said Stephen Roach, chief economist at Morgan Stanley & Co. "It's no wonder voters are cynical about Washington. This is the issue of our generation, and look at the result."

Moreover, Congress's claim that it would balance the budget

by the year 2002 was based on projections that will require discipline that Congress—at least since the 1980s—has lacked. The proof was that just after the Republicans shut down the government, Congress repealed the 1993 gasoline tax increase of 4.3 cents a gallon until the end of 1996. While the price of gasoline had been rising during the year, at an average price of $1.30 a gallon it still was lower than the average in sixteen other countries, including France, Italy, Canada, Great Britain, Argentina, and Chile. The repeal cost the Treasury $2.9 billion in lost taxes, just when the Republicans were claiming balancing the budget was so important that the government had to be shut down to achieve it.

Illogical as the tax repeal was, it was typical of the gimmicky kinds of legislation that Congress turns out. Above all, members want to be reelected. If they can provide voters with goodies now, they are perfectly willing to plunge the country into debt later.

"You know that your opponent in the fall will say: 'Tony Beilenson had a chance to reduce your taxes and did not,'" said Beilenson, who voted against repealing the tax. "Why put up with some additional nonsense by voting [against the repeal]?"

Congress employed the same shortsighted approach to cutting costs in the executive branch. If operated with the efficiency of a profit-making business, the federal government could probably be cut in half. Businesses cut costs by weeding out unnecessary staff, mandating across-the-board cuts, or contracting out jobs that others can do more cheaply. But that requires effort and thought. Instead, Congress took swipes at entire programs and departments. Meanwhile, Congress left largely intact the Government Printing Office, a part of the legislative branch that spends $30.3 million a year. Besides printing the *Congressional Record*, the GPO prints government publications, congressional bills (at least 1,400 copies of each), and stationery and calling cards for members of Congress and their staffs.

"Why do we have to have our own printing presses?" asked Rep. Scott L. Klug, a Wisconsin Republican who has proposed turning the GPO into a procurement office that awards contracts to private printers. "The argument you get [from members] comes down to institutional control. The House and Senate don't want to give it up."

But the Republicans had no compunctions about severely cutting the budget of the General Accounting Office. While the GAO is also part of the legislative branch, it regularly comes up with findings that make lawmakers who want to allocate more money to the Defense Department or to their pet projects uncomfortable. Just before Congress slashed the GAO's budget, the congressional audit agency had released a report showing that cheaper planes performed about as well as the more expensive aircraft sought by the Pentagon.

Through its recommendations and its audits of procurement contracts, the GAO actually returns money to taxpayers. In 1995, the GAO saved the government $16 billion, a return of more than $35 for every $1 spent for the GAO's budget. If the executive branch acted on more of the GAO's recommendations, the savings would be far higher. But Congress slashed the GAO's budget anyway, reducing its staff to 3,700 from 5,325 in 1992. GAO had to disband its program evaluation division, which had issued the report on wasteful Pentagon aircraft.

Arrogantly, the Senate in 1996 refused to perform its most basic function—approve some 120 nominations to boards, commissions, and ambassadorships. Sen. Charles E. Grassley, an Iowa Republican, alone held up eleven ambassadorships because the Clinton administration would not nominate Ann Jorgenson, his choice to fill a Republican seat on the Farm Credit Administration. As a result, such countries as Australia, El Salvador, and Venezuela had no American ambassadors during much of 1996.[232]

The Republican freshmen thought they did not have to compromise. The delegates to the Constitutional Convention in 1787 in Philadelphia approached the task of structuring the government with widely divergent views. Alexander Hamilton wanted a king, while Benjamin Franklin wanted a single legislature. Tempers flared, and negotiations almost collapsed. But the founding fathers cut a deal.

In contrast, the freshmen were ideologues. As a result, while they enacted welfare reform contained in their Contract with

America, the Republicans refused to compromise on other measures, and as a result, few of their initiatives passed. Significant measures that did pass, such as one increasing the minimum wage and another expanding health insurance coverage, were Democratic initiatives.

"This place is dysfunctional," said Rep. Collin C. Peterson, a Minnesota Democrat. "Nobody wants to give. Nobody wants to govern. They just want to play politics. The Republicans make bills so bad that Clinton won't sign them. It's because they want power. The mentality is if they are for it, we are against it."

"The best members are honest brokers who don't try to impose a moral test on people who come to them with issues," said the chief of staff of a House member. "They try to judge the power of the people with complaints and the merit of their claims. They try to cut deals and split the difference and leave everyone with something. Now there's an ideological model. They say they are revolutionaries."

By threatening to default on the government's interest payments, the Republicans further undercut their own credibility. Standard & Poor's Corporation, the agency that rates creditworthiness of debt instruments, said the threat had diminished to some degree investors' faith in the creditworthiness of the U.S. government. It was almost as if the government had been seized by a foreign power.

In shutting down the government, the Republicans cost American taxpayers $1.25 billion in lost federal employee productivity and revenue—three times the GAO's total annual budget of $383 million. Federal workers had to borrow from their families to make mortgage payments. In Russia, U.S. diplomats took a loan to pay their Russian workers. Between twenty thousand and thirty thousand applications for visas by foreigners trying to enter the United States languished. Americans trying to leave the country could not obtain passports even to visit their dying parents.

"The games that people played backfired," said Rep. Constance A. Morella, a Maryland Republican. "They [citizens] lose confidence in government."

As usual, Congress made a special exemption for itself. Thus,

Viewed from the west, the Capitol is framed on the left by the Senate office buildings and on the right by the House office buildings. Behind the Capitol are the Supreme Court to the left and Library of Congress to the right. *(Architect of the Capitol)*

CAPITOL HILL

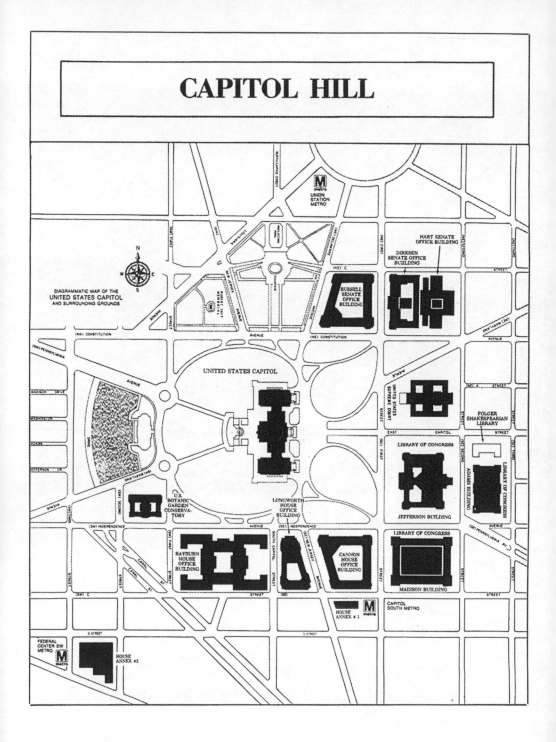

A mural on the ceiling of the first floor of the House wing of the Capitol depicts George Washington laying the cornerstone of the Capitol on September 18, 1793. Today the cornerstone cannot be found.

SOUTHERN CHIVALRY — ARGUMENT versus CLUB'S.

In the Senate chamber in 1856, Representative Preston S. Brooks of South Carolina knocked Senator Charles Sumner of Massachusetts senseless with a cane.

At night, Capitol Police have found members having sex with female staffers in their offices and Capitol hideaways. *(Architect of the Capitol)*

Now considered one of the best legislators, Senator Edward M. Kennedy allegedly once almost ran over a Capitol Police officer. *(AP/Wide World)*

Rita Jenrette had sex with her husband, Representative John W. Jenrette Jr., on the steps of the Capitol. She later posed for *Playboy*. (© Playboy *1981*)

Senator Arlen Specter's staff has nicknamed him Mister Burns, from the television show *The Simpsons*. (*AP/Wide World*)

The Capitol Police, coordinated from these headquarters, have long made it a practice to "unarrest" members of Congress or powerful staffers. *(Ronald Kessler)*

As a prank, Jack Russ, the House sergeant at arms, ordered the Capitol Police to arrest an aide. Russ took pride in being called The Favormeister. *(AP/Wide World)*

Drawing by Steve Lindstrom.

Lobbyist Paula
Parkinson said she had
sex with eight members
of Congress to promote
agricultural interests.
(AP/Wide World)

A blond female Senate staffer who became known as the Attic Girl had
trysts with Senate staffers in the attic of the Senate Dirksen Office Building.
(Ronald Kessler)

Senator Trent Lott, center, enjoying a chuckle with House Majority Leader Dick Armey, left, has the biggest leadership PAC in the Senate and is reportedly one of the stingiest tippers in the members' inner sanctum dining room. A preacher of family values, House Speaker Newt Gingrich, right, divorced his wife when she had cancer and neglected to pay sufficient child support. *(AP/Wide World)*

House Minority Leader Richard A. Gephardt, right, collected more than $1 million in PAC contributions but said he would ban distribution of PAC checks on the House floor so that "members of Congress vote their consciences, not their contributions." According to Capitol Police sources, hundreds of members' tickets each year were fixed—including numerous tickets of Minority Whip David E. Bonior, left. *(AP/Wide World)*

Representative Charles Wilson introduced legislation to cut Defense appropriations after being told he could not take his girlfriend, Annelise Ilschenko, a former Miss USA World, on a Pentagon plane. *(AP/Wide World)*

Teenage female pages used to put on a show for the Capitol Police every night by undressing in front of open windows in this building, which became known as Virgin Village. *(Ronald Kessler)*

After being sworn in by House Speaker Newt Gingrich as chief administrative officer of the House, Scot M. Faulkner found he could not stop members from ordering for themselves ornate custom-made furniture that cost as much as $20,000 per chair. At center is Faulkner's fiancée, Vicki Hunter.

Until the middle of 1996, the House kept track of its own expenditures of hundreds of millions of dollars with pen and ink in a ledger book similar to the one used by the Continental Congress.

Known as one of the dumbest members, Representative Sonny Bono wanted to eliminate what he called "HRD," which turned out to be the Department of Health and Human Services. *(AP/Wide World)*

While she was an intern on his staff, Frédérique J. Sandretto says she was relegated to sorting mail and fetching sodas after she refused Representative Sonny Bono's advances. Bono flatly denies the charges.

Drawing by Handelsman.
*(© 1996 The New Yorker
Magazine Inc.)*

*"Mr. Speaker, will the gentleman from Small Firearms
yield the floor to the gentleman from Big Tobacco?"*

One of the few truly
admirable members of
Congress, Senator
Philip A. Hart was
known as the
"conscience of the
Senate." *(AP/Wide World)*

Gingrich continued to collect his annual salary of $171,500. Majority Leader Richard K. Armey, a Republican from Texas, and Minority Leader Gephardt each continued to get $148,000 a year. The rest of the members of Congress got their pay of $133,600 a year.

Asked on CNN's *Talk Back Live* whether he would support congressional pay cuts during a shutdown, House majority whip Tom DeLay, a Texas Republican, seemed to suggest that he had a divine right to rule. "No, I would not," he responded. "I am not a federal employee. I am a constitutional officer. My job is in the Constitution of the United States."

Travel to and from the United States may have been paralyzed because Congress had shut down the government, but that did not deter members from continuing to take trips abroad at taxpayer expense. Known as congressional delegation trips (CODELs), the trips are ostensibly to gather information to help in formulating legislation. But the same information can usually be obtained without travel, and most members barely disguise that they are vacationing at the taxpayers' expense.

The State Department has long dreaded such trips. Diplomats are forced to ignore their regular duties and become chauffeurs and tour guides for the visiting members. One congressional delegation to Africa drank more than $1,000 in wine and had it billed to the embassy, while other members have demanded military aircraft to fly back furniture they had bought or have requested embassies pick up the tab for their spouses' shopping sprees.[233]

That the government was closed and State Department employees were not being paid did not deter Sen. Arlen Specter from taking an eight-day trip to Africa and Israel. Diplomats scrambled to arrange time at air-conditioned squash courts in each city Specter visited and to set up tours for his wife and the wife of Sen. Richard C. Shelby, an Alabama Republican. Worried that the group might have to return for a budget vote, the senators scrubbed plans to visit Tanzania, Mozambique, and Ethiopia. But a State Department cable noted that the group might still visit Johannesburg, since they had "non-refundable reservations at Mabula Game Lodge." In between squash games, Specter met with PLO leader Yasir Arafat and Israeli prime minister Shimon Peres. Clearly, the senator viewed himself more as an ambassador-at-large than as a member of Congress.[234]

Rep. Gerald B. H. Solomon, a New York Republican, had planned a trip to Russia, Warsaw, Prague, Sofia, and Tuzla. A State Department cable from Czechoslovakia noted, "Since we anticipate no official business will be transacted on this visit, we will use an [alternate account] to secure transportation and the services of a professional guide," according to Al Kamen's account in the *Washington Post*. Because of the government shutdown, Solomon canceled the trip.

Still, during the 1996 spring recess, more than a dozen senators traveled to such places as China, Brazil, Costa Rica, Chile, and Rome. Sen. Ernest F. Hollings, a South Carolina Democrat, and Sen. William S. Cohen, a Maine Republican, decided to take one last dip into taxpayer funds before they retired. They went to Seoul, Bejing, Shanghai, Hong Kong, and Kuala Lumpur. One member—Rep. Joe Knollenberg, a Michigan Republican—spent thirty-two days overseas in one year. During a two-year period, Rep. Stephen J. Solarz, a New York Democrat, spent more than four months overseas.

The cost is astronomical. In 1995, 148 House members flew to sixty-eight countries, spending $1.2 million just for hotels and meals. During that year, thirty-one senators traveled abroad at a cost of $446,900. But these figures do not begin to show the true cost of the trips. Because members fly on military aircraft, the trips cost far more than if members flew commercially. The Defense Department makes it as difficult as possible to obtain figures for such trips. But *Roll Call* learned that one congressional delegation of twenty-one members led by Rep. Dennis Hastert, an Illinois Republican, to Bosnia, Croatia, Italy, Germany, and Belgium cost the military $236,200.[235] A November 1988 trip led by Sen. Robert J. Dole cost $358,849. And nine other trips in 1995 came to nearly $1 million, or an average of almost $100,000 per trip. If such expenditures were charged to

Congress instead of to the Defense Department, the congressional budget would balloon by tens of millions of dollars.

During one such trip, Rep. Charles Wilson, a Texas Democrat, went into a rage when Defense Intelligence Agency officials in Islamabad told him in February 1986 that he could not take his girlfriend on a Defense Department C12 airplane because she was not part of the official party. Wilson wanted Annelise Ilschenko, a former Miss USA World dressed in fox fur and white, high-heeled boots, to accompany him to take a look at the war in Afghanistan.

"Wilson was furious and had a snit about it," said Kathleen Kiely, a Washington-based reporter for the *Houston Post,* who was on the flight. Kiely said Wilson told embassy officials he might consider cutting their appropriations.[236] Sure enough, tucked away in a bill the following year were two provisions engineered by Wilson to cut the number of government airplanes available to U.S. embassies around the world and to reduce the staff of the Defense Intelligence Agency, the Pentagon arm that operated the plane.

Meanwhile, the Republicans, like the Democrats, larded their appropriations bills with pork-barrel projects. They made sure taxpayer funds went to "struggling" companies such as the General Electric Company so it could export products, to agribusiness enterprises that needed subsidies, and to pharmaceutical companies so they could operate in Puerto Rico. Of the amount added on to the defense budget by the Senate Armed Services Committee, 81 percent went to companies in states with senators on the committee or on the Senate Appropriations' defense subcommittee.

In particular, the home districts of two prominent Republicans, Representatives Joseph M. McDade and Bud Shuster, both of Pennsylvania, became the recipients of costly highway projects. Recognizing that money buys pork projects, town leaders in Frederick, Maryland, held a fund-raiser for Shuster because they wanted federal funds to link two interstate highways. Shuster, the chairman of the House Highway and Infrastructure Committee, attended the breakfast event and gave a ten-minute speech on the importance of linking the highways. Sure enough, Shuster introduced a bill to fund the improvement, and Congress enacted it into law.

The Democrats made sure they got their share. Rep. Norm Dicks, a Washington Democrat, obtained $10.4 million to expand the gym at the Puget Sound Naval Shipyard in his state. The expansion had not been scheduled for another five years, and the existing gym, which is little used, is less than a mile away from a YMCA.

When the Democrats ruled, Sen. Robert C. Byrd of West Virginia was known as the King of Pork because of the not-so-subtle way he persuaded federal agencies to move to his state. When the FBI wanted a new fingerprint facility, it had to agree to build it in Byrd's home state.[237]

No member's whim was too trivial for Congress. An avid golfer, Tom DeLay slipped a one-sentence rider on the Interior Department's spending bill to prevent the U.S. Fish and Wildlife Service from barring the construction of a golf course near his home in Sugar Land, Texas. The Environmental Protection Agency had said the new course could harm migratory songbirds, but DeLay wanted to play golf there.

Rep. Jay Dickey, an Arkansas Republican who owns two Taco Bell franchises in Pine Bluff, had an unpleasant experience with the Occupational Safety and Health Administration. The agency fined him $3,600 for violating regulations requiring adequate ventilation at a sign-making business Dickey and his family own. Saying the violation had been "minor," Dickey the next year pushed through a 30 percent reduction in OSHA's enforcement budget and supported riders repealing key safety and health regulations.[238]

Nor did the Republicans stop congressional perquisites to any large degree. The House halted automatic delivery of ice to members' offices, and the Republicans walked around with ice buckets to symbolize that they had saved the taxpayer money. Yet it was another ruse. A total of 356 House members continued to order ice delivered specially. They included 51 of the 73 House Republican freshmen and 10 of the Democratic freshmen.[239] The Senate, meanwhile, continued the outmoded practice of delivering ice, even though little of it was used. Finally, in October 1996, the Senate leadership decided to have ice delivered only to themselves.

While the Republicans tightened reporting and disclosure rules for lobbyists and restricted gifts and meals lawmakers could receive, they made sure the new legislation was full of loopholes.

"The lobbying reform act is a fraud," said Martin Lobel, the former aide to Senator Proxmire. "It opens even more loopholes than before. The enforcement provisions in the new law are almost nonexistent. The law explicitly allows a lobbyist to continue to lobby even if he or she does not comply with its requirements and also eliminates the criminal penalties provided under the old law."[240]

Congress never touched the real issue, which was the need to reform the campaign financing system. A reform bill put together by Senators John McCain, an Arizona Republican, and Russell Feingold, a Wisconsin Democrat, along with Fred Thompson, a Tennessee Republican, would have established voluntary spending limits for Senate candidates—from $950,000 in smaller states such as Wyoming to $5.5 million in larger states such as California. For those who abide by the limits, the bill would have provided for free or reduced-rate television time. The bill would have banned soft money contributions and bundling and would have limited "independent expenditures."

Most important, the measure would have banned PACs. If such a prohibition were found unconstitutional, the bill would have limited PAC contributions to no more than 20 percent of total spending. Because the Supreme Court has linked campaign expenditures to free speech, the constitutionality of prohibitions on contributions has been an issue. But the court has said that if there is a "substantial government interest in stemming the reality or the appearance of corruption in the electoral process," restrictions on financial contributions could survive First Amendment concerns. If Congress can lawfully ban outright corporate contributions, it should be able to ban PACs.

A similar bill introduced in the House by Representatives

Linda Smith, a Washington Republican, Christopher Shays, a Connecticut Republican, and Marty Meehan, a Massachusetts Democrat, would have provided for reduced-rate television and radio advertising to those candidates who abide by a voluntary limit of $600,000 in campaign expenditures.

As might be expected, PACs threatened to cut off members who supported the measures. "Suddenly we had all these new friends in the House, and they were introducing PAC bans," said Steven F. Stockmeyer of the National Association of Business Political Action Committees. "So we put out a report last fall saying, 'Were you aware of this? Here are the people sponsoring the bills. . . . We think it's stupid to support people who want to put your PAC out of business.'"[241]

The caps on spending were disgracefully high. Only about 20 percent of recent congressional candidates have spent more than the proposed limit of $600,000. Yet Congress, during what was billed as "reform week," let the bills die. In the end, neither Republicans nor Democrats wanted to jeopardize the funds that had gotten them elected. Without a scandal involving Congress itself or strong leadership on the issue from the president, members of Congress are no more likely to reform the system than embezzlers are likely to voluntarily stop ripping off a bank.

"All of a sudden Democratic members looked at the campaign reform legislation and didn't want to do it," said Amy Rosenbaum, Rep. Marty Meehan's legislative assistant on campaign finance reform. They said, "We want PAC money. That's where we get a lot of our money from."[242]

The country may have been founded on the principle of political equality, but in the clubby atmosphere of Congress, those who had tried to reform the system so that neither the rich nor the poor had more clout in electing candidates become "pariahs," according to Rosenbaum. The Republican revolution that was purportedly going to drive out special interests had cynically reinforced the existing system.

"Members make wisecracks," Representative Meehan said. " 'Here's the reformer. If he gets his way, he'll put us all in jail.' Foolishness like that. They say it in the cloakroom, on the floor. Half-kidding, half-serious."

"Some of my own friends in Congress view me in a sense as an enemy because somehow I have passed judgment on them and think that what they do is tainted," said Shays.

"The fact is the leadership, Republican or Democratic, doesn't want to get it done," Representative Hamilton said. They "posture without any real prospect of enacting anything into law. That has been going on for the past decade here."

10

$20,000 Silk-Covered Chairs

When Scot M. Faulkner took over as chief administrative officer of the House in December 1994, what he found stunned him. Newt Gingrich and his coterie had handpicked Faulkner to bring modern management techniques to the House. Faulkner had a solid management background, both in government and private industry. But Faulkner, then forty-one years old, had never seen or heard of such a disastrously run, self-indulgent, out-of-control organization. That it was the same organization that initiates taxation and appropriations bills to run a government that spends $1.6 trillion a year made what Faulkner uncovered frightening.

The idea of hiring an administrator to run what was then the $834.2-million-a-year operations of the House like a business went back to 1977, when a commission headed by Rep. David R. Obey, a Wisconsin Democrat, recommended it. As envisioned then, the administrator would control the House's finances and take over many of the duties of the House clerk and sergeant at arms. After the House Bank and House Post Office scandals, the Democrats picked up the idea. They adopted it in 1992 over Republican objections. However, the Democrats never gave the administrator—called the director of nonlegislative and financial services—enough clout to change significantly the way the House operated.

Gingrich had always espoused quality management. As minority whip, he had hired Philip Crosby Associates Inc., a management consulting firm, to train what was called Newt World—the staff of his personal office, whip office, and money-raising operation, GOPAC—in efficient management concepts. Back then, Gingrich wanted to expand the training to the rest of the House, but the proposal died in committee. Both Democrats and Republicans said running the House of Representatives like a business would never work.

Faulkner was the Crosby vice president who had trained Gingrich's people. A straightforward, no-nonsense tactician, Faulkner had worked with Fortune 500 companies ranging from Marriott Corp. and Bell Atlantic to Prudential Insurance Co. of America. Prior to that, he had held management positions in the White House and the General Services Administration, the agency that provides the rest of the government with office space and supplies.

Faulkner was given a beautifully appointed office in the Capitol, with thick blue carpeting, leather chairs, and a cherry-wood desk. On the wall was a painting of Benjamin H. Latrobe, an English architect whom President Thomas Jefferson had appointed in 1803 as surveyor of public buildings in charge of finishing construction of the Capitol.

Unlike Latrobe, Faulkner had little idea of the scope of his new job. The first hint came on December 10, 1994, when he was shown thirty-eight briefing books that described the operations he was about to oversee. Faulkner's next shock came when he saw the books of the House. In any modern organization, financial statements list assets and liabilities so that managers know what bills have been incurred but not yet paid. Such accrual accounting guards against overspending. But the House of Representatives had no need to attend to such niceties. It could always raise taxes and appropriate more money for itself from the people. So the House recorded only receipts and disbursements, as in a giant checking account. What's more, the books of the House were kept by the clerk of the House just as they had been when the Continental Congress first convened in 1774—in a ledger etched with multicolored pen-and-ink entries. Many of the entries had been crossed out and new ones substituted. For example, a sum of $41 million was crossed out and $28 million simply scratched over it.

"Most people's checkbooks look better than this," Faulkner said of the ledger.[243]

Gingrich's transition team decided to hire an accounting firm. It was the only way to make sense of the House's operations. For $3.2 million, Price Waterhouse did an audit that essentially found the patient was too sick to operate on. Officially, the report was made to the House inspector general, a position that the previous Congress had created, giving its occupant a staff of only a secretary.

The worst judgment an accounting firm can render is that it cannot make a judgment. That is what Price Waterhouse said about the House. Never had the accounting firm seen anything like it. Not only could the firm render no opinion on the validity of the House's books, but, the firm found, the House "lacks the organization and structure to periodically prepare financial statements that, even after significant audit adjustment and reconstruction, are accurate." In the polite language of the report, the firm also concluded that the House operated "under rules and requirements that were less restrictive than those of other organizations." Moreover, the House "erred on the side of providing members with the services they wanted without due regard to economy."

"The Price Waterhouse people sat there and shook their heads," Faulkner recalled. "They couldn't believe a place could be as badly run as this was."[244]

Among other things, Price Waterhouse found that members had indeed been overspending their annual office allowances by as much as $250,000 per office. In fiscal 1994, members spent $14 million more than had been appropriated for their offices.[245]

But that was no problem: in supplemental appropriations, the House had simply enlarged the federal budget to cover its overspending. The result was a higher deficit or an increase in taxes.

When Faulkner tried to pin down the House's assets, he learned that records were either inaccurate or nonexistent. Moreover, the House had no contracts to cover many of the goods and services it was receiving. In many cases, the items were not needed in the first place. For example, the House had issued what it called "perpetual purchase orders" so that paper for stationery was regularly delivered, even though the House had enough for years.

"When we first walked in the door, there was dark matter," Faulkner said. "Money was flowing, and we didn't know why. There was no purchase order or contract or voucher. People would say there was a contract, but no one could find it."

Faulkner was in for an even bigger jolt when he traced a rumor that the House maintained a leased warehouse full of perfectly usable furniture. With Rep. Jim Nussle, an Iowa Republican assigned by Gingrich to be in charge of the Republican transition, Faulkner visited the warehouse at First and I Streets in southeast Washington. As it turned out, the House was paying $230,000 a year to lease the 44,860-square-foot building, which covered a third of a city block. Formerly owned by the *Washington Star*, the building was now owned by the *Washington Post*. Yet the House had no record of the lease; Faulkner had to obtain a copy of it from the *Post*.

When Faulkner and Nussle toured the building, they could not believe their eyes. Crammed into five floors were four thousand pieces of furniture—either custom-made for members and discarded or new and still in packing crates. Some of the new desks, sofas, armchairs, and lamps had been delivered as far back as 1962. Price Waterhouse determined the total original value of the forgotten furniture to be $12 million.

"It was custom-made furniture and systems furniture," Faulkner said. Systems furniture snaps onto office partitions. "There was no inventory. You had members going back to the sixties who wanted something different, bought systems furniture, and then sent it back. The bill of lading was still on the furniture."

Faulkner decided the only way to keep track of the rest of the House's money was to sign every check and voucher himself. In that way, he found out that members were able to buy the furniture in their district offices for ridiculously low sums.

"I received this reimbursement check for fifty dollars," Faulkner said. "A member had overpaid for the district office furniture. Attached was a price list of one dollar, two dollars for each item. I'm sitting there going, 'Two dollars for a desk that I know was probably five hundred dollars to buy?' The signal was that there was something grievously wrong with the furniture policy."

Faulkner found that the House had intricate procurement rules and restrictions on how members could obtain supplies and services for their offices, but ignored them all.

"Procurement rules were a joke, so members got waivers from the Committee on House Administration to do almost anything they wanted," Faulkner said. "People had to get waivers just to function. Because they issued the waivers, the power of the members of the administration committee was enhanced. If you do things through waivers, then your core system is irrelevant."

Contained in a manual almost four inches thick, the House rules prescribed what kinds of letter openers could be ordered and what model number and brand of copying machine or television set could be bought.

"It was like living in the old Soviet Union," Faulkner said. "There were only three TV sets you could have. Members got written waivers to buy television sets at Circuit City at one hundred dollars less than what was on the prescribed list."

In fact, "the rules were so prescriptive that members could only spend two hundred and fifty dollars a year for subscriptions," Faulkner said. "If they got *The Economist*, they were already over the yearly limit. So they had to obtain a waiver from the Committee on House Administration. Members would say, 'I want *The Economist*, the *Wall Street Journal*, and *Time*.' That would be a waiver."

In other cases, the rules were simply ignored. "That is why we had money going out the door with no invoice, contract, purchase order, or voucher," Faulkner said. Moreover, "no one enforced the rules. You had a fifty-four-person finance shop with no certified public accountants. Only three people had any accounting training."

Everywhere Faulkner and Price Waterhouse looked, they found waste and duplication. Rather than buying existing computer software, the House had spent $5 million to develop its own program for eventually mechanizing its financial system. The new system never worked. Even if it had, it would have produced only seven of the thirty-four categories of information required by government accounting guidelines. The House had been overpaying employees or duplicating their benefit payments by as much as $76,000 a year. Overall, the House was paying workers $4 million more than people in the private sector were being paid for comparable jobs. At least $5 million was being wasted because the House staffed such antiquated functions as the folding room, which mailed newsletters, at the same level regardless of what the demand was.

In the first place, said Faulkner, "They were using 1850s technology." But the real waste occurred because the operation employed enough people to handle 2 million pieces of mail a day. In some months, the folding room handled half a million pieces of mail in an entire month.

"We were paying as much as four hundred and eighty dollars per thousand pieces of mail for some of those months," Faulkner said. "We averaged forty or fifty dollars per thousand. The private sector was doing the same job for fifteen dollars or even eight dollars per thousand."

Running a simple supply store was beyond the grasp of the House. The store stocked and stored 2,114 items—pencils, paper clips, stationery. More than 80 percent of the items accounted for 5 percent of sales. A new House gift shop that opened in 1994 to sell House mugs and sweatshirts was losing an estimated $270,000 a year. One reason was that the number of employees per $1,000 in sales was three times higher than in the private sector. Moreover, controls over the cash were nonexistent.

When Faulkner looked into the House's parking policies, he found a disaster. On congested Capitol Hill, nothing is as important as parking. "Eliminating parking spaces on the east front of the Capitol was a much bigger issue than providing funds for education or even military expenditures," said Alan S. Novins, a former Senate staffer.[246]

Despite all the perquisites Congress provides for itself, Congress had made no provision for parking for the public. Citizens who want to see their congressman or senator have to take the subway or hire taxis. Nearly all street parking on Capitol Hill is either restricted for members or their staffs or limited to no more than two hours.

Faulkner found that just as in the financial area, the lawmakers ignored the rules they had made for themselves. Thus, while House rules permitted members only eight parking spaces for themselves and their staff—five in garages and three on nearby streets or lots—157 members had more than eight spaces.[247] Indeed, as Faulkner privately reported to the Committee on House Oversight in April 1995, Herbert H. Bateman, a Virginia Republican; Tom DeLay, a Texas Republican; Vic Fazio, a California Democrat; and Matthew G. Martinez, a California Democrat, each had eleven spaces. Members who had ten parking spaces included Richard H. Baker, a Louisiana Republican; Thomas M. Barrett, a Wisconsin Democrat; Tom Bevill, an Alabama Democrat; John Bryant, a Texas Democrat; John D. Dingell, a Michigan Democrat; Anna G. Eshoo, a California Democrat; Martin Frost, a Texas Democrat; Sam Gejdenson, a Connecticut Democrat; Benjamin A. Gilman, a New York Republican; Bob Inglis, a South Carolina Republican; Dale E. Kildee, a Michigan Democrat; Peter T. King, a New York Republican; Scott L. Klug, a Wisconsin Republican; Floyd Spence, a South Carolina Republican; Louis Stokes, an Ohio Democrat; James A. Traficant Jr., an Ohio Democrat; Curt Weldon, a Pennsylvania Republican; and Frank R. Wolf, a Virginia Republican.

Checking spaces and permits against license tags, Faulkner found that fifty of the additional spaces had been given to former members who were now lobbyists.[248] Like much of what Faulkner found, that fact never saw the light of day.

"Some members had all eight spaces inside," Faulkner said. "Some members who probably got on the wrong side of the leadership had all but the member's space outside. In one case, we had a staffer's Jaguar in long-term storage in a lot. We found a Bentley on blocks in a garage. Every few years, Congress had acquired more land for more parking, even though there was no need for it. This was outrageous. People were being told there weren't parking spaces, and then we ran across this."

Because of security concerns, the implications were more than financial. "The Hill is not as safe a place as we would like it to be," Faulkner said. "There have been rapes up here. A year ago, a woman cut through an alley and turned in the wrong direction and got raped. So parking is a security issue." So that tighter security could be imposed on garages, Faulkner handed the parking operation over to the sergeant at arms.

As in the financial area, all of the special privileges had been handed out through waivers, according to the Price Waterhouse report. "There were four thousand written waivers a month issued by Charlie Rose, chairman of the Committee on House Administration, that allowed members to circumvent the public rules of the House," Faulkner said.[249]

When Faulkner told members they could no longer give their spaces to lobbyists, some complained. Many members had had the inside track on other privileges such as fancy computers or programs because they had cultivated certain employees. When they found they were being treated equally, they complained as well. But because Faulkner had the support of Gingrich, members realized they had little chance of overturning his decisions. "They complained to the leadership that they couldn't do what they had done before," Faulkner said. "The leadership said, 'You shouldn't have been doing those things before.'"

"If we had had forty years of Republican rule, I think some of the same things might have gone on," Faulkner said. "The process was so loose and so unaccountable that anyone in power for a long period of time would have succumbed to the temptations.''

By requiring members to abide by their own rules, and by reducing parking spaces to the prescribed number for House committee staffs and other House offices, Faulkner freed up a total of 786 spaces. As a result, Faulkner was able to add another inside space to each member's allotment. Members now have six spaces inside instead of five, and two outside instead of three.

Because members now had the prescribed number of spaces, two outside lots were no longer needed. Faulkner canceled the lease on one lot that was owned by the District of Columbia government. He turned the second, 225-space lot over to the public. To this day, that lot at South Capitol and D Streets SW is the only congressional lot open to public parking. The Senate has yet to see fit to provide public parking. As a rule, Americans who drive from Missouri or New Hampshire to see their elected representatives still must scout for two-hour restricted parking.

One reason the parking operation was such a mess was that it was operated by the Architect of the Capitol. The Architect constructs and maintains the Capitol and its office buildings and grounds. A separate duchy within Congress, the Architect reports to both the House and the Senate and is therefore largely immune from accountability. Yet the Architect employs 1,545 people and has a budget of $159 million a year. Under legislation approved in 1989, the architect is appointed for a ten-year term by the president, with the advice and consent of the Senate, from a list of three candidates recommended by a congressional commission.

President George Washington appointed the first architect, William Thornton, in 1793. From 1971 to 1995, George M. White served as the architect. Appointed by President Nixon, White was the ninth to hold that position. He was a gracious man with degrees in electrical engineering, law, and management. But White did not have the toughness needed to run an organization of such magnitude. Of all the congressional fief-doms, the Architect's office is known as the most wasteful.

An April 1994 General Accounting Office study found that the Architect did not employ many accepted modern personnel management techniques, contributing to a "demoralized and distrustful" working environment. Compared with private industry and the rest of the government, the Architect had a higher percentage of white men in high-paying jobs. Conversely, women and minorities tended to have low-paying jobs.[250] At one point, Sen. Barbara Mikulski, a Maryland Democrat who had requested the GAO study, called for White to resign.

"They had twenty people working a job that four in industry would do," said Leroy Tolbert, who was a laborer in the Architect's office and has also worked for private industry. "They would clean the floor or move something. It would take thirty to move what ten could do. They would work slowly. The work ethic was different. They worked, but worked real slowly. If someone worked fast, they would fire your ass. If you work one way and they work another, they can't go for that."[251]

"There are many support people who do nothing," said Sgt. John A. Gott of the Capitol Police. "At night you see people who work for the Architect in shops sleeping in the garage."[252]

In 1993, the Architect of the Capitol paid nearly $500,000 in taxpayer funds to settle a sexual harassment lawsuit brought by two kitchen workers whose complaints to managers over a three-year period about their supervisor's sexual advances were ignored.

"Some supervisors have relationships with some of the maids who clean up at night," said Mark A. Watkins, a former laborer in the Architect's office. "In return, they get better jobs."

In 1994, the Architect's office installed an $18-million subway system that periodically traps members in the cars. The subway connects the Capitol with the Hart and Dirksen Senate Office Buildings. The architect called the new subway a "state-of-the-art people mover." But if a passenger holds a door open, not just the affected subway car stops: all the cars operating on the line stop. Twice during April 1995, Senate votes were delayed because the subway had trapped senators. Sen. Frank R. Lautenberg, a New Jersey Democrat who was caught, said of the subway, "I think it stinks. It's too complicated."

But Sen. Hank Brown, a Colorado Republican who was trapped and freed himself by tripping an emergency lever, said the new system was a great improvement. He had to walk the rest of the way to his office. It gave him "more exercise."

"All indications are that if Price Waterhouse weighed into the Architect, they would find many times over what they found here," Faulkner said. "The Architect has a lot of accounts that slosh around and need to be looked at."[253]

The lack of reliable information is symptomatic of the way the Hill operates. "There is an enormous amount of paranoia on Capitol Hill," said Terry Eisenberg, who was commander of the Capitol Police's employee development bureau for nine years. "People are concerned about who is going to stab them in the back. There is very little trust to either do what is right or work cooperatively with each other. I have never been in an atmosphere or known of an atmosphere which is as mean-spirited and dishonest as the atmosphere on Capitol Hill."[254]

As a result, "either I got no information or misleading information. . . . You spend fifty percent of your time doing your job, and the rest of the time covering your ass," Eisenberg said.

To get the House into shape, Faulkner and the House Committee on Oversight, formerly the Committee on House Administration, discarded the thick book of rules and replaced it with one that is only a third of an inch thick. The new rules allowed members to buy whatever they wanted from their office allowances. So long as they did not overspend, the assumption was they would buy economically.

"Now you have, in effect, a chief executive officer with a budget of about nine hundred thousand dollars," Faulkner said. "Whatever they want to do with it, they can do with it, as long as it is documentable within broad guidelines. If they have worked with a computer vendor before, they can use him. In the real world, this stuff is commonplace. Here it is revolutionary. . . . You are dealing with two hundred and five years of dysfunction."

Instead of operating a folding room, Faulkner let members hire printers to do their mailings. If they were from Montana, they would then save considerable sums by hiring lower-cost printers in their districts. Since postage for such material is based on distance, members could save additional money by mailing newsletters to their constituents from their home states rather than from Washington. The net savings to taxpayers was $2.6 million a year.

Faulkner held an auction to get rid of some unneeded furniture, bringing in $140,000. Other furniture is being used. Faulkner was able to cancel the lease on the warehouse. Rather than using the House's Rube Goldberg software to track its finances, Faulkner adopted a computer software system developed by the U.S. Geological Survey that was already working. While some glitches occurred when the new system took over and some payments were delayed, the problems were overcome within a few weeks.

Faulkner awarded a contract to Pitney Bowes to sort the 42 million pieces of mail that go in and out of the House each year, replacing the discredited House Post Office. For $1 a year, the U.S. Postal Service took over window operations at thirteen locations throughout House office buildings and the Capitol. The change saved $1.4 million a year.

Referring to the House Post Office scandal and the use of stamps to embezzle money, Faulkner said, "When you have an outside vendor, the possibility is less he will be intimidated by a congressman who says he will cut its funding or he can get you fired if you don't do what he wants."

Overall, the House budget went from $834.2 million to $755.6 million a year—a savings of nearly $80 million. These figures include what Congress has declared to be "permanent" budget authority, which naturally includes members' salaries. Two-thirds of the savings came from cutting House committee staffs by a third. The rest of the savings came from more efficient operations.

Because Congress passed the Congressional Accountability

Act on January 23, 1995, Faulkner had to begin paying overtime to employees. For more than two hundred years, Congress had passed laws to regulate the workplace but had always exempted itself. Thomas Jefferson wrote that the constitutional framers had taken care to "provide that the laws should bind equally on all, and especially that those who make them shall not exempt themselves from their operation." Yet members had enacted employment and civil rights laws that applied to everyone in the country but them.

The new law applied eleven existing statutes to Congress. But as usual, Congress made sure that when it came to laws its own members had to follow, there would be a cornucopia of loopholes. So Congress decreed that the Accountability Act would apply to Congress only as an exercise of its "rulemaking power." Thus, the provisions of the law can be changed at any time, and members who violate the workplace laws—for example, by sexually harassing or discriminating against an employee—suffer no consequences.

"If, after a convoluted internal process, a legislator is found to have violated one of these rules, no monetary penalty can be assessed on the individual," according to Robert Turner of the University of Virginia Center for National Security Law. "Instead, the much-heralded law provides that all fines or damages—as well as the legal fees of the culprit—will be conveniently picked up by the American taxpayer."[255]

As soon as the rules that Congress had imposed on private employers began to chafe, Congress began carving out exceptions for itself. The Capitol Police claimed unions should be barred from organizing its members because they are engaged in "sensitive activities of the government, and their work directly relates to the protection and preservation of the government." Likewise, the House Oversight Committee recommended that most professional and legislative staffers be prohibited from joining unions. At least eleven members defied the law and exempted their entire staffs from the overtime requirement. The members included Rep. James Barcia, a Michigan Democrat who ironically had always voted for the positions endorsed by the AFL-CIO, and Rep. Bill Thomas, a California Republican who is chairman of the House Committee on Oversight and thus has jurisdiction over the new law and its enforcement.

To reduce overtime, Faulkner rearranged workers' schedules to conform with Congress's schedule. Whenever possible, he also made sure employees took compensatory time instead of overtime.

By July 1996, Price Waterhouse had completed a second audit and certified that the books of the House accurately presented its financial condition. But after almost two years in the job, Faulkner was still confounded by some mysteries. One was the existence of a Western Union office in the Cannon House Office Building. With fax machines, electronic mail, and overnight mail delivery, Faulkner could not find out why the House needed a Western Union office in the first place. Nor could he figure out how Western Union had gotten there or what financial arrangements it had with the House.

A visit by the author to the office in Room 242-A shed little light on the riddle. Hearing a visitor, a clerk in a back room came out to the front counter. He seemed astounded to see anyone. Asked his name, the clerk paused and said, "John Smith." Asked how many customers he has, "Smith" became more enthusiastic. "At least a couple a day," he said.

"Western Union has been operating in Cannon for eighty years, and there is no documentation on who brought them in and whether they were ever paid or whether they were paying us," Faulkner said. "Given that Western Union is an endangered technology, we are looking at whether it makes sense to have them here."

But the reformist zeal of the Republican leadership had its limits. While they approved most of Faulkner's changes, they would not give up some perquisites. To this day, both the House and the Senate provide members with elaborate furniture made by dozens of congressional cabinetmakers and upholsterers. In the House, the specially made furniture is available to the leadership, officers, and committee chairmen—roughly two hundred members. In the Senate, any member can order it. When they leave office—often to become lobbyists—the members buy some of the furniture at ridiculously low prices. Often, members order wet bars, refrigerators, and custom cabinets and bookcases installed as well.

Faulkner got his first hint of how regally members decorate when he and some of Gingrich's lieutenants saw a Capitol hideaway used by House Speaker Tom Foley and his wife, Heather. "You walked in the door, and there was her desk and a small room," Faulkner said. "No one was allowed behind that desk. Some of us went past that desk. We found a stairway that had been built at Foley's instruction to the second floor. In essence, it was an apartment, with a wet bar, a bedroom, a full bath. It had a kitchen unit. Even some of the Democrats didn't know about it. We were able to attribute at least sixty-eight thousand dollars to the construction of that space. No one knew it existed. It was not in the blueprints."[256]

By the time Faulkner saw the hideaway, Foley was out of office, and the furniture had been removed. Faulkner never found out what had happened to it. Asked what became of it, and if he took it, under what authority, Foley did not respond.

Like most House and Senate leaders, Foley had ornate furniture made for his office as well. A former House cabinetmaker said he made a stereo cabinet for Foley to the tune of $12,000 in labor and materials. It would have cost a fraction of that if purchased from a manufacturer.

"We made it per his specifications," the former House employee said. "My boss went over it with him, and the architect drew up drawings. . . . It was nine feet high. It took me four months to make it. I was making thirty-five thousand dollars a year. It was solid mahogany."

Even the new Senate page dormitory was royally outfitted. Instead of buying ready-made furniture, a cabinetmaker spent nearly a year making eighteen solid-oak bunk beds, along with bookshelves and desks, for the new dorm.

"Anything a member wanted, they would put in a request, and they got it," a cabinetmaker said. "They're like little gods. They talk a bunch of stuff about saving money until it hits home for them."

Like many other employees, the cabinetmaker was appalled by the waste he saw in Congress. "Many times we did an office and did it again a year later when a new member came in," the cabinetmaker said. "We stripped out everything, including carpets."

"There is a lot of waste," said Steve C. Alder, an elevator mechanic. "So much is thrown in the trash that could be sold. To recycle or bring something back into the system, there's an attitude that there's too much paperwork. They throw out furniture, computers. You name it, it goes in the trash."[257]

Daniel J. Kreitman, a former Senate upholsterer, said members buy new furniture and have Senate employees remove the covering and replace it with far more expensive fabric. "It's all leatherwork; the wood is hand-carved," Kreitman said. Moreover, the leather chairs in the Senate chamber are not only custom-made, the wheels they sit on are custom-made, too.[258]

"One man finished twenty chairs a year for the chamber," said David W. Clements, a former Senate cabinetmaker. "He is paid about forty thousand dollars a year. That comes to two thousand dollars a chair."[259]

When senators leave, they can buy their chairs for $100. "The wheels probably cost more to make than they sell the chairs for," Kreitman said.

Price Waterhouse determined that the House alone was spending $1.3 million a year for custom furniture. Besides the furniture, House leaders often order custom-made draperies, upholstery jobs, and carpeting.

"Members say they want silk damask with tassels for drapes," a House financial officer said. "We have seen amazing prices. It could be forty thousand dollars for a couple of chairs covered with silk. Or special custom drapes made with special fabrics woven to order."

These luxuries are charged to the overall budget of the House, instead of to members' office allowances. Thus, members have no incentive to order less expensive furniture. Nor does the cost show up in any public financial record.

Faulkner proposed requiring members to pay for their furniture, upholstery jobs, carpeting, and draperies out of their allocations, but the House Committee on Oversight never approved it. Nor would the committee approve requiring members to pay the true replacement value of furniture they are allowed to take home with them—their desk, desk chair, and district office furniture. Allowed or not, many members also take home the rest of their furnishings.[260]

"When a member asks for a cherry cabinet, the shop builds it," said Raymond Carson, who retired from the Capitol Police as a lieutenant in February 1997. "Then when they leave, they might have thirty thousand to forty thousand dollars' worth of furniture, and they bought it for six hundred dollars or a thousand dollars. There were conference tables and desks going out to some lobbyists' offices."

To make members accountable for such extravagances, "we proposed that they would be charged the difference between upholstery that costs twenty thousand dollars instead of one thousand five hundred and ninety-nine dollars," Faulkner said. "That proposal has been before the committee since November 1995."

Rebuffed, Faulkner instructed his staff to diplomatically show members the differences in cost between the custom work they wanted and the prices of similar goods maintained in the House inventory. "We are here not only to serve our ten thousand customers, but we are also stewards of the public funds," Faulkner said. "To tell members we will do all of these things, but they should also think about the tax dollars involved, is a new concept up here."

That worked only about half the time. As if the custom work defined their own importance, half the members continued to order the more expensive items even when told of the price differences. Faulkner's records depict the waste: A member ordered furniture that cost $17,610 and would have cost $627 from stock. Another member ordered office furniture that cost $14,875 and would have cost $626 from a manufacturer. Draperies that would have cost $1,902 from the House inventory cost $12,107. Carpet that should have cost $3,222 cost $9,338. Upholstery available for $248 cost $3,120.

Those ordering such outrageous custom work include the House Republican leadership—House Speaker Newt Gingrich of Georgia; Majority Leader Richard K. Armey of Texas; John

Boehner of Ohio, the chairman of the House Republican Conference; and Majority Whip Tom DeLay of Texas—along with David E. Bonior of Michigan, the minority whip.

Thus the same members displaying ice buckets on television to show they had cut out a wasteful perquisite; who railed against government waste and deficits; who had advocated cutting Medicare and Medicaid; and who had shut down the government in an effort to cut the budget were secretly ordering for themselves custom-made $20,000 silk-covered chairs and other items that cost as much as 2,713 percent more than the cost of furnishings available from the House inventory. Many of the items would put Buckingham Palace to shame.

Yet in terms of total money wasted, the real scandal was that both the Senate—which has a budget of $446 million—and the Architect of the Capitol continued to operate much as the House had operated before Faulkner came in. The Senate, for example, continues to maintain its own post office. Despite interest shown by leaders appointed by Sen. Trent Lott, the new majority leader, in what Faulkner had done, "trying to do something very simple like buying a laptop computer for the senator gets frustrating," said Matt Raymond, communications director to Sen. Conrad Burns, a Montana Republican. "We've had to go to the rules committee. Even though we might have the money, we can't spend it to improve the way this office operates." Moreover, "only certain software packages are approved. Everything up here has to go through an incredible vetting process. . . . There is a lot of passing of the buck. There's a lot of that in Congress."[261]

"This should run similar to a city management government," said Sen. Frank H. Murkowski, an Alaska Republican. "It is internally inefficient."[262]

Even finding out how much each senator spends for his or her office is virtually impossible. A call to the Senate Rules and Administration Committee, which oversees such matters, is met with the suggestion that the information can be found in a Senate report. But the report only lays out the formula for allocating money; it does not list the amounts. Stuart F. Balderson, the Senate's chief financial officer, did not return telephone calls.* Unlike in the rest of the government, no Freedom of Information Act requires Congress to provide such information. Reformed or not, Congress was still unwilling to apply to itself the FOIA, among other laws. In its public reports, the Senate even scrambles the names of employees to make it more difficult for outsiders to look them up.

"There hasn't been much change in the Senate," Faulkner said. "It's a much more tradition-bound body. I have had encounters there. I think Price Waterhouse could put together a similar report on the Senate."

As for the House, members could only take so much reform. After the November 1996 election, Bill Thomas, the chairman of the House Committee on Oversight, demanded that Faulkner report only to him, not to Gingrich. All along, Thomas had blocked many of Faulkner's reforms. When Gingrich acquiesced to the change, Faulkner told him he did not want to continue.

In fact, after swearing him in, Gingrich had had no further contact with Faulkner. While Gingrich occasionally bumped into him at receptions and sat in on a few meetings that Faulkner attended, the Speaker never called Faulkner or met with him alone. Representative Nussle, rather than Gingrich, had provided Faulkner with most of his support. When it came down to a choice between continuing reform or returning to the House's self-indulgent ways, Gingrich chose to turn back the clock, leaving Faulkner out to dry.

The purpose of appointing Faulkner was to take politics out of the management of the House. Yet as soon as he left, the House fired ten of his immediate staff, giving them two weeks of severance pay. Two weeks before Christmas, Gail F. Henkin, Faulkner's executive assistant, said she had to move from her apartment because she had no job. The message was clear: the much-touted Republican reform of the House was not only dead, it was in disrepute.

---

* The author was able to obtain the figures anyway because Rep. Lee H. Hamilton asked the Congressional Research Service, which normally does not respond to specific queries from the media, to cooperate on the research for this book.

"They don't want to be accountable to the taxpayer," said one of Faulkner's assistants. "We supposedly elect representatives for us. Once they get that little power, forget it. It has to do with their egos. They do what they want, not what the constituents want. It's this trip that they're on. They want to go back to the way it was. They don't want the taxpayers to know what they're doing. It's disgusting."

11

The Packwood Papers

"Had an apple and a hamburger and milk, and then went out shopping at the Safeway," Sen. Bob Packwood wrote in his diary on January 14, 1993. "God, it's such a much better store than the Giant—the 'Social Safeway' in Georgetown," he wrote. "Then, stopped at Myer-Emco to look at their receivers. They had some modest-priced receivers in the $300–$400 range, but God, they were not as user-friendly as that new Sony that I bought."[263]

On February 2, 1992, Packwood wrote, "Went home. Thought I'll buy those two wall-mounted telephones this afternoon and put them in. So I went to Hechinger's. I was looking for AT&T equipment. I still find it the best equipment around for telephones. And I said, will these mount on the wall? They said yes. So I bought some connecting cord—although it's that round cord, and what I really needed was flat cord. As a matter of fact, it seems to me that I . . . can drill a couple of holes in the very thin plywood and mount it there with no great difficulty."

When Packwood's diaries became public during an ethics

investigation, voters may well have wondered how a U.S. senator, who was later chairman of the powerful Finance Committee with oversight over tax laws, could have found the time to write about the pleasures of shopping at Safeway. But Packwood's vapid prose and his obsession with the boring minutiae of his personal life point to a more alarming fact: many members of Congress are compulsively self-centered and not very bright.

"Here is a U.S. senator who thinks his thoughts on hair-care products or Safeway versus Giant are important," said a Senate staffer. "That is actually representative. They think that because they worry about it, and it came out of their heads, it is important."

Moreover, while Packwood's diary does not shed light on the issue, many members are remarkably passive individuals who blame everyone but themselves for what even they concede is the dysfunctional, mendacious way Congress operates.

Most Americans form their impressions of Congress by watching members expound on television shows, give speeches on the floor, or mouth canned lines in campaign commercials. But television is selective. According to one study, 90 percent of network coverage of Congress focuses on fewer than 3 percent of the members. Forty percent of House members never make it onto the network evening news.[264]

The reason the same members keep appearing week after week on the air is that "the lesser known members are too dumb to put on," according to a producer at *Fox News Sunday*. "They are orchestrated by their staffs and can't discuss the issues."

Interviews with members bear that out. Away from their staffs, many do not understand questions. Some give wandering, stream-of-consciousness answers. Others contradict themselves. They may look good on television, but away from the Capitol, most members of Congress would not stand out as leaders.

Fearful of how he might respond to questions from high school students in Omaha, aides to Jon Christensen, a Nebraska Republican, gave some students prepared questions to ask during his 1994 campaign. So Christensen would know to call on them, the aides instructed the student plants to hold up a pen when they asked a question. But word got out, and soon most of the students were raising pens. Christensen took ten questions from the students; only two were from the plants.

In 1831, Alexis de Tocqueville characterized the House as "remarkable for its vulgarity and its poverty of talent." Today, the same could be said of both houses. As if to underscore the point, after Bill Clinton's 1994 State of the Union message, an open microphone caught then representative Martin Hoke, an Ohio Republican, remarking on the anatomy of Conus Communications producer Lisa Dwyer. Dwyer was wiring Hoke for a reaction to Clinton's speech. Turning to Rep. Eric Fingerhut, an Ohio Democrat, Hoke said, "She has the *beeeeg* breasts."[265]

At the close of Rep. Don Riegle's 1976 Senate race, the *Detroit News* ran tapes of his intimate conversations with Bette Jane Ackerman, a staffer in his office, who tape-recorded their conversations.[266] During one telephone call, Ackerman said, "Don, I love you, and I'll always love—"

"And I'll always love you," Riegle interrupted. "I—I, God, I feel such super love for you. By the way, the newsletter should start arriving."

While Riegle's affair was consensual, Sen. Bob Packwood regularly forced himself on female staffers, kissing them fully on the lips, forcing his tongue into their mouths, or rubbing their breasts or buttocks. Citing eighteen such cases between 1969 and 1990, the Senate Ethics Committee concluded in May 1995 that Packwood had engaged in a pattern of sexual harassment and misconduct. In the face of the committee's recommendation that he be expelled from the Senate, Packwood resigned.[267]

During his eight years in the House, Rep. Jim Bates, a California Democrat, regularly propositioned female staffers and commented on the size of their breasts. One woman said Bates fondled her leg while discussing legislative business.[268] Rep. Mel Reynolds, an Illinois Democrat, not only had sex with a former campaign worker when she was sixteen and tried to acquire nude pictures of a fifteen-year-old, he then tried to induce witnesses to recant testimony against him.[269]

"PAC reform is a small part of the problem [in Congress],"

said Rep. Jim Leach, an Iowa Republican and one of the more respected members of Congress. "The larger problem is the kinds of people who run. One has the sense that the very best people in America do not participate in the democratic process. A congressman or senator ought to be the quality of a top partner in a law firm, or of the executive vice president of a top company, or a first-class entrepreneur, or a first-class teacher or labor union leader. Most people in Congress today would not have made those positions."[270]

Leach, who attended Princeton University, Johns Hopkins University, and the London School of Economics, said he respects as decent, honorable people only about two dozen members of the House and fewer than a dozen members of the Senate.

"The type of people who are good at getting elected are generally not good at representation," said Leach, meaning people who are slick on television may not make good representatives. Leach usually wears a ratty sweater, and his administrative assistant, Dill Tate, said, "I can't even get him to comb his hair."

"A pretty face and being good at raising money do not necessarily mean they can represent you well," Leach said. "I know very few instances today when a congressman is one of the fifty most superior people in a district."

Lawyers predominate in Congress, followed by businessmen, politicians, teachers, and journalists. Corporate executives rarely run for Congress. Many members are druggists, morticians, or real estate agents. Eleven percent of members of Congress never graduated from college. The average age of members is fifty-three. A quarter of the members are Catholics, followed by Protestants. Jews account for 8 percent of the members. Ten percent of members are women, and 7.5 percent are African-Americans.[271]

Male members gave way to women members grudgingly. In 1967, three women members invaded the members' gym in the Rayburn Building, demanding equal access to the swimming pool. Because men insisted on swimming nude, they had allowed women members only ninety minutes a day in the pool.

The male members refused to put on their trunks but agreed to extend women's swim time to fourteen hours a week.

Yet it was a woman, Sen. Margaret Chase Smith of Maine, who was the first Republican who had the courage to take on Sen. Joseph R. McCarthy. McCarthy, a Republican from Wisconsin, viciously attacked officials in the executive branch, claiming—without evidence—that they were Communists. In June 1950, Senator Smith startled her colleagues by rising to say, "I do not like the way the Senate has been made a rendezvous for vilification for selfish political gain at the sacrifice of individual reputations and national unity."

By September 1996, the House finally agreed to a resolution sponsored by Rep. Constance A. Morella, a Maryland Republican, that moved a nine-ton marble statue of three women suffragists from the crypt in the Capitol to the Rotunda, where it had first made its appearance seventy-five years earlier. Chiseled by Adelaide Johnson, the statue depicts three busts emerging from an unfinished base. It has been dubbed "Ladies in Bathtub." The base is supposed to represent constraints placed on Lucretia Mott, Susan B. Anthony, and Elizabeth Cady Stanton, the women who sought ratification in 1920 of the Nineteenth Amendment to the Constitution, allowing women to vote. In moving the statue to the Capitol's most prestigious hall, Congress underscored the importance of women voters.[272]

Under the best of circumstances, a legislator's job is demanding. "There are six hundred thousand people in the district," said former representative Anthony C. Beilenson. "They are always badgering you about this or that. They're not even sure half the time what they want you to do. You don't know if they would be for this bill or against it if they heard the arguments for and against it. You're trying to be a sensible, thoughtful person who weighs the evidence, trying to do what is right, trying to represent the majority viewpoint of the people you represent. After all, that is your job. You're not even sure how many people even know or care about this issue. In a sense, you are elected to make the judgments on their behalf."

Yet under the system Congress has fashioned, performing that job properly is nearly impossible. Scheduling Congress so that members have enough time to do their work and study the issues is beyond members' capabilities. In a survey taken in 1992 by the Joint Committee on the Organization of Congress, nearly 90 percent of the responding members said Congress needs "major and procedural organizational improvements." More than 70 percent favored simplifying the cumbersome budget approval process. And most wanted to spend more time "studying and reading about pending or future legislation or issues."

Yet with the exception of some streamlining in the House under Newt Gingrich, members have made few of the changes they themselves say are necessary. Most striking of all is that, while members alone are in a position to change the way Congress and America operate, and most of them recognize the need for change, the majority of them have resigned themselves to accept the system as is.

"It's a bizarre lifestyle," said Rep. Scott L. Klug, a Wisconsin Republican who is a former television newscaster. "The hardest part about this job is you have no control over your schedule. Historically, we are off the week of Memorial Day. So I had all kinds of plans for that week. Visits to schools, business tours, a day to golf with buddies. It all got blown out of the water. We had to come back Tuesday for votes Wednesday, Thursday, and Friday. Yesterday at four, they said we're going to vote late tomorrow night. No votes on Friday. Well, that's fine, except I had all kinds of appointments back here in Washington. Then they announced yesterday we won't have votes on Friday, but instead of having votes Tuesday, we'll have them on Wednesday. So I have to be back on Tuesday."[273]

Most of the time, Klug said, he feels as if he is in an airplane sitting on the runway, waiting for a thunderstorm to stop so the plane can take off. "I have no control or power over it," Klug said. "I think that is different from many businesses I've been involved in. When I worked in TV, you knew you would be on at eleven every night. You knew what the patterns were during the year."

Like most members, Klug flies back to his district almost

every weekend, usually to raise funds. Because members go home so regularly, the House usually schedules business for only two or three days a week. Often, the sessions go beyond midnight. Committee meetings are crammed into the remaining time, and their scheduling is constantly in flux.

Because of a lack of funds, a handful of members such as Klug sleep in their offices. Perhaps nothing illustrates so well how dysfunctional Congress is.

"It's been tough on me and on my three little boys at home," Klug said. They are four, seven, and eleven. "They know I'm going to be gone. They are used to that. Most Tuesday mornings, Dad is going to be gone until Thursday night. But the frustrating part is when I said I'll be back on Friday because they have games, I can't get back because we have votes. It's disappointing to the kids, and it drives a lot of folks out of here."

In contrast, former representative Anthony Beilenson flew back to California once a month. "The majority fly back to California every week," Beilenson said. "They are out of their minds. If you are an hour or two away, that is different. . . . Most of the members let themselves live lives they should not let themselves live. . . . Too many members let their staff overschedule them or respond too much to demands from back home. You don't have enough legislators spending time on legislating."

Most members carry their schedule with them. "Some have a computer printout a foot long with twenty-three items on it per day," Beilenson said. He brought out a piece of light green paper. "Here I have, 'House convenes at ten A.M., doctor's appointment at eleven, some people stopping by at noon, Ron Kessler at one-thirty P.M.'"

For most members, meeting with constituents and lobbyists and raising money leaves little time to attend hearings. "They can't sit at their committee hearings for more than fifteen minutes," Beilenson said. "We had fifteen members on the intelligence committee, and six or seven were usually there."

"We would be better off if there was a sector when we knew we would be here," said Sen. Russell D. Feingold. "Senators are constantly setting up things and canceling and disappointing people."[274]

During an interview with the author, an aide interrupted Rep. Robert S. Walker, a Pennsylvania Republican, at 11:30 A.M.

"Your oversight meeting is now at eleven forty-five A.M., instead of at one P.M.," the aide told him.

"Well, I can't be there at eleven forty-five," Walker said grumpily.

"It's only going to be a half an hour long," the aide said.

"They can't do this," Walker responded.

"That's the kind of thing that goes on all day long," Walker said. "Whatever schedule you have in place is subject to someone else's schedule change. . . . It's maddening and frustrating."

Yet even though he was one of Gingrich's lieutenants and one of his closest friends, Walker portrayed himself as helpless to do anything about it.

"I don't know how you change it," Walker said. "There are always going to be those pressures, no matter how you change the process."[275]

Walker said the Republican leadership explored broadening legislative sessions, shortening weekends, and adhering to a more regular schedule. "I have sat in leadership meetings where we try to work this out," Walker said when he was still in Congress. "You find members saying, 'Well, if you're going to give me Friday at home, you have to get me out at two P.M. on Thursday afternoon, so I can have a full Friday at home on the coast.' Then they say, 'To get a full day Monday, you have to schedule votes after five P.M. on Tuesday.' All of a sudden, you have one legislative day in Congress. You can't do the committee work with that schedule."

In some cases, "members want time for a golf tournament on Monday," Walker said. "That is something they see as important to them. If you have ten percent of the Congress that wants to do that, the leadership has to pay attention to it. If we blow them off, you have angry members. Then you have individuals who will have their own agenda. They expect all four hundred thirty-five members to accommodate their schedule. They say,

'My daughter has a wedding on Friday. I thought we would not be in session on Friday.' You have to accommodate that. You have four hundred thirty-five independent operators who make their own plans."

Walker enjoyed being in Congress. "You work with people who have perennial problems that they want congressmen to solve, and you become interested in some of the most fundamental issues facing the globe," Walker said. "Sometimes you do those things within minutes of each other. So there's constant variety. It's a constant challenge, and that generates enthusiasm." But Congress is a "very human institution. What you have is five hundred thirty-five egomaniacs who have been elected. Maybe that's too strong a term—five hundred thirty egoists. Welding those people together to go in the same direction even on something as fundamental as schedules is very difficult. They each operate within their own fiefdoms."

Looking over his schedule for the day, Rep. Floyd D. Spence, a South Carolina Republican, recited a litany of back-to-back meetings. At night, he was scheduled to attend three fund-raising receptions for other congressmen. At the same time, the House was expected to be in session.

"The House might be going until midnight," Spence said. "I'll be going back and forth. Sometimes we've been here all night. I hardly ever get away from here until eight or nine."[276] Spence, who is chairman of the National Security Committee, which oversees the Defense Department, said, "I can't get my work done. I don't have a whole lot of time to think. . . . The staff often works all night. The defense bill is four inches thick. Then there are annexes that are volumes."

"I always felt they were disorganized," said Robert B. Thomas, a former reporter of debates, mostly in the House. "It was constant turmoil. . . . They put everything off until the last minute. They do nothing on Monday. They piddle around on Tuesday. Then about Wednesday, maybe you'd be there until one or two A.M. Then on Thursday and Friday, they wouldn't do anything. They spin their wheels. If a bill is going to expire on March 31, they don't get anything done until March 29."[277]

"You are dealing with one hundred egos," said Sen. Frank H.

Murkowski, an Alaska Republican. "You can see that some members are motivated by their press offices to make their speeches at a certain time and tie up the Senate. . . . The only discipline is when you are approaching the weekend when people have commitments. We have thirty amendments, and pretty soon by Friday morning, they start dropping off. By one or one-thirty P.M., it's done. That's the sixth-grade mentality. If you don't finish your homework, you'll have to stay through recess."

Even debates on the floor—the bread and butter of Congress—have become public relations gambits rather than part of the legislative process.

"The idea of debate has radically changed in the past several decades," said Rep. Lee H. Hamilton. "It used to be that members would come on the floor to explain the bill, to advocate and defend it. Today the whole process is much more political. Each party gives out talking points to their members, sound bites in essence. They want you—as they will tell you in caucus—to repeat it over and over again. Forget the substance, forget the details of the legislation. 'Make these following three points and do it twenty times in the course of the afternoon, or forty times.' So that's what you see—an enormous amount of repetition."

"The debates rarely change the minds of members," said Rep. Bob Inglis, a South Carolina Republican. "My guess is that, with the advent of C-SPAN, the debate is mostly designed to change the minds of the American people."

"The one thing that most members of Congress will agree to is that time to read, digest, and ponder is a luxury. It should be a requisite," said Rep. Constance A. Morella, a Maryland Republican. "Most members are not at committee meetings. Sometimes you have two subcommittee and one major committee meeting at the same time. You stay for the opening statement, try to get to the other one, and you've missed the initial statements. The staff tries to fill you in on what you missed. Then you are called over to vote."[278]

Somehow, the discipline that state legislators impose on themselves eludes members of Congress. "When I was in the state legislature, all committees met at a certain time. Then the House of Delegates was in session. That way you could plan. There were also fewer committees," Morella said.

Asked how Congress can be so passive, Morella underscored the problem. "What can you do?" she responded.

During an interview, Rep. Jim Kolbe, an Arizona Republican, kept shifting uncomfortably in his chair. He explained that he had a bad back, and the chair he chose to sit in was making it worse. Normally, he said, he sits in another nearby chair. Kolbe's failure to get up and change chairs seemed symbolic of members' passivity.

Without backbone, most members spend their days attending fund-raisers, traveling to their districts to raise money, preparing for the next election, and responding to constituents who encounter difficulties with the executive branch. The Constitution gives Congress legislative and impeachment powers. It says Congress may determine its own rules and punish or expel its members. Congress may collect taxes, borrow money, regulate commerce with other nations, coin money, establish post offices and roads, declare war, provide for an army and navy, establish courts, and protect authors and inventors by giving them the exclusive right to their works. But the Constitution makes no mention of solving constituent problems. Nevertheless, Congress has been devoting an increasing share of its resources to that function. Since 1972, the proportion of members' staffs assigned to their district offices—where most constituent service is done—has more than doubled. While helping constituents may be laudable, it is but another way members win reelection and detracts from the time members need to serve the country as a whole. Moreover, it usually means that one citizen's problem is solved at the expense of another's, whose application is moved lower in a pile.

"There are no more than one hundred at most, maybe fewer, members who work hard at being legislators," Beilenson said with frustration. "The public doesn't understand that. The public probably doesn't care. It probably doesn't make too much difference to them. But it makes a lot of difference. We don't have enough people left here who are serious legislators. That is the primary part of our job. We have to run for reelection so often, we have to raise so much money, we have to meet with constituents. There are so many pressures on us. It makes it difficult to put in the time to be an effective legislator."

That has changed since 1976, when Beilenson was first elected to Congress. Back then, members had time to legislate rather than be politicians. "The difference is the need to raise money, and the fact there were fewer challengers then," Beilenson said.

Of all the pressures, none looms as large as the need to raise money. In years past, "there was an unwritten rule that you didn't start fund-raising in the Senate until two years before your term ended," said Roy L. Elson, the former administrative assistant to Sen. Carl Hayden. "Now they raise money all the time."

Aside from its corrupting effect, most members acknowledge that the campaign finance system prevents Congress from operating more effectively. Even the proliferation of committees and subcommittees goes back to the influence of money. The more committees members sit on, and the more committee chairmanships they win, the more likely they are to receive donations from the special interests affected by those committees. Yet, just as members seem incapable of rationally scheduling their time, they are unwilling to step off the treadmill and reform the campaign finance system.

"Just about every member I've talked to hates the current system," Feingold said. "I come back with these guys at eleven P.M. from fund-raisers. They are just dragging. If they could wave a magic wand, they would eliminate fund-raisers."

If members refuse to devote sufficient time to legislating, it is because money drives the agenda. "I'd say three out of four members agree the current system of financing campaigns is a bad way to run a political system," said former representative Peter H. Kostmayer. "I think members know it's wrong. . . . I think partly the dysfunctional scheduling is because there is not much leadership. The leadership is afraid of the membership. If they take a real initiative to change the system, the membership will say, 'You are depriving us of the resources we need to get reelected.' The real power is outside of the institution with the

PACs, which have a narrow financial interest in what is happening."

This has not been lost on the public. In polls, an overwhelming majority say special interests rule Congress. Most of the time, the public thinks Congress is doing a poor job. A *Wall Street Journal*/NBC poll showed only 36 percent said they approve of the job Congress is doing. During the House Bank and Post Office scandals, the approval rating sank to 17 percent.

Rather than reform itself, Congress often responds by blaming the media. Asked why most people have such a negative opinion of Congress, Representative Spence said, "I think it's media driven. Most people believe what they read. They are told that, and so they believe it. The polls say that is what people think, so they react that way. If you asked them about their own member, it wouldn't be nearly as bad as for the overall institution."

Thus when Rep. Wes S. Cooley, a Republican freshman from Oregon, had to drop a bid for reelection in 1996, he blamed the media. The local press had disclosed that Cooley had lied about serving in Korea during the war and about when he was married, allegedly so his spouse could continue to collect her late husband's military survivor's benefits. Railing against the media, Cooley said on the floor, "We have very few publications in this country that are very, very conservative, that really try to report the news objectively. It is always slanted."[279] In December 1996, a Marion County grand jury in Oregon indicted Cooley for falsely claiming on an election pamphlet that he had served in the Korean War.[280] Cooley pleaded not guilty to the charges.

The tendency to blame the press is not new. A century ago, Frank G. Carpenter, who covered Washington for the *Cleveland Ledger*, described the press corps as one of two Congresses on Capitol Hill: "One sits on the floor of the House and the Senate; the other has seats in the galleries. One makes its speeches to the members of the two lawmaking bodies, the other talks to the nation. . . . The latter criticizes the former and praises or condones its actions. It has much to say of the future of great men."[281]

"I read no newspaper now but [Thomas] Ritchie's [*Virginia Patriot*], and in that chiefly the advertisements, for they contain the only truths to be relied on in a newspaper," Thomas Jefferson wrote to North Carolina representative Nathaniel Macon on January 12, 1819.

In 1839, Sen. John M. Niles asked, "Who are these persons who style themselves reporters?" He answered, "Why, miserable slanderers, hirelings hanging on to the skirts of literature, earning a miserable subsistence from their vile and dirty misrepresentations of the proceedings here . . . venal and profligate scribblers, who were sent here to earn a disreputable living by catering to the depraved appetite of the papers they work for."

In 1890, Charles E. Kincaid, a reporter for the *Louisville Times*, wrote a story accusing Rep. William P. Taulbee, a Kentucky Democrat, of impropriety. As a result, Taulbee was defeated.

"When Taulbee ran into him, the congressman beat the reporter up," Donald A. Ritchie, associate historian of the Senate, said. "The next time they met, Taulbee lunged for Kincaid, and Kincaid took a pistol from the congressman and shot him." Taulbee died of his wounds.

A marble step on the House side of the Capitol is said to be discolored by the congressman's blood. But the architect of the Capitol has said the apparent stain is part of the marble grain and had nothing to do with the shooting.

Today, politicians rail against the press for being too cynical and quick to jump on failings—so-called "gotcha" journalism. Yet the complaints are often self-serving efforts to cover up misdeeds. Predictably, the members who are most uncomfortable with press coverage often turn out to be the ones engaging in the greatest abuses. And those same members are most facile at stonewalling. Thus, after Florence George Graves, a freelance journalist, brought to the *Washington Post* allegations about Packwood's sexual misconduct, Packwood initially told her and *Post* reporter Charles Shepard in a wounded voice, "I am so hesitant of anything at all that I just, I don't make any approaches [to women]." He added, "It's simply not my nature with men or women to be forward."

If anything, the press could be more aggressive in covering what goes on behind the scenes in Congress. While beat reporters cover Congress under difficult circumstances with extraordinary skill, they are faced with daily deadlines. Reduced to trying to obtain self-serving comments from congressional leaders such as Gingrich in the men's room off the Rotunda, they cannot be expected to uncover the kinds of abuses that require months of dogged investigative work. Yet at most newspapers, investigative reporting as practiced by Bob Woodward and Carl Bernstein has become a relic.

If Watergate demonstrated the power of the press, it also impelled politicians to embrace the media. Instead of being outsiders, the press became part of the establishment and thus less willing to take on powerful interests or to burn its bridges with those who feed it tips. Even though rarely successful, libel suits have further dampened the press's enthusiasm for exposing wrongdoing.

Pressures to suppress critical coverage are "greater today than almost any time in the past, except the McCarthy era or the sixties," Dan Rather has said, referring to Sen. Joseph R. McCarthy's witch-hunts against imagined Communists in government. "And I think in the last fifteen years, some of the spine has gone out of journalists. It's self-censorship, really," Rather said.[282]

"What bothers me is the press often is not cynical enough to see through [what happens in government]," said Representative Klug, the former television newscaster. Too often, Klug said, the press focuses on who is ahead in a race rather than what he stands for. "In my own race, what is going on is largely handicapping," Klug said. "There is very little discussion of issues." At the same time, Klug said, voters are often bored by stories that probe issues. "So I understand the frustration of the press."

In the end, the tendency to blame the press is but a manifestation of members' passivity and disinclination to take responsibility for their actions. That goes back to the kinds of people who run for Congress and the docile, herd mentality they acquire as members.

"When you come back in January, it reminds you exactly of how you felt coming back from vacation as a kid in the fall. You see all your friends again, although it's sad to see some not come back because they lost the election," former representative Beilenson said. "They are the only people in the entire country who understand. There are four hundred thirty-five in the House who more or less understand what your life is like. What you have to put up with from your constituents. How difficult it is for you to cast votes. How difficult it is for you to go out and raise money. So you share these things. You are thrown closely together with them on a daily basis. They are friends and colleagues."

Because of that bonding, Beilenson said, he develops an accepting attitude about members who take PAC money, or who won't vote for campaign finance reform because it would jeopardize their jobs, or who vote for repealing the gasoline tax because giving out money may win them reelection. "It's hard to be judgmental of one's colleagues, understanding the situation they come from," Beilenson said

Yet members of Congress are not homeless people in need of sympathy and understanding. They were elected to run the country. Once they enter the club, they develop a self-protective, us-against-them mentality. In the unreal, conformist atmosphere they have created for themselves, members adopt perquisites and the arrogance of power to compensate for their feelings of powerlessness.

"Some members who are passive bubble with rage underneath, and some convert it into a feeling of entitlement," said Dr. Bertram S. Brown, the former director of the National Institute of Mental Health who has often been consulted about members of Congress. "The feeling of entitlement is a reaction to the loss of self-esteem they feel because they are passive."

Many candidates who choose to run in the current system "have a need for celebrity," Dr. Brown said. "They get their highs when the eyes in the room come on them. That's when they get their political orgasm. These are people who become addicted to celebrity and power. They have a need to be seen, to be noticed."

These members "often confuse recognition with respect," Dr. Brown said. "The high they get when all eyes are focused on them sometimes gets internalized so they expect every Capitol Police officer to recognize them on sight." When they need an ego boost, "a few members go out into the corridors just to be recognized, just to have the public ask for their autographs."

This type of personality often lacks substance and character. The need to rationalize acceptance of PAC money places them in a "quasi self-delusional state," Dr. Brown said. "Trying to convince themselves that taking this money has no influence on their behavior or their vote leads to some of them saying to themselves, 'I'm above the voters. I'm better than them. I can treat them as children and fool them.' In other words, they feel superior to the voters, and by manipulating them, they feel powerful. They are outmanipulating them and outfooling them."

Yet in therapy, many depressed or anxious members turn the contempt they feel toward the people they are manipulating inward toward themselves, Dr. Brown said. "They feel self-contempt, shame, and low self-esteem. When you sit them down, they acknowledge their hubris. They feel so ashamed. Occasionally, this breeds a vicious cycle of being demanding and being brittle. That is when they feel they are between two worlds of feeling very powerful and very weak. On the one hand, they are powerful, making laws, taking money, manipulating. The next minute, they feel powerless. They can't get as good a parking space as another member. This shows up as a brittleness and in loss of temper. On occasion, they realize they have gone too far and they will apologize."

The syndrome can also lead to a sense of entitlement. "They think, 'My pay as a congressman is not enough,'" Dr. Brown said. "'I'm so great. I'm entitled to perks, that's why I launder stamps or kite checks or demand custom-made furniture.'"

Thus, the irony is that members elected to run the country are so self-absorbed and acquiescent, so lacking in substance and principle, so fixated on glorying in public recognition, that they become impotent. The most fundamental reason for that is they are so corrupted and subsumed by money that everything else becomes unimportant. They acknowledge that the present system has a calamitous effect but refuse to change it.

Under the present system, members spend "all of their time grubbing for money and making the kinds of at least implied commitments that destroy their ability to be good legislators," former senator William Proxmire said.

"I think the existing system is corrupt," Beilenson said. "I think it's corrupting good members even if they don't think they are being corrupted or want to be corrupted. They hate the system often. They don't know what else they can do."

"Clearly they can do something about it," former representative Kostmayer said. "If they can't, who can? What members are not prepared to do is foreclose the possibility of being re-elected."

12

Animal House

The Senate Park is a favorite of television crews, who tape stand-ups along its perimeter so that the Capitol dome appears as a backdrop behind reporters. Bordered by D Street and Delaware, Constitution, and Louisiana Avenues, the park faces the west side of the Russell Senate Office Building. Under it is the Legislative Garage, built for members of Congress and their staffs. A block from Union Station, the park features a reflecting pool and a grand fountain that shoots water through the sculpted mouths of six stone lions.

One weekday afternoon in August 1995, a television crew from Washington's Channel 4 was filming as usual when a woman reported to a Capitol Police officer cruising the area that something strange was going on in an expensive car parked on D Street adjacent to the park. It was five o'clock. The policeman left his cruiser and looked inside the car. The television crew could not see exactly what was going on. But to the officer, it appeared that, in broad daylight, a woman who looked like a prostitute was giving oral sex to the man in the driver's seat. As he approached, they tried to straighten themselves.

Normally, such activity would result in arrests for disorderly conduct. In this case, the officer did not actually see enough to make an arrest, but as he later told supervisors, he would have investigated further and would probably have made an arrest if it were not for one fact: the man was a former congressman, once chairman of the National Republican Congressional Committee, which coordinates fund-raising and campaigning. When Congress is involved, different rules apply.

"As soon as the member saw the officer approaching, he reached under his seat and pulled up his expired congressional license tag—which is of no value," a high-ranking Capitol Police official said.

If the former member had not displayed his expired congressional tag, the officer said he would have asked him to step out of the car. When he stepped out of the car, if his sexual organ was exposed, the officer would have arrested him. Or if the man had been intoxicated, the officer could have arrested him for driving while impaired.

"Because the former congressman displayed the tag, [the officer] felt there might be some congressional immunity, and he felt his supervisors would have a problem with making an arrest," the Capitol Police official said. "The placement of the tag on the dashboard squashed his zeal to pursue it further. When he put the tag up, the officer said, 'I know that stuff isn't going to stick.' He knew that [arresting him] would have a deleterious effect on his career."

In fact, Supreme Court decisions have established that members of Congress are not immune from arrest. "It's outrageous," a Capitol Police official said. "You don't do that at five in the afternoon." Still, "some officers wouldn't arrest anyone powerful because they are afraid of repercussions."

The fear is justified. "You can be one hundred percent right and still be wrong because of who the staffer or member is," the Capitol Police official said. "Even though you do everything right, you'll still get reassigned or something will happen to you."

If the incident next to the Senate Park sheds light on the character of members of Congress, it also suggests that little has changed on Capitol Hill since the days when Lyndon Johnson bedded secretaries in his hideaway offices, lobbyists brought wads of cash into congressional office buildings, and the Capitol Police unarrested drunken members and altered police reports to cover up their crimes. Members of Congress and their staffs often claim that congressional abuses are a thing of the past. According to these claims, the media are so vigilant that no member, past or present, would risk engaging in improper behavior. Alternatively, the excuses go, if any abuses do occur, it is only because members are representative of the people.

The claims are but another way to cover up what goes on in Congress. If a corporate personnel director said he wanted to hire criminals and imbeciles to reflect the percentage of miscreants and idiots in the population as a whole, he would be fired. The fact is that, while sexual indiscretions are not as blatant as they were in the 1960s and 1970s, they continue on Capitol Hill, as do other congressional abuses. Like Mafia chieftains, members are aware of their colleagues' misdeeds but maintain a code of silence. As Bob Dole remarked, only half in jest, to several hundred students in Hanover, New Hampshire, Congress is like "Animal House."

In particular, the Capitol Police remain a scandal, a microcosm of the way Congress as a whole operates. To be sure, over the years the Capitol Police have become more professional. Under House sergeant at arms Wilson (Bill) Livingood, a former Secret Service agent, for example, the Capitol Police became more sophisticated at assessing threats against members. But Congress still requires the Capitol Police to engage in cover-ups and improper behavior. As in the past, the Capitol Police maintain two standards—one for the powerful, and one for everyone else.

"It used to be that if you were a member, you could get away with anything. Now we would still make every effort not to arrest a congressman," said Richard W. Micer, who recently retired as a Capitol Police inspector.[283]

"If they say they're a member, you have to drop it [an arrest],"
said Edward P. Percival, who retired from the Capitol Police in
October 1995. "If you press it, they won't stand for it. They
control the situation, and they know it. You better drop it or
you'll get yourself in all kinds of hot water."

In fact, the one time the Capitol Police arrested a member of
Congress without later unarresting him, back in February 1981,
they first obtained permission from Tip O'Neill, the Speaker of
the House. As a Democrat, O'Neill had no reservations about
approving the arrest of Republican Jon C. Hinson of Mississippi. Hinson later pleaded no contest to a charge of attempted oral
sodomy. The offense took place in a rest room on the sixth floor
of the Longworth House Office Building with a male Library of
Congress employee.[284]

When Gary L. Abrecht became Capitol Police chief in April
1992, many Capitol Police officers thought the force would
improve. A graduate of Yale University with a degree in economics, Abrecht (pronounced *AH-brekt*) originally taught ninth
grade Latin. Abrecht, who wears glasses and has a mustache, is
fluent in French and knows German. Abrecht joined the Metropolitan Police in Washington, where he was an officer for
twenty-three years. When the Capitol Police Board—which
consists of the sergeants at arms of the House and Senate and
the architect of the Capitol—chose him to be chief, Abrecht was
a deputy chief and commander of the first district, which
includes most of Capitol Hill.

Despite this background, under Abrecht, whose salary is
$109,016 a year, many of the abuses that Congress has always
expected of the Capitol Police have continued. One example is
the practice of using Capitol Police cruisers as a congressional
taxi service. Upon request, cruisers pick up members and
discharge them at restaurants and drive them to and from
airports. If members requested it, until at least 1995, individual
dispatchers or watch commanders approved using sirens and
flashing lights. The cruisers traveled up to eighty miles per hour
and ran red lights.

Back when James J. Carvino was chief from 1984 to 1987,

David A. Curry, who recently retired as a captain, wrote him a memo pointing out the dangers of using police emergency powers to shuttle members to and from the airport. In Capitol Police parlance, the practice is known as "running code," or Code One, which means flashing lights and sirens are used. Curry had checked with the Commonwealth's Attorney in Arlington, Virginia, which is located on the way to Washington National Airport: What would happen if a Capitol Police cruiser hit and killed someone while exceeding the speed limit or running a red light so a congressman or senator in a hurry could make his plane or return home after a trip?

"He said emergency vehicles can only be used in that way for emergency situations, a matter of life or death," Curry said. The prosecutor warned, "If you run into someone, you're liable."

"I told him [Carvino] that running congressmen to the airport with sirens going was setting us up for liability in a lawsuit," Curry said. "If we kill someone, what's the emergency? This is often in rush-hour traffic. You get other cars out of the way."[285]

Carvino had been shocked to see a Capitol Police cruiser running a member to the airport with its siren wailing. Agreeing with Curry, Carvino ordered the runs stopped. But acquiescent sergeants at arms circumvented the chief and continued to give members a quick lift to the airport. Jack Russ, for one, considered it part of his job to do what members wanted. "If you have any smarts, you'll continue to do it," Russ would say.

"You run code, at sixty or seventy miles an hour, with lights and sirens all the way to Dulles Airport with all these staffers," said Capitol Police sergeant John A. Gott, who often performed the escort service in years past. "It's a dangerous thing to do."[286]

In guarding the president, the Secret Service exceeds the speed limit only for security reasons. By slowing down and then speeding up, Secret Service agents try to make it difficult for would-be assassins to predict when the presidential motorcade will arrive at its destination. The likelihood that the vice president will be assassinated is considered far lower. Because of that, to protect the public, the Secret Service generally stays within speed limits when transporting him.

Congress has had no such concerns. Gott said he has even used sirens and flashing lights when driving members of Congress to Andrews Air Force Base for junkets. Occasionally, his superiors have told him not to use emergency signals, but members or staff have insisted on it.

"The staff will say, 'The congressman is in a hurry to get there. Can you use lights and sirens?'" Gott will call the dispatcher for permission. "So they say to run code. I turn on my lights and sirens and run all the way up Pennsylvania Avenue," a congested thoroughfare.

Curry said even friends of congressmen have received the free, high-speed escort service. In fact, "one time we expedited a suitcase," Curry said. "I got the call. They had landed at Andrews Air Force Base and expedited a congressman. He had forgotten his luggage. So we sent that Code One."

"Members would ask to be picked up at the airport and to have us bring the Sunday paper," said Raymond Carson, a former Capitol Police lieutenant who retired in February 1997. Often, they were members of the congressional leadership. They would never bother to reimburse officers for the $1.50 cost of the Sunday paper.

In the past, when picking up members at the airport, Capitol Police exceeded the speed limit by thirty miles an hour or more. "They're lucky we haven't hit anyone," Carson said.[287]

While the Capitol Police normally use unmarked cruisers for airport runs, they sometimes use marked cruisers. "We used to get complaints sometimes if we took a marked car," Curry said. "They asked why it was racing at seventy-five to eighty miles per hour. We would say, 'We had a member of Congress in there.'"

The use of sirens to the airport continued until at least 1995, according to Curry. Because requests for use of sirens are individually approved on the way to airports, it is difficult to determine with certainty if the practice continues. If use of sirens is approved, it does not appear in daily reports. What is clear is that Congress still requires the Capitol Police to provide free taxi service to and from airports.

Another continuing abuse is checking on members' homes

when they are out of town. The service, known as a D Check, is performed in Washington. Curry said the Capitol Police serves at least thirty members in this way. A Capitol Police official said that when members are away and their wives are at home, they occasionally have the Capitol Police drive to Virginia or Maryland to check on them. At times, Capitol Police have driven to Baltimore to check on members' homes, Curry said. This detracts from their law enforcement and security duties and requires the hiring of more officers to take up the slack.

"Why should the taxpayers pay for that?" Curry asked.

Capitol Police officers typically make $40,000 a year. With overtime, many make much more. A sergeant makes roughly $50,000 a year.

While the Capitol Police are not supposed to provide a protective detail unless a member has been the target of a threat, when members demand protection, they usually get it, regardless of the circumstances, according to former captain Curry. Often, that means sending officers all over the country with them. In addition, even if members live on Capitol Hill, the Capitol Police are expected to pick them up during snowstorms.

When Capitol Police officers do engage in law enforcement, some claim they are often unable to obtain legal advice because John T. Caulfield, the general counsel of the Capitol Police, is inebriated. Caulfield, who has a Capitol Police badge, has been general counsel since 1985. He previously was counsel to a House subcommittee.

"As far as I was concerned, I thought he was a drunk," said former captain David Curry, who often dealt with Caulfield when Curry was assistant commander of the Capitol Police patrol division. "I always thought he was useless. He was never there when we needed him. I always smelled alcohol on him, in the morning. I'd pass him in the corridors, and he would smell."[288]

"The joke in this department is, if we have a legal question and we call the legal counsel [Caulfield], we might get a return call in six months," said Sergeant Gott. "The result is we don't call."[289]

Animal House

"I know he had a drinking problem," said Micer, the recently retired Capitol Police inspector, referring to Caulfield. "We called his office 'the Black Hole.' What went in never came out. I worked internal affairs for four years," Micer said, referring to the unit that investigates allegations against officers. "At one time, all cases were passed through his [Caulfield's] office for review after they were completed. Then, we stopped doing it. We got permission from the chief, because they never came out. It never got done. . . . We couldn't punish a guy now for something that happened two years ago."[290]

"John shows up when he shows up," a Capitol Police official said of Caulfield, who makes $109,016 a year. "He has three-to-four-hour lunches. Then he pops back in and leaves around six."

One morning, Caulfield showed up late for work and spent the morning throwing up in a bathroom across from the police chief's office on the second floor of Capitol Police headquarters, which was then at 331 First Street NE, a Capitol Police official said. "The U.S. Attorney's office wanted to discuss a last minute change in a proceeding," the official said. "We were trying to find him. He wasn't at home. He had lost his pagers. Finally, he called in at ten A.M. He was slurring his words. He was already shit-faced at ten A.M." Later, Capitol Police officials found Caulfield in the bathroom. "He had locked himself in and had passed out," the official said.

Frank A. Kerrigan, who was Capitol Police chief at the time, said he was told about the incident. "He [Caulfield] was sick, I guess, from drinking," Kerrigan said. "He had a drinking problem. At times, you could smell he had been drinking. He had alcohol on his breath in the morning."[291] Asked why he didn't fire Caulfield, Kerrigan said he couldn't because Caulfield reported both to the Capitol Police Board and to the police chief. When Jack Russ was House sergeant at arms, he and Caulfield were friends. Caulfield continues to be friendly with members of Congress.

When the Capitol Police arrested a lobbyist who knew Caulfield for driving while under the influence of alcohol in January 1989, Caulfield advised him not to take a Breathalyzer test. The

197

Capitol Police were infuriated. "He was our department lawyer, yet he advised a criminal suspect under apprehension," the official said. "The guy is supposed to be working for us, and he gave him advice like this."

More recently, Curry said, police in Alexandria, Virginia, arrested Caulfield: "He got drunk, got picked up, and the police charged him with public drunkenness."

"John was drinking, as he frequently does every night, this time at the Penalty Box in Alexandria on King Street," a Capitol Police official said. "He was getting loud and rowdy and had been asked several times by the bartender to get hold of himself. The manager told him to leave. They got in an argument. The manager said, 'Buddy, you're out of here.' He punched the manager. The police locked him up. . . . He was placed under arrest. When they saw the police identification and his badge, they called the Capitol Police watch commander."

Court records show Caulfield was arrested in Alexandria on October 6, 1994, for appearing drunk in public.[292] The Commonwealth's Attorney chose not to prosecute, and the charge was dropped on December 28, 1994.

In an interview, Caulfield denied he had a drinking problem or that his work was impaired because of it. He said he is often away from his office because of his dual role of providing legal advice to both the Capitol Police and the Capitol Police Board. In fact, the board, which meets irregularly, rarely requires legal advice. In addition, each member of the board has his own counsel. But when Russ was sergeant at arms, Caulfield cited his dual role and was awarded a pay increase.

Caulfield denied that internal discipline cases are dropped because he is slow to review them. "It gets delayed because it's a serious matter, and I don't take lightly the fact that someone could lose their job," Caulfield said. He also denied that Capitol Police officers do not call him for legal advice because he never gets back to them. He pointed out that the Capitol Police Board had just bestowed on him its highest award—one for displaying "extraordinary leadership over a period of time which has had a profound effect on the organization."

Caulfield declined to discuss his advice to the lobbyist who had been arrested by the Capitol Police for drunk driving. "I spoke to him as a lawyer," Caulfield said. "I think it's a privileged conversation."[293]

Asked if it was not a conflict of interest for the general counsel of the Capitol Police to advise a suspect arrested by the Capitol Police, Caulfield said, "It is a conflict to give advice. That's what I tell them [people who ask for his advice]. That I can't give them particular advice concerning their particular case. They can get a lawyer, and I'll be happy to recommend three or four people." Caulfield did not explain why the conversation, if it did not entail dispensing legal advice, was "privileged."

Caulfield denied that he was sick in the Capitol Police headquarters bathroom because he had been intoxicated. "I have a bad stomach anyhow," he said. "I've had four major surgeries in the last three years. It wasn't from coming in hungover and sick."

The allegation by Chief Kerrigan and other officers and police officials that he often comes to work in the morning smelling of alcohol is "total bullshit," Caulfield said. "Because of the position I have, there are people out there obviously who are saying these things who don't particularly care for me. That's nonsense."

Caulfield called the incident at the Penalty Box in Alexandria a "misunderstanding." The manager "pushed me, and I pushed him back," Caulfield said. "That's all that happened."

Caulfield claimed he wasn't sure why the public drinking charge against him was dropped: "I think it was dropped basically on a procedural thing. I don't recall exactly what happened. I had an attorney, and he handled it. The officer didn't show up, or something like that."

Caulfield later appealed "person to person" to be dropped from this book.

"I'm a big defender of the First Amendment," Caulfield said. "You can write whatever you feel is appropriate. But I don't believe that writing anything about me enhances any story you have. I don't consider myself anything other than a legal bureaucrat. I don't make policy recommendations." At another point, he said, "I have the personal skills and knowledge, if this isn't right and if this is personal, to protect my family and my reputation."

In the second interview, Caulfield called his problems with drinking "ancient history." But in November 1995, the Metropolitan Police found Caulfield with a gash on his head wandering around Thomas Circle at Massachusetts Avenue and Fourteenth Street NW in Washington. Saying it was part of an "alcoholic incident," a high-ranking Capitol Police official said the Metropolitan Police found Caulfield's Capitol Police credentials in his pocket and called the Capitol Police.

"We went up to George Washington University Medical Center where they were trying to treat him," the official said. "He was very belligerent and refused to be cooperative. One of our cruisers wound up driving him to his home in Alexandria. He insisted on being dropped two blocks away from his home so he would not be seen being taken home in a cruiser."

"That's basically a mugging situation," Caulfield said. After going to the nearby Post Pub, "I was hit over the head, that's all I know. I went to the hospital." Asked if he was drunk, Caulfield said, "I don't think I was."[294]

Caulfield said the Capitol Police have never required him to enter an alcohol treatment program. "It's not a problem," he insisted. As for his arrest, "It wasn't a big deal."

To some of the Capitol Police, Caulfield's conduct is a big deal.

"When an officer gets arrested for alcohol-related problems, he is sent for help and disciplined severely," Sergeant Gott said. "To have the general counsel not held to the same standards quite frankly pisses most of us off."[295]

If Abrecht has done nothing to discipline or fire Caulfield—in fact, he gave him an award—some feel he has been less than aggressive in investigating criminal conduct on the Hill. In May 1983, Joseph A. Califano Jr., special counsel to the House ethics committee, accused the Capitol Police of failing to follow up "significant leads" about congressional employees and Capitol

Police officers themselves selling marijuana, cocaine, and PCP.[296] Califano recommended that other law enforcement agencies assume the job of policing Capitol Hill. Congress, of course, was not about to let others police it. But the Capitol Police, responding to Califano's criticism, created a drug investigation unit. The unit consisted of fifteen plainclothes officers who could infiltrate rings on the Hill without arousing suspicion.

But early on, it seemed as if Chief Abrecht began to undo the small reform Califano's investigation had produced. He insisted that investigations and surveillance end when suspects leave Capitol Hill. As a result, the Capitol Police often cannot make arrests because they have not caught suspects in the act of making a drug deal. In other cases, Abrecht has insisted that after Capitol Police have already developed enough evidence to make arrests, the Metropolitan Police in Washington make the arrests. Because the Metropolitan Police are underfunded, deferring to them sometimes means no arrests are made and criminals go free. Abrecht also cut back on the number of officers assigned to criminal probes and continued cutbacks ordered by previous chiefs in the number of officers assigned to the drug unit.

In January 1996, Abrecht disbanded the drug unit altogether. By then, it had only four officers. At the time, Congress was controlled by Republicans who were furiously attacking the Clinton administration for allegedly failing to deal forcefully with the national drug problem. In particular, they targeted Clinton's own admission that he had once tried marijuana but had not inhaled.

"It sounds to me that we have a drug problem everywhere in the world but on the Hill," said Micer, the recently retired Capitol Police inspector. "When Abrecht first came in, I heard good things about him. There were big hopes. But those hopes have gone down the tubes. Officers think he doesn't have the balls to do what is the right thing. Instead, he'll do whatever is best for him to keep his position. I would think disbanding the drug unit is part of that."[297]

Even before Abrecht disbanded the unit, officers felt that by restricting their investigations he had made it difficult for them to make cases. "He forced them not to be productive," former inspector Micer said.

Even with the restrictions, Franklin C. Shelton, a former deputy chief of the Capitol Police, said the drug unit made as many as ten arrests a year. "In my opinion, they were productive," he said.[298]

In one case, Abrecht appeared to minimize allegations of drug dealing on Capitol Hill. In November 1993, an anonymous tipster called the Capitol Police and said kilos of cocaine and heroin were being sold through the House folding room, which sent out newsletters. The tipster said a Capitol Police officer was involved. In the past, anonymous tips with less specific information had led to major arrests. But Abrecht demurred, according to a Capitol Police official.

"The normal thing to do is to place an undercover person in," the official said. "It could take a few months or a year, but eventually he will be exposed to it. So the chief was told about it. 'Naw. It's anonymous. Who knows if it's true or not?' he said."

One official pointed out to Abrecht that major drug cases had recently been made with even less initial evidence. Another said that whenever an officer is implicated in a crime, the department is obligated to pursue it. It would look bad if it got out that the Capitol Police had suppressed an investigation, they told Abrecht.

"One day, you would have one set of facts and he would give you one decision," an official said. "A week later, you would give him almost the same set of facts, and he would give the opposite conclusion."

After a delay of several months, Abrecht agreed to seek approval for the drug investigation from the House sergeant at arms. But that was not the end of the politicking. To insert an undercover officer into the House facility, the Capitol Police have to inform the head of the affected department. While he had been warned to keep the investigation a secret, the department head let others in his department know what was happening. Eventually, then representative Charlie Rose, a North Carolina Democrat who headed the House Administration Committee, heard about the investigation. As a way of keeping the Capitol Police under members' control, Rose often claimed the Capitol Police were spying on members. He also tried to require the Capitol Police to notify Congress before telling the executive branch that a House member or employee was under criminal investigation.[299] Saying they should have obtained his permission before proceeding, Rose ordered the Capitol Police to stop the drug investigation.

More recently, after a woman driver had failed a Breathalyzer test, Abrecht questioned why she had been arrested. While the alcohol level in her blood was not high enough to warrant charging her with driving under the influence, it was high enough to charge her with driving while impaired.

"Abrecht said, 'We should be cutting our losses. Why should this woman be processed?'" an official recalled. "It was lunacy."

Three years earlier, the District of Columbia City Council had toughened the law against drunk driving. In line with the new law, Abrecht had sent a memo to the force ordering "zero tolerance" for drinking and driving. According to the memo, drivers found to be driving while impaired should be prosecuted. After Capitol Police officials showed the memo to Abrecht, he dropped his opposition, and the prosecution proceeded.

Abrecht appeared to be similarly "clueless," according to one Capitol Police official, at a retirement party in the Capitol for Inspector Michael E. Hupp on November 15, 1996. Former inspector Micer praised Hupp for his integrity and loyalty to his officers, adding that he only wished that Hupp had been promoted to a higher level.[300]

"Everyone started standing up and clapping, and Abrecht did, too, as if he had had nothing to do with it," the official said. "It was because of him that he had not been promoted."

Of all Abrecht's orders, none produced as much fury and amazement as when he minimized a purposeful attempt to run over a Capitol Police officer in late April 1996. Two Capitol

Police officers had spotted a stolen car being driven near Union Station. When the officers tried to stop the car, it drove directly toward one of the officers.

"The guy looked the officer right in the eye, and when the officer tried to jump out of the way, the guy hit him," a Capitol Police official said.

The second officer radioed for help. After pursuing the car around Capitol Hill, Capitol Police arrested the driver. They found drugs in the car.

"Abrecht shows up on the scene," an official said. "He said, 'We're making much ado about this. I don't understand what's going on. At best, you have him leaving after colliding. Even that's pushing it.' The sergeant on the scene said, 'Ah, I don't think so. We have an assault on a police officer, at a bare minimum.' Abrecht pooh-poohed it. He continued at headquarters along that track. Fortunately, a sergeant was aggressive enough to go toe-to-toe with the chief.

"To put it mildly, the officers who heard this were outraged," the Capitol Police official said. "Here's someone who ran over one of our officers and could have killed him, and he just wants to charge him with a minor traffic offense."

As it turned out, one of the officer's legs was broken, and two of his teeth were chipped. After learning of the officer's injuries, Abrecht agreed to charge the driver with assault on a police officer. When the U.S. Attorney's office in Washington got the case, prosecutors decided the conduct had been even more serious. They upped the charge to assault on a police officer while armed, meaning the vehicle had been used as a weapon.

"Abrecht is a joke," said Capitol Police sergeant Gott. "He's a political pawn."[301]

So concerned was Abrecht about the material being gathered for this book that he met with his top officials to discuss the author's investigation. He then issued an unprecedented written warning to every officer not to speak with the author.* During roll calls, police officials also warned officers.

---

* Abrecht's memo appears as an appendix to this book.

Abrecht himself declined to be interviewed. Through Capitol Police spokesman Daniel R. Nichols, Abrecht confirmed that many of the incidents that relate to him took place, but said that in police work disagreements are common and Abrecht's intervention was properly part of his job as chief. Thus, when an officer was struck by a car at Union Station, "there was discussion as to which charge would be appropriate, given the totality of the circumstances," Nichols said. "That was between the chief of police and the supervisors on scene."[302]

While Nichols said Abrecht did not specifically recall the arrest of the woman who had failed a Breathalyzer test, he said several such cases had led Abrecht to question whether arrests should be made when alcohol levels in the blood show the driver was impaired. "The chief expressed concern if a person is arrested on the street for poor driving coupled with poor psychomotor tests. We bring them back to the station, and they have a low reading, how should they proceed with those cases?" Nichols said. "The chief consulted with Mr. [Howard R.] Horowitz of the D.C. Corporation Counsel and was informed we should go ahead and place the charge and put them through the system. . . . The chief has never interfered with any arrest by any officer or tried to get the prosecution stopped."

Nichols said Abrecht disbanded the Capitol Police drug unit "because we were downsizing our sworn personnel to assure we were using our personnel in the best manner toward our primary mission," Nichols said. "The chief made a decision that the drug unit would be integrated into the criminal investigations division. It was reduced in size by one or two members. We will still pursue drug investigations. It will have no effect on the operational ability of the police department to investigate drugs."

Nichols said the Capitol Police must sometimes hand over cases to other police departments because of lack of jurisdiction. In response to the tip about drug activity in the House folding room, Nichols said Abrecht approved placing an undercover officer there. "Soon after, her cover was blown," he said.

Moreover, Abrecht said John Caulfield, the Capitol Police general counsel, is doing a "good job." Rather than having been impeded by page supervisors, the investigation into who painted a swastika on the page dormitory petered out because of "insufficient evidence."

While the Capitol Police check on members' homes when they are out of town, it is because the Capitol Police "serve the congressional community," Nichols said. "Just about any police department provides that as a service to their community. When they are on vacation, they notify the police department, which will give them extra attention." Nichols denied that the Capitol Police routinely check on members' homes in Virginia or Maryland.

Nichols said the practice of taking members to and from the airport using sirens "has long since been discontinued. It's no longer allowed by the U.S. Capitol Police Board." Nor would an officer accede to a request to turn on sirens in such circumstances. "We don't take direction from members of Congress or staff members on this issue," Nichols said. "Our policy is clear. It's not done. . . . If an officer did it, it was in clear violation of our policy."

Finally, Nichols said the officer who spotted a former congressman in his car near Union Station told his superiors he did not actually see any illegal activity. "Nothing of an illegal nature was going on," Nichols said. "Otherwise, the officer would have placed a charge. He told his supervisor that much." Nichols acknowledged that if the officer had investigated further, he could have spotted a violation. "I don't know what was in the officer's head," he said.

"The chief takes allegations of interference in the arrest or the progress of any criminal investigations, or allegations he tried to have anyone unarrested, or in any way obstructed a criminal investigation, very seriously, and if such allegations are made, he would not discount the possibility of taking legal action," Nichols said.

Nichols said Abrecht's memo was not meant to prohibit officers from talking with the author. "The problem was people were complaining you were calling them at home. Officers felt their phone numbers were being given up publicly." Nichols added, "It looks like our people are talking to you pretty readily."

Asked when the practice of using sirens on the way to airports stopped, Nichols said it was in 1992, before Abrecht became chief. But Curry, who was second in command of the patrol division, which provided the service, said that during the nearly four years he served under Abrecht, the practice continued. "I didn't see any difference [after Abrecht became chief]," said Curry, who retired in 1995.[303]

Asked about that, Nichols said, "If an officer takes it on himself [to use sirens] because he feels pressure from the member, that is against our policy." Similarly, if Capitol Police officers direct mentally deranged individuals to bother the president in the White House, "they shouldn't be doing that," Nichols said.

In claiming that his decision to disband the drug unit has not harmed investigations, Abrecht glossed over the fact that the purpose of having a separate unit was to allow officers to infiltrate drug rings by working undercover.

"The whole reason for a separate unit was they were lodged in a facility separate from the Hill, so when there are undercover operatives, these people will not be seen talking to someone who is known to be a police officer," said a Capitol Police official. "We lost that facility. He wants to have the same person directing a drug case one day and then investigating a theft in the same facility the next day. You can't do it."

Before Abrecht took over, fourteen officers were assigned to criminal investigations and four to the drug unit. Now, nine officers are assigned to criminal investigations, and there is no drug unit. As for the claim that the Capitol Police lack jurisdiction, "we go all over the country doing various things," a Capitol Police official said. "That's a red herring."

Contrary to what Abrecht said, a high-ranking Capitol Police official said the investigation into vandalism at the page dorm was impeded by the refusal of page supervisors to allow interviews. "When you can't conduct an interview, it's pretty hard to reach any conclusion," he said.

While no official questioned Abrecht's honesty, many felt he was not aggressive enough in pursuing investigations. There are exceptions. For example, a member reported thefts from his office and demanded that the Capitol Police immediately install a video camera to catch the thief. Even though some said installing a camera at that point was premature, Abrecht readily acceded to the member's request.

"We hadn't even had the crime reported," said a Capitol Police official. "We hadn't interviewed anybody or taken a theft report: 'Well, the sergeant at arms wants it.'"

Abrecht does not improperly interfere with investigations but rather appears to try to "avoid criminal investigations or the orderly arrest process by throwing these crazy roadblocks out," an official said. "For example, if blood alcohol level is less than a certain percentage: 'We'll let the drunk drivers go.' Or, 'I'll wait three or four months before I seek approval from the sergeant at arms to place somebody undercover in the House folding room. Maybe by then it will go away.' Maybe it's not direct interference, but it's certainly not enabling, as a chief of police should act."

Nichols responded, "The fact is we pursue allegations of criminal conduct. When we do so, we want to make sure we have a solid foundation to work from."

If the FBI had delayed looking into leads in criminal cases, covered up for past and present administration officials, disbanded a unit that was making good drug cases, run Cabinet officers to airports at high speeds using flashing lights and sirens, unarrested suspects because of their connections, used agents to check the homes of administration officials, and tolerated a general counsel who had been arrested for appearing drunk in public, as the Capitol Police have done over the years, Congress would be outraged and demand the dismissal of the FBI director, if not the attorney general and the president. But Congress makes the rules. The Capitol Police may make a mockery of the criminal justice system, but that is the way Congress wants it.

"We call it the Land of Oz," a high-ranking Capitol Police official said of Congress. "It's unlike any other place in the world. Congress is just a cesspool. The biggest chunks rise to the top."

If corruption and abuse of power continue on Capitol Hill, so does sexual harassment and inappropriate sexual behavior.

"I think every young female reporter has a story to tell about members," said Lisa Wolfington, who covered Capitol Hill as a radio correspondent for six years. Wolfington, a pretty blonde, said she was leaving a party in a House office building when a Southern congressman followed her. "He took my hand and tried to kiss me. I just pulled away. I told him, 'I'm a reporter, and I cover your district,'" Wolfington said. "He acted like he was going to kiss me on the lips."[304]

Another House member told Wolfington she was "stacked." When Sen. Strom Thurmond, the South Carolina Republican, saw Wolfington with another female reporter on the night the Senate voted to confirm Clarence Thomas as a Supreme Court justice, Thurmond put his arms around both of them. "If I kiss you on the cheek, would you accuse me of sexual harassment?" Thurmond said to both of them.

On another occasion, Wolfington said, "I was on an elevator, and a congressman asked if I was the elevator operator. I said no. Then when I got on a subway car going to the House in the Capitol, he got on it. He said, 'If you were on the elevator when Buz Lukens did what he did, I can understand why he did it.'"

Donald E. (Buz) Lukens, an Ohio Republican, resigned from Congress in 1990 rather than face ethics sanctions. One allegation was that Lukens had fondled and propositioned an elevator operator in the Capitol. Lukens had previously been convicted of contributing to the delinquency of a minor by having sex with a sixteen-year-old girl.[305]

Contrary to claims that members today are too afraid of the press to behave inappropriately with their own staffers, Frédérique J. Sandretto asserts that while she was an intern on his staff in June 1996, Rep. Sonny Bono, the California Republican, sexually harassed her.

Sandretto, an attractive, twenty-seven-year-old whose black

hair is as long as Cher's, was pursuing a Ph.D. at the Sorbonne in Paris when she won a Fulbright Scholar fellowship to study in the United States. Under the auspices of the American Political Science Association and the Franco-American Commission, Sandretto, who was born in Lyons, came to Washington in October 1995. In November, the Senate Judiciary's subcommittee on terrorism, technology, and government information, headed by Sen. Arlen Specter, selected her as an intern. In that capacity, Sandretto prepared a report on terrorists' possible use of weapons of mass destruction.

After finishing the report in March 1996, Sandretto heard that Bono was looking for an intern. Sandretto had heard of Sonny and Cher and had heard them sing "I Got You Babe." But she was taken aback when one of Bono's staffers interviewed her and asked, "Is the president of France de Gaulle?" referring to the late Charles de Gaulle, who left the French presidency in 1969.[306]

Sandretto landed the job and began in Bono's office on May 8, 1996. While considered an intern, her official title was congressional fellow. Under the fellowship arrangement, the United States Information Agency and the Franco-American Commission, funded by the French government and French organizations, paid her tax-exempt salary of $2,000 a month.

The *Hill* ran an item on Sandretto's joining Bono's staff. "In France, a former entertainer . . . will never be able to have a political position," she was quoted as saying. "In America, things are different, if you think of President Reagan and Congressman Bono."[307]

Sandretto found that Bono was programmed by his staff, who in turn snickered about him behind his back. When Bono spoke in his high-pitched voice on the floor of the House, and colleagues referred to him as the "distinguished gentleman from California," his staff watched on television and commented on his nervous, inarticulate remarks.

"Sonny Bono would say what his staff said he should say," Sandretto said. "They would say, 'You do that,' and he would do it." When it came time to vote, Bono, a self-described conservative Republican, followed Gingrich. "If Newt Gingrich voted yes, he voted yes. He wanted to please Gingrich." Despite the fact that Chastity, Bono's daughter by Cher, has proclaimed herself a lesbian, Bono espoused Gingrich's position on family values.[308]

When Sandretto was selected, Bono's staff told her she would be working on terrorism. Instead, they had her answering telephones, sorting mail, bringing coffee, and buying Cokes for Bono. Sandretto kept asking when she would begin her work. The French government and the USIA were paying her to study in the United States, not to be a receptionist. Finally, on Tuesday, June 18, Bono called her into his office.

Bono, who sat on the House Judiciary Committee, told Sandretto he would like her to prepare a report on terrorism. When Sandretto asked Bono what aspect of terrorism she should work on—domestic, foreign, the threat of nuclear proliferation—Bono said, "Work on anything you like." Bono had "no idea what he wanted to do," Sandretto said. When Sandretto suggested she might work on domestic terrorism, Bono said, "Okay. That's good."

Sandretto wondered if Bono would even remember what they had agreed upon. "I would tell him something, and then he would forget," she said. "It was astonishing."

Bono wanted the report before the November 1996 election. He wanted to tell voters he had conducted research on the issue. Sandretto pointed out that her visa expired before the election, but Bono told her he could help her obtain an extension. Bono also thought the terrorism report would help win him a seat on the House Select Committee on Intelligence.

"All he wanted was to be reelected," Sandretto said. Bono also had his eye on the Senate again. In 1992, he had lost a primary election for a Senate seat. "He would ask, 'What can I do to be reelected?' He had no idea of what to do," Sandretto said.

In a memo she wrote later in June, Sandretto recorded what happened next.

"At the end of the discussion [about the report], he asked me an inappropriate question, which surprised me," Sandretto wrote. Bono, sixty-one years old, asked, "For how long have you been growing your hair? I like long hair; it is so beautiful."

"I looked at him strangely, and after a pause I finally said,

'Ten years, why?' I was wondering if, because of his . . . career in show business, this type of question was just the commentary of an outgoing man who liked to know about his staff." Perhaps this is to be expected of Californians, she thought. "I did not see it as a first sign of harassment," she wrote.

Bono invited Sandretto to have lunch with him the next day. "I was convinced I would work on the project," she wrote. "I brought a large part of my research, including articles, reports on terrorism."

The next day, Bono asked Sandretto to come into his office ten times. "Instead of talking about the report, he asked me personal, inappropriate questions about my private life," she said. "Do you have a boyfriend?" Bono asked. When Sandretto said she did, "he wanted to know exactly how I met him, if I wanted to marry him." Sandretto told Bono that they planned to marry once her friend, who was separated from his wife, obtained a divorce.

"He laughed and started to tell me about his own experience with his respective wives!" Sandretto wrote. "I felt extremely embarrassed, not knowing why he wanted to open up his life and ask me to do the same."

Bono's fourth wife, the thirty-three-year-old former Mary Whitaker, called him often at the office. She had worked for Bono's Italian restaurant, called Bono. They have two children.

Bono, Sandretto, and a staff member had lunch in the Capitol. "He remained correct, simply alluding to how difficult divorces were," she wrote.

After lunch, Bono continued his personal questions. Bono "constantly interrupted me, asking me to follow him to the Capitol, to the votes, to different receptions, to pictures with his constituents," she wrote. She felt the staff started to look at her strangely. The legislative director said, "You are going to take my job, aren't you?" Other staffers smiled at her and said the congressman "really liked" her. "I did not know how to respond," she wrote.

On Thursday, June 20, Bono called Sandretto to his office. He told her he would help her to have her visa extended so she could work on the terrorism project. Sandretto suggested that

Bono attend a briefing on terrorism at Los Alamos National Laboratories in New Mexico. As part of his congressional duties, Sandretto's boyfriend would be attending as well.

"Where are we going to sleep?" Bono asked the intern. "I said, 'In a hotel.' It was awkward."[309]

Late that afternoon, Bono asked Sandretto to accompany him to the Capitol for three votes. Usually, Bono's legislative director, chief of staff, or a staff member who was an expert on the issue accompanied Bono to votes. This time, "he insisted on me coming with him and nobody else," she wrote.

During one of the votes, Bono sat with Sandretto on a sofa in a reception area. As he talked, he placed his hand on her shoulder. Again, Bono asked questions about her personal life: Does she like her boyfriend? Does he have children? How old was his wife?

"I didn't have the courage to say, 'Excuse me, Congressman, you shouldn't be asking me about this,'" she said.

"Can I tell you something personal?" Bono asked. Staring at her, Bono said he found Sandretto "extremely attractive."[310]

"I felt ill-at-ease and looked down, not knowing what to answer. I felt terribly confused," she wrote. But Bono's purpose appeared clear to her, she said later. She felt as if "he was trying to seduce me."[311]

As it turned out, Bono was so busy speaking to Sandretto that he missed one of the three votes—House Vote 263, on an amendment to an appropriations bill. Favored by the Republicans, the amendment prohibited the Bureau of Indian Affairs from transferring federal land into a tribal trust unless non-Indians were required to pay state and local taxes on retail sales there. Bono was one of sixteen members who did not vote. But the amendment passed anyway, a close 212 to 206.[312]

At about 7 P.M., Bono asked Sandretto to come to his office.

"Are you Catholic?" Bono asked.

"Yes," Sandretto said, surprised that he would pry into her religion.

"I have something for you," he said.

Bono took a box from his desk. "This is for you," he said, showing Sandretto a gold-colored ring with a crucifix on it.

Bono warned her not to mention the ring to her boyfriend or to staffers.

"I cannot accept it," Sandretto said.

Bono insisted. "Take it. It is for you."

Ignoring her protests, Bono placed the ring in her hand. Before she could return it, he left. "I was scared, not knowing what to do," she wrote. "I was paralyzed."

When Sandretto's boyfriend met her for the drive home, he noticed that she was pale and looked shaken. He asked what was wrong. Sandretto showed him the ring.

"That's so ugly," he said. "Who gave you that?"

"It was Sonny Bono."

"No, come on. Who gave it to you?"

"Yes, I swear to you."

Her boyfriend looked at her. "My God," he said, laughing at the absurdity of it.

The next day—Friday—Bono was away. When Sandretto came to work on Monday, June 24, staffers treated her coldly and barely said hello. It was clear to Sandretto that something had changed. When she asked what was going on, staff members told her she had been taken off the project, and the trip to Los Alamos was canceled. Bono was said to be "too busy" for the trip. No reason was given for taking her off the project. One staffer jokingly said she had made Bono miss a vote.

Sandretto went into Bono's office to ask for articles she had given him on terrorism. "I understand the trip is canceled," she said.

"I am sorry, I cannot get to Los Alamos," he said. Then he walked out the door.

She believes that she was removed from the project because "he tried to give me the ring, and the consequence of rejecting him [by saying she could not take it] was I was removed from doing the report," she said. Once again, Sandretto was sorting mail and fetching coffee and Cokes.

According to Sandretto, a House staffer saw her crying in a hallway and consoled her. The House staffer said she was aware of what had been happening and suggested that Sandretto complain to the House Office of Fair Employment Practices, which then handled complaints of discrimination. The staff member, who declined to be quoted by name, confirmed to the author Sandretto's account.

But the House Fair Employment Office was another joke. In 1993, Representatives Pat Schroeder, a Colorado Democrat, and Olympia Snowe, a Maine Republican who is now a senator, observed that only a handful of complaints were filed with the office each year. It was not that Capitol Hill was free of unfair labor practices. Rather, the complaint process does not work. Since being established in 1988, the office had received twelve hundred inquiries but only seven formally filed complaints.[313]

The office told Sandretto it could not help her legally with her complaint because the USIA and the Franco-American Commission paid her, rather than the House of Representatives. That was an incorrect interpretation of the law, according to Pamela B. Stuart, a former assistant U.S. Attorney in Washington who helped defend Bob Packwood before the Senate ethics committee and has also successfully represented victims of sexual harassment. Stuart said the office should have accepted a case like Sandretto's because Congress is considered a "joint employer" with the USIA and Franco-American Commission.

After being given the facts recited by Sandretto without the name of the congressman or his version of events, Stuart said, "The congressman exercised control over her and what she did. He could hire and fire her. He would be seen as a joint employer, and she could proceed against him in a civil suit."

Stuart remarked that in a case such as this, an implication can be drawn that she was removed from the project because the congressman didn't want her around anymore after she didn't respond to his overtures. Stuart explained that a case in which one is stripped of assignments and turned into the mail girl without any other complaints about performance could be construed as what is known as quid pro quo harassment, meaning that her refusal to be seduced was the basis for an employment decision that adversely affected her employment. In other words, the alleged victim suffered discrimination because of her gender.[314]

To be sure, if Sandretto sued and was successful, Bono would pay nothing. The taxpayers would foot the bill for all the congressman's legal fees and damages imposed on him.

Joseph P. Horn, a staff attorney with the Fair Employment office, said he could not comment. The office's duties have since been taken over by the Office of Compliance.[315]

In contrast to the way Sandretto said she was treated after she rejected Bono's overtures, Sandretto's supervisors on the Senate Judiciary Committee were pleased by her work. Sandretto is "very bright, enterprising, industrious, tenacious, and hard-working," one of them said. She is also "truthful," her former supervisor said.

Three days after Sandretto had been removed from the project, she quit. "They had me go back to the mail," she said. "I did that for two days. I asked, 'Will there be anything else to do?' They said no. I said, 'I'm leaving.'"

Bono declined to be interviewed. "He was pretty indignant when I mentioned it to him," Frank Cullen Jr., Bono's press secretary, said. "He said, 'That's crazy. We certainly wouldn't stand still if someone is going to make that kind of accusation. But there's no reason for me to address it because it's completely false.'"[316]

Cullen said he checked with other staffers, who attributed Sandretto's charge to her "frustration" because she had not been allowed to work on terrorism issues. While the staff "probably considered" her as a "resource" on terrorism, Cullen said, "it was never assigned to her. At no time was this etched in stone." Ultimately, the staff decided that because she was not an American citizen, Sandretto should not work on sensitive issues "from a security standpoint."

Cullen said Sandretto was also perturbed that Bono had not helped her with her visa problem. "The day she left we were all aware she left mad," Cullen said. "She was not happy about not being given that opportunity or getting a paid job. On top of that, she was frustrated that she was given work that a high school graduate could do."

Cullen said Bono has a large supply of rings of the kind he gave to Sandretto. "He did give a lot of those rings out," Cullen said. He said no other staffer has complained of advances. "We have a position that there is no past pattern. It seems unusual that she did not go to the chief of staff. . . . We've had a lot of interns come through this office. We've never had a complaint."

Cullen added, "She is someone who had her own motivations and, in our mind, is not credible in terms of what her charge is. . . . He is being put in a bad spot on this deal by someone who feels she did not get what she wanted out of this office."

In contrast to what Cullen said about security concerns, the Senate subcommittee where Sandretto worked had no such reservations. Classified information can only be shared with people who have appropriate clearances, regardless of their citizenship. While working for the Senate, Sandretto had attended unclassified briefings given by the FBI and other sensitive government agencies.

Told of Cullen's response, Sandretto asked why Bono had not consented to an interview to confront the charge himself. "If he is above reproach, he would say, 'Okay, come here tomorrow.'" She said she was a Fulbright Scholar and was not interested in a permanent job with Congress.

After the incident with Bono, Sandretto confided what had happened to two other people besides her boyfriend and a House staff member. One was a Senate committee counsel, who advised her to write down what had happened. The other staffer, who also works for the Senate, had been the target of sexual advances by a senator in years past. All four congressional employees confirmed to the author that Sandretto had told them in June 1996 of Bono's advances and of her belief that she suffered retribution when she rejected them.

Based on the advice some of the congressional staffers gave her, Sandretto decided against taking further action. As a member of Congress, Bono could retaliate and make her life miserable, they told her. In the same way, none of the staffers harassed by Packwood over the years ever complained. Only when the *Washington Post* learned of the incidents did some of them agree to talk.

Since the House had erroneously advised her that she could not file a sexual harassment complaint against Bono, Sandretto thought her only recourse would be to go to the press. She was unaware that she could also have complained to the House Committee on Standards of Official Conduct. Composed of House members, it could have censured Bono or recommended his expulsion.

"At first, I thought, 'Let's tell the local newspaper,'" Sandretto said. Then she began to think of the implications of going public. Would Bono besmirch her reputation? Would people think she had led him on? Why hadn't she confronted Bono immediately? Given his power, Sandretto feared that Bono could do almost anything to her.

Sandretto decided to do nothing. Three months later, when writing this book, the author learned about her experience from others. When asked for an interview, she readily agreed.

"I thought I didn't want to be that kind of woman," Sandretto said of her initial decision to keep quiet. "In the country I come from, sexual harassment happens. We don't have, like you have in America, women's protections. If it happens to a woman, we say in France it's her fault."

13

Reform

In 1830, Sen. Daniel Webster described the Senate as consisting of "men of individual honor and personal character, and of absolute independence. We know no masters, we acknowledge no dictators."

Whether that was ever entirely true of the Senate or House is debatable. Three years after Webster made his remark, he complained to the privately owned Bank of the United States about the size of his retainer.

But what is clear is that what once occurred sporadically has engulfed Congress. By legalizing contributions of hundreds of millions of dollars from special interests, Congress has corrupted itself and made a mockery of the democratic process.

The system is self-selecting. Few candidates with integrity want to run. Those who choose to run perpetuate the system once they are elected. Then they spend as much as half their time seeking more money. The need to conceal how money influences them generates deceit in other areas. Hypocrisy, lying, and criminal conduct become commonplace. The fact that members succeed with the charade breeds arrogance and contempt for the people they serve. Members become so brazen that they distribute PAC money on the floor of the House and corrupt the institutions of Congress itself. From the House Post Office and Bank scandals to the corruption of the Capitol Police, the way Congress operates its own fiefdoms reflects the character of the members as a whole. Rather than electing legislators who will honestly represent them, Americans are literally electing to Congress the best fund-raisers.

"Some say they don't like raising money, but a lot do," said Rep. Jim Leach, an Iowa Republican who refuses PAC money.

"I taught at the University of Louisville Law School," said former representative Romano L. Mazzoli. "Not many law students think very highly of the election system. It just doesn't look clean. It's not something they want to do, kowtowing to people."[317]

"Few decent people want to subject themselves to the kind of grueling abuse candidates take when they run," said Dr. Bertram S. Brown, the expert on congressional psychology. "Many of those who run crave superficial celebrity. They are hollow people who engage in abuses more easily. They have no principles and simply want to be reelected."[318]

Today, so few members of Congress are truly honorable, decent individuals that one must look back in time to find examples of admirable legislators. One such man was Sen. Philip A. Hart, whose name graces the Hart Senate Office Building. A three-term senator who died in office in 1976, Hart, a Michigan Democrat, took on powerful interests without fear or favor. From the oil and banking industries to the insurance and newspaper industries, Hart held probing hearings on antitrust violations and other issues affecting consumers and developed legislation to correct abuses. Even the auto industry, the keystone to his state's economy, came under Hart's scrutiny.

When Hart felt he had been wrong, as when he supported a federal housing program that turned into a scandal, he apologized publicly. When Hart attended a campaign dinner that recounted on the program his impressive war record, Hart became upset. "I want it clearly understood that I just happened to be there on D-day," he told the gathering. "What happened to me happened to other people." He told his aides he never wanted his war record discussed.[319]

"There was a kind of spirit of goodness about Phil Hart that tended to elicit a more noble response from other people," said Harrison Wellford, an aide. "You were ashamed to be narrow and polemical and partisan in his presence because he gave you the impression that he was so much more than that himself."

An advocate of campaign finance reform, Hart persuaded his opponent in the 1970 election to agree to a self-imposed limit on advertising expenditures.

From Bob Dole and segregationist Sen. James O. Eastland to Sen. Ted Kennedy, members looked up to Hart and considered him their friend. Just before a vote, senators would gather on the floor to find out what their party recommended. Then, "they would cluster around Phil to find out what the right vote was," recalled Sen. Ernest F. (Fritz) Hollings, a South Carolina Democrat.[320]

Above all, Hart had "incorruptible integrity," as the inscription to him above the main entrance of the Hart building says. Hart was known as the "conscience of the Senate."

Patricia Bario, a former aide, said that Hart "got so uptight about what was proper that not only could we not accept things like drinks, but when the office staff got a box of chocolates at Christmas from a reporter, he had us return it. There were forty staff members, and each would have gotten one piece of chocolate."[321]

Because of the cost of today's campaigns, unless candidates are independently wealthy or without family responsibilities, they are usually forced to take PAC money. Rep. Martin T. Meehan, a Massachusetts Democrat who ran without PAC money, said he was able to do so only because he was not married and was willing to part with most of his assets.

"When the election was over, I was two hundred and fifty thousand dollars in debt," Meehan said. "I sold my car. I cashed in my pension with the state. You shouldn't have to do that to get here."

"The ability to raise big money and buy saturation television ads has become the dominant theme of our political races," former senator Sam Nunn, a Georgia Democrat, said.

Even if some members retain their integrity against the tidal wave of money, the system creates an appearance of corruption, suggesting that everything Congress does is bought.

"The money becomes a corrupting influence," said former senator Gaylord A. Nelson, a Wisconsin Democrat. "Even when it isn't, it appears to the public to be. Pretty soon the people start to lose confidence in their elected officials. Once that happens, in a free society like ours, you are threatening the very basis of our system. You don't have to have confidence in the Politburo; it doesn't matter. It does matter in our system."[322]

"I wonder if James Madison could be elected to Congress today," said Rep. Lee H. Hamilton, an Indiana Democrat. Considered the father of the Constitution, Madison was a House member before becoming president. "Would he want to run? I think he probably would not want to run and could not get elected if he wanted to," Hamilton said.

Few members are so audacious and obtuse that they publicly oppose campaign finance reform. Instead, they give lip service to the concept of reform and make empty promises while picking away at one feature or another in an array of reform measures. When the time comes to take a stand, they let the measures die noiselessly.

Thus, on June 11, 1995, Bill Clinton and Newt Gingrich, speaking from the same podium in Claremont, New Hampshire, shook hands on a pledge to support a nonpartisan commission to reform campaign financing. The agreement came in response to a question from Frank MacConnell Jr., a member of the audience. MacConnell said, "After the health care reform failure, the very, very large disappointment of the past two years . . . is that the special interest groups really are running the country. Let me ask you both, gentlemen, a question. Would you be willing to have the same type commission as a [military] base closure commission to review" the campaign finance system?

MacConnell was referring to the bipartisan Commission on

Base Realignment and Closure, which Congress created in October 1988. Because members did not have the backbone to do it themselves, Congress charged the commission with producing a list of military bases to be closed or reduced in size. Neither the administration nor Congress could amend the list; they had to accept or reject all the recommendations. Once the commission made its recommendations, Congress gave itself forty-five days to decide. In the event of a veto by the president, Congress would have needed a two-thirds vote to override it.[323]

Clinton responded that he would support the appointment of such a commission to reform the campaign finance laws. Newt Gingrich then jumped up and said, "I accept. Let's shake hands here in front of everybody."

But the word of a member of Congress is about as good as a con man's. While Clinton kept making overtures, by August, Gingrich was telling reporters, "We have not had the mental energy this summer to do anything besides the appropriations bills and Medicare." A few days later, the House Speaker said the subject of money in politics was "too serious to play narrow, cheap political games with." Then in November, Gingrich said the commission should have sixteen members, eight from each party, and should report by May 1, 1996. But in the same statement, Gingrich said, "One of the greatest myths of modern politics is that campaigns are too expensive. The political process, in fact, is underfunded."[324]

As might have been expected, that was the last anyone heard from either politician about a commission. Later, Gingrich even compared the amount spent on campaigns to soap ad campaigns and claimed that political advertising educates and informs the public.

The truth is just the opposite. Negative campaign ads—along with the perception that the system is corrupt—tend to turn off voters and discourage them from voting at all. And rather than serving to educate the public, most campaign ads are either inaccurate or misleading.

In one ad during the 1996 Republican presidential primary campaign, Bob Dole claimed that as governor of Tennessee, primary candidate Lamar Alexander had raised the sales tax by 85 percent. In fact, he had raised the sales tax 22 percent, according to an analysis by CNN's Brooks Jackson.[325] President Clinton ran an ad claiming, "Republicans cut school lunches, Head Start." In fact, Congress ultimately increased funding for both programs. A Dole ad said that under Clinton, the typical American family pays more than $1,500 in additional federal taxes. While the typical family did pay more taxes, that was because the average family had $6,000 more in income. An ad by Republicans against Sen. Paul Wellstone, a Minnesota Democrat, attacked him for being soft on crime because of his vote on three bills. What the ad did not say was that Minnesota's Republican senator at the time, David F. Durenberger, had voted the same way. In fact, on one of the bills, more than half the Republicans in the Senate voted as Wellstone did.

"You develop a theme, and you communicate it in thirty-second spots. Not a great way to educate people about who you are, what you stand for, and why you are running," said former representative Mel Levine, a California Democrat.

If members of Congress find it too risky to publicly oppose reforming the system, a few academics and columnists have had no hesitation. Their arguments only demonstrate how flimsy the case against reform is. Writing in *Newsweek*, Robert J. Samuelson claimed, "In politics, money is not the root of all evil, though many people think it is."[326] Saying campaign spending is only 0.05 percent of the gross domestic product, Samuelson concluded this "hardly seems a high price for democracy."

But the concept of democracy means everyone has an equal say in the political process. Allowing special interests to purchase more influence is the antithesis of democracy. Moreover, money that buys misleading advertising promotes fraud, not democracy. And comparing the amount spent on campaigns to the gross domestic product is meaningless. From corrupt bribes and theft to sales of chocolate, almost anything is dwarfed by the gross domestic product.

The amount spent on campaigning might be a high price to

pay if campaign money were "thoroughly corrupting," but it is not, Samuelson wrote. In his view, campaign contributions "probably" protect tax breaks given to large contributors such as Dwayne Andreas and his Archer Daniels Midland Company. But, Samuelson claimed, Congress initially passed the tax breaks because farmers supported them. In other words, he seemed to be saying, money does buy influence, but only to protect special breaks already enacted.

"The necessity of money would be troubling if it settled elections—if candidates could buy victory. They can't," Samuelson said. Many issues decide elections, Samuelson wrote. In 1994, eight of the twenty House candidates with the largest total contributions lost, he said. Yet more impressive was that twelve of those candidates won.

Obviously, money is not the only factor in elections. Voters weigh many factors in making their decisions. But to discount the role of money in any human enterprise is to live in an unreal world. If contributions do not buy elections and influence votes, why did individuals and PACs contribute $2.7 billion to federal candidates in the 1996 election?

The evidence is clear that the money is well spent. In the 1996 election, nine out of every 10 House candidates and eight out of every 10 Senate candidates won after spending more than their opponents. No candidate who was outspent by more than five to one was victorious. The average winning candidate for the House spent $490,216; the average loser spent $197,695. The average winning Senate candidate spent $3.4 million; the average loser spent $2 million. The amounts spent were obscene: Rep. Newt Gingrich spent $5.4 million to beat challenger Michael J. Coles; Sen. John F. Kerry spent $10.7 million to beat Bill Weld. The system favored incumbents, who received four times more money than their opponents and won 95 percent of all congressional races.

Once in office, the winners did the bidding of their benefactors. Restaurants and pizza delivery companies contributed $2.5 million and got a new tax credit buried in the minimum wage bill. Auto makers and dealers contributed $4.2 million and got a phase-out of the automobile luxury tax. Pharmaceutical and computer companies contributed $9.8 million and got a reversal of a tax on corporations' overseas earnings. These breaks alone, passed in 1996 by the supposedly budget-conscious 104th Congress, will cost taxpayers more than $590 million over 10 years, according to the Center for Responsive Politics.

If the evidence of the impact of money on politics is clear, so is the perception that money corrupts it. Acknowledging that, Samuelson wrote that a *New York Times* poll found 79 percent believed "government is run by a few big interests." But Samuelson suggested that is because groups such as Common Cause, along with journalists and politicians themselves, persist in proclaiming that campaign money is corrupting.

If politicians cannot be believed when they say that money does, in fact, corrupt them, who else is in a position to know? According to Samuelson, that person is Herbert E. Alexander, a political scientist at the University of Southern California. Alexander, director of the Citizens' Research Foundation, which tracks campaign finance issues, has said campaign contributions are not attempts to gain "special favors." Indeed, Alexander has said that elections are actually "improved by well-financed candidates able to wage competitive campaigns."[327]

As if campaign spending is somehow necessary to run the government, Alexander has said that total expenditures for election campaigns represent only 1 percent of all government spending. At other times, Alexander has compared campaign expenditures to the advertising budgets of companies such as Procter & Gamble, a view Gingrich later adopted.

Summarizing Alexander's position, Samuelson said it's not easy for bankers to buy liberalized regulations because their competitors, the brokers, give to political campaigns also. Thus, according to Samuelson, money does buy influence, but only when it happens to neatly cancel out someone else's money: the money from brokers counterbalances the money from bankers. It is true, as Rep. Lee Hamilton put it, that "money often fights money." That is a sad commentary on American democracy. The loser is the American voter, who does not get the benefit of disinterested regulation and legislation.

If Samuelson's argument is specious and Alexander's naive,

their positions are also belied by the facts. As far back as 1983, the impact of PACs had become clear to those who are in the best position to know: members of Congress themselves. "Congress is literally being bought and sold by PAC contributions," said then representative Leon Panetta, a California Democrat who later became Bill Clinton's chief of staff. "These new PACs not only buy incumbents, but affect legislation," Rep. Barber B. Conable Jr., a New York Republican, said. "We are the only human beings in the world who are expected to take thousands of dollars from perfect strangers on important matters and not be affected by it," Rep. Barney Frank, a Massachusetts Democrat, said. "Fund-raising has a corrupting effect on all of us," according to former senator Paul Simon, an Illinois Democrat. "The only reason it [PAC contributions] isn't considered bribery is that Congress gets to define bribery," said Rep. Andrew Jacobs Jr., an Indiana Democrat.[328]

Indeed, as former representative Bob Eckhardt, a Texas Democrat, said, "The process has all the advantages of bribery and none of its risks." Former senator Russell B. Long, a Louisiana Democrat, said the difference between a PAC contribution and bribery is a "hair." And former senator S. I. Hayakawa, a California Republican, called PAC money "a huge, masked bribe."[329] Even Bob Dole, who swam in PAC money, once referred to the present system as "campaign sewer money." If that is so, how can more campaign spending be beneficial?

Thus, the comparison with the advertising budgets of companies such as Procter & Gamble is fallacious. By and large, a company is able to devote large sums to advertising because it sells a product that people buy because they consider it worthwhile. If consumers did not consider a product worthwhile, the company that made it could not generate enough money to continue to advertise it. If a company runs false or misleading advertising, the Federal Trade Commission can force it to stop. If a company spends too much to advertise a bad product, it will eventually go bankrupt. If a company is successful, it will create more permanent jobs and add to the economy.

In congressional campaigns, the incentives are reversed: the more a member sells out his vote to special interests, the more money he receives from those interests to buy more advertising. If a member runs false or misleading advertising and it is believed, he is more likely to be elected. If elected, he will likely hand out special tax breaks and subsidies to the special interests that helped elect him, increasing the deficit and corrupting the system further.

Americans are not fooled. The majority believe that half or more of the members of Congress are financially corrupt.[330] A 1995 poll for Campaign for America, a group that advocates campaign finance reform, found that 92 percent of those surveyed believed that special-interest contributions affect congressional votes. Only 4 percent said such contributions do not make a difference. The survey also found that 87 percent of the respondents favored limiting the amount of money candidates can spend on campaigns.

Asked if they would favor a candidate who refused PAC contributions, 71 percent of Americans surveyed in a 1996 Roper poll said they were more likely to vote for such a candidate. Finally, a USA Today/CNN poll found 83 percent of Americans want Congress to pass campaign finance reform, and 64 percent favored public financing of elections.

Nor are PAC managers fooled. They know that money buys influence. When campaign finance reform legislation was being considered, a number of corporate and trade-association PACs said they would withhold contributions from those lawmakers who voted to ban PACs.[331] "We take it real personally when people bash PACs and then come to us for money," said Katie Maness, director of political affairs at Union Pacific Corp., whose PAC gave nearly $300,000 to congressional candidates in 1995. Privately, PAC managers joke about what their money has bought them. Describing how much time he spends with President Clinton, the Washington representative of a major financial firm's PAC said, "I paid enough for it."

Instead of encouraging ordinary citizens to participate, as proponents of PACs suggest, the vast quantities of money in the campaign process turns them off. "Without PACs, people would be more likely to participate [in the political process]," Representative Leach said. "Why would you want to give ten dollars to a candidate when a PAC just gave ten thousand dollars?"

That fewer than half the eligible voters turned out for the 1996 presidential and congressional election is a shocking symptom of this malaise: it was the lowest percentage since 1924. When presidential elections do not coincide with congressional elections, the turnout rate is even lower. In the 1994 election, only 36 percent of eligible voters participated in the House election. As it is, the United States has one of the lowest participation rates in the world. In their most recent elections, 79 percent of those eligible in Israel voted, 82.2 percent in Brazil, 69.7 percent in Canada, 77.7 percent in Great Britain, and 78.9 percent in Germany. In America, winners represent only a majority of a minority. Moreover, only about 7 percent of the U.S. population contributes money to political candidates or to PACs, suggesting that the claim that PACs encourage little people to participate is another myth.

"The most critical failing of our current system is that much of the public is turned off by campaign financing and campaigns themselves," Sen. Fred Thompson, a Republican from Tennessee, said. "Many think the system reeks of special interests and favors bought and sold. This undoubtedly contributes to our low voter turnout."

"Whether we are beholden to these special interests or not, it certainly appears that way to the general public," said Rep. Wayne T. Gilchrest, a Maryland Republican. "Doesn't that alone undermine the public's confidence in our electoral process?"

Perhaps the most damaging effect of the present system is that it creates an air of unreality about the political process. Candidates appear on television to argue a position without disclosing that they have received money from one side of the argument. Journalists pretend that the answers they are given are sincerely motivated. In debate, members refer to themselves as "honorable" and "distinguished" when they know that because of the money they are taking and the influence it buys, they are anything but. The entire political process becomes a charade.

"If I were running C-SPAN, I would put a caption underneath each member detailing how much they've gotten from different industries," former representative Pat Schroeder, a Democrat from Colorado, said after she announced her retirement. "You sit there in the conference committee and think, 'Oh, that's the one that got umpty-ump thousand from such-and-such interest group.' It's outrageous."

Whether voters would prefer to see captions disclosing how much a candidate received from special interests is debatable. It would only remind them that members of Congress do not truly represent them. Moreover, the credibility of the candidate's comments would be so undermined that viewers would switch to another channel.

In reviewing videotapes taken by surveillance cameras during bank robberies, FBI agents are often startled to see the bizarre reactions of some customers waiting in line. Instead of looking frightened, they smile or look bemused as they watch robbers demand money or even fire weapons. According to agents, these people hope that if they do not acknowledge what they are seeing, it will mean it is not happening.[332] In other words, they are in denial.

Today, the same could be said of American voters. As if to underscore the point, during a discussion of campaign finance reform on CNN's *Crossfire*, former White House chief of staff John Sununu asked David Axelrod, a Democratic Party consultant, "Aren't we all fouling our own nest here when we give credibility to the idea that the campaign contributions really have that kind of influence?"[333]

In other words, wouldn't it be better to pretend that money has no influence, lest we all look bad? If the subtext of what happens in Congress is the exchange of influence for money, what is the point of discussing weighty political issues? If America's elected representatives are corrupt, what does that say about Americans?

To be sure, voters are not fully aware of how out of control members really are. But they know enough to take a dim view of Congress and the American political process. Poll after poll shows that Americans generally do not approve of the job

Congress is doing and believe special interests control Washington and dominate the legislative process. Yet when asked specifically about their own congressman or senator, voters across the country generally have a more favorable opinion. Whereas 92 percent of those surveyed for the Campaign for America poll thought special interest contributions affect congressional votes, only 60 percent thought such contributions affect their own members' votes.

Despite their disappointment in them, the electorate keeps returning the same politicians to office. Over the years, voters have come to ignore the track records of candidates, to accept their dissembling, and to look the other way when confronted with evidence of their character flaws, including candidates' acceptance of PAC money. Instead, they focus on candidates' promises—which they usually break once in office—and how well they come across on television. Sonny Bono may lack brains, but he has name recognition, which has become all-important in winning elections. In effect, Americans vote for accomplished actors rather than smart, honorable people. By supporting flawed candidates who lack integrity, voters guarantee that their representatives will perpetuate the corrupt-money system. The problem is not Washington; the problem is every state in the union.

In training FBI agents at the FBI Academy in Quantico, Virginia, the Bureau teaches that the best indicator of future behavior is past behavior. "No man can climb out beyond the limitations of his own character," Maximilien Robespierre, the French politician, said.

Before television, voters received most of their information about candidates from newspapers. Because of the nature of the medium, that meant candidates' track records and past conduct assumed far more importance than they do today, when a winning appearance on TV may suffice. To be sure, in those days, evidence of corruption and unethical conduct was suppressed far more often. For example, it never came out that the FBI found substantial evidence of vote fraud in the 1942 Democratic primary election that returned Wilbur D. Mills to Congress. The FBI found "unsigned duplicate ballots, similarly written signatures, missing ballots, absentee ballots unsigned," as well as evidence that "Mills received considerably more votes than were cast for him," according to an FBI memo.[334] A federal grand jury concluded the fraud did not violate federal laws, and the matter never came to light.

Yet in years past, when improprieties did come out, the perpetrators generally were taken to task. In 1958, Sherman Adams, a special assistant to President Dwight D. Eisenhower, was forced to resign because he had accepted hotel accommodations, a vicuña coat, and the loan of an expensive rug from Bernard Goldfine, a Boston industrialist. There was an implication, never proven, that Adams had used his influence to help Goldfine.

Compared with the millions of dollars members of Congress receive, the incident seems trivial. Whether politicians receive money for personal or campaign use is immaterial. They still become beholden to their benefactors. Yet back then, the Sherman Adams scandal "rocked the capital," as the Boston Globe put it. Meade Alcorn, the chairman of the Republican National Committee, told Adams that Eisenhower wanted him to resign. Three days later, he did.[335]

Today, there is no sense of shame about betraying the public trust. Unless they are indicted, cabinet officers involved in unethical conduct continue to serve. Government officials responsible for billions of dollars in waste do not lose their jobs. The Defense Department stores $36 billion in unneeded inventory. The Interior Department fails to collect $1.2 billion in oil royalties. The Internal Revenue Service fails to collect $125 billion in delinquent taxes. The Department of Energy spends $29 million to design and construct accident-resistant containers for the Air Force without bothering to ask the Air Force if it wants them. (It doesn't.) Those in charge are never held to account.[336]

Like a spreading inkblot, this moral neutrality colors history as well. Despite the fact that J. Edgar Hoover engaged in illegalities and harassed Martin Luther King, his name remains on the FBI's headquarters building. Despite the fact that key officials of the Johnson administration lied about why the

United States was involved in the Vietnam War and about the war's progress, none of them is today held in disgrace. Having been named an unindicted co-conspirator in the Watergate cover-up, Richard Nixon went on to advise presidents and pontificate on foreign policy. Although Spiro T. Agnew was forced to resign as vice president over a charge that he had accepted bribes of more than $100,000 in cash while serving in three different elected offices, the architect of the Capitol, in May 1995, unveiled a bust of Agnew in the Senate wing of the Capitol.[337]

To be sure, an 1896 Senate resolution dictates that every former vice president is entitled to such an honor. But the Senate could have changed the resolution. Instead, the Senate brushed aside the fact that Agnew had brought disgrace on his office and betrayed the public trust. When Agnew died, former senator Bob Dole eulogized him as a hero—a man who "earned the support of millions of his countrymen because he was never afraid to speak out and stand up for America."

In the same way, when they elected Gingrich, Georgia voters had to blind themselves to the fact that he espoused family values after having divorced his wife when she had cancer and refusing to pay sufficient child support. Most Americans would never choose such a person as a friend, hire or promote him in a job, or place him in a position of trust. When it comes to choosing politicians, the electorate tolerates hypocrisy and bad character, which inevitably lead to duplicity once candidates assume office. Thus, given his demonstrated ruthlessness and dishonesty, it should have come as no surprise that Newt Gingrich would shut down the federal government, threaten to plunge the country into default on its debts, and renege on an earlier promise to seek campaign finance reform.

Over and over again, the electorate has ignored signs of bad character and regretted it. When he was a candidate for vice president, Richard Nixon became embroiled in an ethics issue when the *New York Post* revealed he had secretly accepted $18,000 from private contributors to defray his expenses. It should have come as no surprise that he would end up being driven from office by the scandal known as Watergate. Ronald

Reagan was an actor given to facile promises. It should have come as no surprise when he ran up the biggest government deficits in history. Given Bill Clinton's compulsive philandering while governor of Arkansas, it should have come as no surprise that he would turn out to be a spineless leader whose word was not trusted. That, in turn, has diminished his effectiveness: a leader who is not respected cannot lead. The fact that Clinton felt he had to declare in April 1995 that the "president is relevant" demonstrates what happens when voters elect politicians lacking in substance.

In examining what is known about most members of Congress, similar ethics controversies and evidence of poor character are apparent. Often, the signs are in their faces. Many members have hard, power-hungry looks and smarmy, darting eyes. In person, most members cannot look an interviewer in the eye. Yet made up for the cameras, most of them look presentable on television. If people's faces illuminate their character, America is in trouble. The tendency to overlook the warning signs is but another demonstration of denial.

"The character of Congress has changed because of too much money," said former representative John E. Moss, a California Democrat who was in Congress for twenty-six years. "They are bought. They are put up by strong interests in the district. These are people whose main objective is to remain in office. That's a horrible disease to get. You have to be able to live without the aura of the office. You have to convince yourself you have things you want to do, and you do your damnedest to do them. When you are dependent on your own resources, you tend to be a little more considerate of the other person. When you think you have enough dollars to empower you, you don't worry about other people. When you get the money out of the picture, you'll start getting good character in Congress."[338]

Instead of focusing on character and track records, many voters have bought into the politicians' whining counterattack: that American voters have become too cynical and mistrustful, that bringing out personal flaws discourages good candidates from running, that the sanctity of the country may be threatened if the truth comes out.

"Reporters now just wait for a gaffe, a boneheaded statement, a profanity, then they chop your head off—and love it," Sen. Alan Simpson, a Wyoming Republican, said after he announced his retirement.

Almost as if they feel they do not deserve honest politicians, Americans fall for the phony distinction that so long as they do not influence public acts, flaws in candidates' private lives should be disregarded. This is another display of denial. Human beings do not consist of two spheres, a public and a private one. Poor judgment, hypocrisy, deceit, arrogance, and corrupt tendencies displayed in one's personal life inevitably surface in official acts. To deny that is to guarantee that candidates will engage in wrongdoing once they are elected.

"The best way to measure a candidate's character," according to Prof. James Barber of Duke University, author of *The Presidential Character*, "is by looking at the signs he gives in private—how he talks and acts around the people closest to him, like his staff, in unguarded moments—when the press isn't watching."[339]

Contrary to the claim that it is difficult to find people without character flaws, the truth is that most Americans are decent, honorable people, but many—such as Colin Powell—do not want to run in the present system. Others are thought to be unpresidential for the very reason that they are too much like Boy Scouts. From lawyers and doctors to electricians and plumbers, every other profession and trade is expected to adhere to ethical standards. In the political arena, honesty and purity of motive are considered liabilities. Those who point out that the emperor has no clothes are said to be too cynical and are accused of discouraging good candidates from running. So long as Americans embrace these attitudes, they will be disappointed in their public officials, and the present corrupt system will continue.

"You misunderstand PACs if you think PACs are the principal problem," Rep. Jim Leach said. "Decency and quality are."

The reelection of Newt Gingrich as speaker in January 1997 was a stunning demonstration of how base Congress has become. Lying to the government is a criminal offense, one that should result in expulsion. Yet House members not only did not expel Gingrich, they re-anointed him—albeit narrowly—as their leader. They took the step even *before* hearing all the evidence against him.

The support was to be expected: they saw themselves in Gingrich and excused him. Vindictively, the Republicans informed the nine Republican House members who had not voted for Gingrich—including Jim Leach—that they would not be welcome at a dinner honoring Republican National Chairman Haley Barbour. Then it turned out that despite an agreement with the ethics committee that he would refrain from shaping strategy on how his case would be presented to the public, Gingrich and his attorney discussed the timing of party action on the news from the committee and the language that the leadership would disseminate, according to their intercepted cellular phone conversation. They even conceded in their conversation, revealed by the *New York Times*, that by plotting strategy, they were violating their agreement with the committee.

While Gingrich agreed with the House ethics committee's determination that he should pay $300,000 to cover the cost of the investigation, Gingrich was said to be considering whether to pay the fine from campaign funds or from a special collection. Either way, the sanction would become yet another payoff by special interests to bail out the speaker. As for the law against lying to the government, Congress, with its usual foresight, had made sure that—according to a recent court ruling—the law would apply only to false statements made to agencies or departments of the executive branch, not to Congress.

Just as voters adopt a defeatist attitude about electing people with good character, many claim it is too difficult to reform the campaign finance system. The excuses are endless: Money will always find the loopholes. The Supreme Court will reject any change that infringes on the First Amendment. Enforcement is too difficult. The last effort at reform resulted in the proliferation of PACs. Disclosure is the only answer. Somehow, America had the fortitude to fight Communism and Nazism, but passing an airtight law so that Americans will have a clean election system is considered too difficult.

"Money is going to get involved in political campaigns no matter what you do," said Rep. Floyd D. Spence, a South Carolina Republican. "You want to know where money comes from. As long as it is made public, people can make their own judgment on whether they should support a candidate."

But lists of hundreds of thousands of dollars in special interest contributions to candidates convey no meaning except that the system is corrupt. If nearly every candidate accepts such contributions, the voter is left with the sole alternative of voting for flawed politicians.

In another effort at obfuscation, Sen. Mitch McConnell, a Kentucky Republican who has been the leading opponent of campaign finance reform in the Senate, has claimed that the First Amendment precludes reform. In fact, the Supreme Court's key decision on the issue made it clear that Congress could impose campaign financing restrictions as long as wealthy candidates still had the option of spending their own money to finance their own campaigns.

In *Buckley v. Valeo*, the Supreme Court in 1976 upheld the limits set by Congress on how much individuals and PACs may contribute to candidates. It also upheld public funding of presidential elections. But, on the grounds they violate the First Amendment, the court rejected campaign spending limits imposed on candidates who spend their own money unless the candidates agree to the limits in return for receiving public funding. Thus, the court's ruling permitted spending caps as part of an optional public-funding arrangement. In any case, a wealthy candidate who spends his own money is not in the same category as one who accepts money from special interests. When a candidate spends his own money, he is not subject to being influenced.

More recent Supreme Court rulings striking down limitations on expenditures by so-called independent groups pose a separate problem. The court has said that to prevent independent groups from running ads for candidates they support would violate the First Amendment. But the problem is not the ruling; the problem is that the campaign finance laws passed by Congress are so porous and enforcement is so lax that candidates routinely control the efforts of "independent" groups that support them. Thus, the groups are not truly independent. The solution is tighter laws and better enforcement. Moreover, the Supreme Court has indicated it might pose no objection to even more limitations on campaign financing if there is a "substantial government interest in stemming the reality or the appearance of corruption in the electoral process." That clearly is the case today, so limits imposed even on independent expenditures could well be upheld.

There is no need for a constitutional amendment to permit campaign finance reform, as Sen. Trent Lott and others have suggested. Such a radical remedy would never be adopted; it is but another clever charade to postpone reform. What Congress needs is the will to enact reform. Enforcement of campaign finance laws is difficult because Congress purposely wrote them vaguely.

"There is a lot of First Amendment rhetoric going on in Congress, but to the best of my knowledge, none of the members of Congress who are worried about the First Amendment think that campaign finance reforms are a good idea," said Frederick Schauer, Frank Stanton Professor of the First Amendment at Harvard University's Kennedy School of Government and a visiting professor of law at Harvard Law School. "That should tell you something about whether the First Amendment rhetoric is real or transparent. I believe it's the latter."[340]

Just as the Supreme Court is used as a shibboleth by those who would avoid reform, so is the commonly made claim that the 1972 campaign finance reforms allowed PACs to flourish. While the change that allowed PACs to flourish was contained in a reform package, groups such as Common Cause opposed the measure. Rather, business interests and labor unions supported the change.

While PAC money is the biggest problem, under the present system contributions from individuals who comprise an interest group—the trial lawyers, labor union members, or insurance industry employees—can also have a powerful effect on members.

"Singling out PACs as the sole or primary source of the problem is a gross oversimplification," said former representative Eric D. Fingerhut, an Ohio Democrat. "The solution is to limit the size of individual contributions so no one party can be too influential in the process. The solution is to find other sources of funding. I support public funding and tax credits on smaller contributions. Also you can get in-kind contributions like free TV time. You want to guarantee that a candidate has a sufficient amount of money to be heard."[341]

In his State of the Union message in 1907, President Theodore Roosevelt proposed public financing of all federal elections and a ban on private contributions. He was responding to charges during his 1904 campaign that he had received large corporate contributions from prospective government contractors.

As always, Congress is expert at spotting flaws and fashioning remedies, but is unwilling to apply those remedies to itself. Thus, acknowledging that money corrupts campaigns, Congress passed a plan to provide for public funding of presidential elections. That law, which took effect in the 1976 elections, allows taxpayers to designate on their tax returns whether they want to contribute $3 to a fund that supports presidential campaigns. The system provides optional public matching funds during the primary election and full public funding for the major candidates in the general elections. Candidates who accept public funds agree to adhere to spending limits in both the primary and general elections, thus passing First Amendment tests. Soft money has been allowed to creep into presidential campaigns, but slightly more than half of the funding for the 1996 presidential election still came from public funds.

In polls and in referenda, voters overwhelmingly support the idea of public financing of elections, usually combined with limits on total expenditures. Such limits are just as important as public funding. The bulk of campaign money goes for television advertising, whose cost is the main reason elections have become so expensive. But television advertising is the least desirable way of depicting the differences among candidates. Voters should judge candidates not by their promises, charisma, and positions on issues, but by their track records and reputations for integrity. Those who recall flip-flops on taxes by Presidents Bush and Clinton know just how meaningless candidates' enunciated positions usually are.

Between 1972 and 1994, voters in forty-two state and local jurisdictions succeeded in placing referendum questions on ballots to achieve election reform, and thirty-three of the questions passed. Of the sixteen that set up public financing, twelve succeeded. As of 1995, twenty-three states—almost half—provided some form of public financing to candidates. Some of the plans allow voters to designate the party to which they want their money to go.[342] More recently, election reforms have passed in Maine, California, Colorado, Arkansas, and Nevada.

Maine's plan is a model. Over the past decade, the Maine legislature had considered campaign finance reform measures and rejected them forty times. Finally, a coalition backed by the League of Women Voters, Common Cause, the American Association of Retired Persons, the AFL-CIO, and other groups gathered sixty-five thousand signatures to place the question on the ballot. "Remember when democracy was something we believed in, not something for sale?" the campaign literature asked. In 1996, Maine voters adopted the Clean Elections Act— question three on the ballot—by 56 percent.[343]

Tailored to meet Supreme Court scrutiny, the Maine plan gives candidates for state representative, senator, and governor the option of either continuing to raise private funds or accepting public funds. Just as in congressional elections, those who rely on private funds must abide by limits on individual donations. In Maine, besides individuals and PACs, corporations can also give to campaigns. But the limits on those donations were reduced to just $250.

To become eligible for money from the Maine Clean Elections Fund, candidates have to show they have broad public support by receiving from individuals a prescribed number of $5 checks made out to the fund. Candidates for state representative need

Reform

50 such checks; candidates for senator have to solicit 150 checks. That money, plus an annual appropriation from the legislature of roughly $2 million a year and tax money contributed through a $3 checkoff option on state tax forms, will support the fund. The plan includes no tax increases. On the theory that incumbents use their offices to supplement their campaigns, the appropriation for the fund will be offset by a reduction in legislative and executive-branch office budgets. An increase in registration fees charged to lobbyists will help give more enforcement powers to an Ethics Commission that will administer the fund.

The plan takes effect in the year 2000. Each candidate who qualifies will receive from the fund an amount 25 percent lower than the average spent in the previous two campaigns for that office. Based on current spending, the public funding will be $3,100 for House races and $19,000 for Senate races. Maine voters are not used to shelling out large sums for campaigns. At the expected funding levels, Maine campaigns will not be waged through TV ads, just as they are not now. In return for the funds, candidates also must agree not to begin campaign spending until the start of the election year.

Shortening campaigns is crucially important. Because of their grueling demands, some of the best candidates are discouraged from running. Longer campaigns also raise the cost of running and cut into the time incumbents spend doing their jobs. Ideally, primary elections—which few voters participate in anyway—would be eliminated. Instead, as in years past, political parties would choose their candidates in caucuses.

Besides receiving public funds, under the Maine plan candidates have an incentive to accept the limits imposed because they would be labeled "Clean Elections" candidates, drawing more votes. If a candidate who chooses to receive private funds spends more than a Clean Elections opponent, the amount of public funding provided to the Clean Elections candidate can be increased to as much as twice the normal amount. In making that determination, so-called independent expenditures spent on behalf of the candidate who receives private funds can be taken into account.

241

Thus, the Maine plan promises to be a simple yet effective way of cleaning up the election system. The *Boston Globe* called the plan a "blueprint for national change, enabling Americans to take back their democracy." A national poll by the Mellman Group found that 68 percent of those surveyed favored a system modeled after the Maine plan. The support was bipartisan: liberals and conservatives, Democrats and Republicans, strongly favored the idea. According to David Donnelly, the manager of the Clean Elections campaign, "At least ten calls a day come in from other jurisdictions interested in trying the plan."

Among twenty Western countries, the United States is the only one that places no restrictions on the total amounts that may be donated to legislative races. Canada, France, New Zealand, and Great Britain limit candidates' campaign spending. Most of the countries have some form of public financing for legislative elections.[344]

"I think the system needs to be changed," said William F. Hildenbrand, a former secretary of the Senate. "Public financing is probably the only way to fix it. It now takes most of a member's time after he is reelected to raise enough money to get reelected. We need equal access to television. . . . Part of the reason Congress is not respected is the campaign financing system."[345]

"Congress must pass campaign finance reform, so our legislators can be free of endless fund-raising and indebtedness to special interests," former senator Warren Rudman, a New Hampshire Republican, said.

Yet members of Congress are not about to risk being replaced by clean candidates. Congressional interest in investigating foreign money in campaigns is but another diversion to deflect attention from the real problem. In a meeting of Newt Gingrich's PAC after the November 1996 election, Sen. Mitch McConnell, a Kentucky Republican, made it clear that reform is "not going to happen in the 105th Congress. You can write it down."[346]

As disclosures of improper fundraising activities by the Clinton re-election campaign became almost a daily occurrence, Clinton dropped a few lines in his 1997 State of the Union address calling for campaign finance reform by Independence Day—July 4, 1997. The deadline had as much chance of being met as the dates tossed around by Clinton and Gingrich after they shook hands on supporting campaign finance reform in New Hampshire in June 1995. In fact, even as members sanctimoniously began investigations of Clinton fundraising efforts, they became even more determined to block any real reform that might diminish the size of their own funds.

A February 1997 *Washington Post* survey found nearly nine in 10 Americans favor overhauling the election finance system. But Senator McConnell vowed to "kill" the Band-Aid approach of the bipartisan reform bill reintroduced by Senators John McCain and Russell Feingold and by Representatives Chris Shays and Marty Meehan. Employing true congressional doublespeak, McConnell—who wraps himself in the First Amendment to justify his opposition to limiting campaign funds— said the reforms that Republicans would favor are *increasing* the ceilings on individual contributions and *removing* limits on political party expenditures.

"Those who have once been intoxicated with power, and have derived any kind of emolument from it, even though but for one year, never can willingly abandon it. They may be distressed in the midst of all their power, but they will never look to anything but power for their relief," Edmund Burke, the Irish philosopher and statesman, said.

"After eighteen years in the Senate, I can say with certainty that no matter what promises have been made, Congress alone, even Congress and the president, will never be willing to give up the system that most have mastered," former senator Bill Bradley, a New Jersey Democrat, said.

"It's like a drug, and everyone's hooked," according to former senator David L. Boren, an Oklahoma Democrat.

As a way of forcing members to accept reform, some have proposed creation of a bipartisan commission similar to the one Clinton and Gingrich agreed to in New Hampshire. While the idea is appealing, in reality the appointments would likely be weighted so that the commission would propose only window dressing.

"All the formulations for a commission have the members appointed by the same people who have killed reform in the last sessions," said Don Simon, executive vice president of Common Cause. "To have them appointed by Trent Lott, Newt Gingrich, and Dick Gephardt is not a way to advance the ball."[347]

Nor are limits on congressional terms a solution. "Term limits are a gimmick to overcome the money," said Michael R. Lemov, a former House Commerce Committee chief counsel. "Term limits would diminish the experience and thus the power of Congress by eliminating members with extensive knowledge of the legislative process, making them even more dependent on special interests which write the legislation. It's up to our leaders to come up with reasonable solutions to the campaign financing problem, and they have failed, both the Democrats and the Republicans."[348]

In his book *Everyone Is Entitled to My Opinion*, David Brinkley suggests locking politicians in a Goodyear blimp and sending them away, launching them into orbit in space, or letting them fall through a trapdoor behind lecterns at conventions. Short of these whimsical solutions, how can voters force politicians to end the corrupt money system and substitute public funding?

Unlike states, the federal government has no provision for referenda. In the end, American government derives its power, as the Declaration of Independence states, "from the consent of the governed." The only way to achieve real reform is to vote into office honorable candidates pledged to vote for public funding similar to the Maine plan. In judging whether a candidate is honorable, Americans must look at their track records and reputations. It would be unrealistic to expect voters to conduct research into candidates. But in the normal course of events, voters form impressions about candidates by following political and legislative news. When candidates have had ethics problems or lied or broken their word—as Gingrich did in pledging to support a campaign financing reform commission— voters should automatically vote against them.

Equally important, first-time candidates who do not pledge support for public funding of congressional elections similar to

Reform

the Maine plan should be defeated. Voters should reject incumbents who have not voted for public funding. If Congress fails to vote on the issue, the electorate should vote against the entire membership—with the exception of candidates who themselves reject PAC money. If public interest groups distributed lists of those members who match these criteria, and if voters disciplined themselves to follow the lists, the electorate could defeat candidates who do not support reform. If that does not happen, the public's anger at the present system could well lead to formation of a third political party pledged to establish clean elections, according to respected political journalists David Broder and Haynes Johnson.[349]

America does not need charismatic actors to run the government; it needs honest people with good judgment and character. Only by applying to their voting choices the same standards of integrity and honesty Americans use to select friends, business associates, tradespeople, lawyers and accountants, and employees will they get the kinds of leaders they merit. Those kinds of honorable people, in turn, can be expected to vote to end the corrupt money system.

"Ethics must be reintroduced to public service to restore people's faith in government," Walter Cronkite said. "Without such faith, democracy cannot flourish."

The press must play a part. There is no need to require free television time for candidate debates. Debates promote the most accomplished actors. On the congressional level, they usually draw negligible audiences in any case. "I don't think I've ever heard a debate on television," former representative Moss said. "I've heard a presentation of opposing views. Debates are meaningless. They are for show. Sometimes the most eloquent is the biggest louse."

The mainstream press needs to realize that campaign financing and candidates' character are intertwined issues that require more aggressive coverage. The *Washington Post* considered it front-page news that Indonesian businessman Mochtar Riady, whose relatives and associates had provided hundreds of thousands of dollars to the Democrats, had written a 1993 letter to Bill Clinton outlining policy initiatives he wanted.[350] Yet lobbyists and PACs responsible for bringing in far more money make such requests of members of Congress every day. Such requests, considered routine, rarely make their way even to the inside pages of newspapers.

Similarly, even if they document candidates' hypocrisy, the mainstream media are reluctant to break stories about candidates' personal lives. The *Star*, a tabloid, broke the story of Gennifer Flowers's affair with Clinton when he was governor. That tabloid and the *National Enquirer* revealed White House consultant Dick Morris's relationship with a prostitute.[351] The *Washington Post* and *Time* decided against breaking the story of Bob Dole's extramarital affair during his first marriage. Yet after others had reported on these matters, the *Post* and other papers were perfectly willing to run stories about them.[352]

"The *Star* has broken more news than the *Chicago Tribune*," commented Evan Thomas, *Newsweek*'s Washington bureau chief. "In the last two campaigns, they have broken two of the biggest stories. It's embarrassing that a supermarket tabloid is breaking these big stories. On the other hand, the establishment press rightfully doesn't like to be first on these sorts of stories."

Yet the press cannot have it both ways, claiming that stories illuminating candidates' character are not news before they come out, but become news when others have reported them.

Too often, television interviewers display the same tendency to shy from embarrassing questions about character or the relationship between PAC money and voting records. Often, these questions make both interviewers and interviewees uncomfortable. Interviewers do not want to risk the possibility that guests may refuse to appear again on their shows. When interviewers do ask probing questions only to get evasive answers, they usually allow candidates to get away with it.

While newspapers run numbing lists of PAC contributions and follow foreign-funding controversies, they rarely devote the same kind of space to coverage of campaign finance issues as they do to calling the front-runners in congressional races. Coverage of the Maine plan, for example, was almost nonexistent. While the *New York Times* explored the plan before the election, by the end of November 1996, it had not reported that the plan had passed. The *Los Angeles Times* ran only a few lines about it. The *Washington Post* ran no stories; nor did the newsmagazines.

"If the media discussed these issues and put good questions to the candidates, that can help," former representative Moss said. "The media has to do more to focus attention on the problem, in depth."

In the movie *Dave*, the White House chief of staff secretly replaces a disabled president with an ordinary citizen who looks like him. Free of obligations to moneyed interests, he proceeds to balance the budget and make honest, commonsense decisions. The people love him. In real life, Dave could not get elected.

Instead, the genuine patriots of our day—reformers such as Fred Wertheimer, former president of Common Cause; Ellen S. Miller, the former executive director of the Center for Responsive Government who has started Public Campaign, which will promote public financing of elections; Ann McBride, president of Common Cause; Joan Claybrook, president of Public Citizen; and sponsors of reform legislation in Congress—are seen as pesky dreamers. In the same way, Samuel Adams, Patrick Henry, Thomas Jefferson, and others were seen as radicals when they formed committees of correspondence that became the underground of the resistance movement against England. In fact, while the reformers privately favor public funding, most have had to settle for advocating lesser improvements, including limiting or banning PAC money and capping campaign spending at obscenely high levels, as the only realistic way of achieving change.

"The bill I really like . . . is public financing," said Sen. Russell D. Feingold, a Wisconsin Democrat who has cosponsored reform legislation. "I don't think we should have campaign contributions. It adds nothing. It cheapens the process. But that's a dream I have."[353]

To say that the system does not work is to overstate the case for reform. The fact that America continues to elect its leaders democratically means the system does work. Because of the freedoms Americans enjoy, the country functions in most spheres without the intervention of government. In those areas, America is the envy of the world.

Nor is Congress without its achievements. Each session produces some worthwhile legislation. "This institution is responsive to the American people," Rep. Lee Hamilton said. "Maybe it doesn't register every blip, but over time, if the American people feel strongly about something, Congress responds."[354]

At the same time, money "has an impact on every bill," Hamilton said. "If you have big checks and you are willing to distribute that money widely, you get results."

From crime to health care, from crumbling inner cities to deteriorating public schools, from government waste to a bloated federal bureaucracy, America today faces problems that Congress could help solve if it were not controlled by special interests. In particular, the deficit represents Congress's failure to do its job and its lack of accountability.

Money magazine estimates the average American spends an extra $340 a year because the states do an abysmal job of regulating the insurance industry. That is so because the industry's financial clout has stopped Congress from imposing federal regulation.[355]

"Before he was even sworn in as chairman [of the Commerce Committee], Rep. Tom Bliley said, 'I'm going to stop these hearings on tobacco,'" said Rep. Martin Meehan. "He was taking more PAC money from tobacco interests than any other member. We shouldn't allow that in this country."[356]

The principle that the laws should apply equally to all was at the heart of the American Revolution. The Fairfax County Resolutions, produced in a 1774 meeting chaired by George Washington, said England had denied the colonies a legal system with representatives "chosen freely by themselves, who are affected by the laws they enact equally with their constituents."[357]

James Madison wrote in *The Federalist Papers* that one check on governmental abuse was that the House of Representatives could make "no law which will not have its full operation on themselves and their friends, as well as on the great mass of society." Without such equality between the ruled and the rulers, "every government degenerates into tyranny."

By exempting itself from the laws and standards that apply to every other facet of American life, members of Congress have created for themselves a haven of power and privilege without precedent in America. By refusing to enact for themselves the public funding plan they created as an option for presidential candidates, members have deprived citizens of honest representation. From turning the Capitol Police into a corrupt force to legalizing bribery for themselves, members have institutionalized dishonesty and deceit. By providing themselves with $20,000 custom-made silk-covered chairs while shutting down the government to cut the budget, members have engaged in obscene hypocrisy, pampering themselves like kings and queens in a monarchy. In displaying ice buckets to show how they have cut out perquisites, these same members demonstrate how much contempt they have for the public.

As documented by the insiders quoted in this book, the unreal atmosphere that members have created for themselves enhances their lack of accountability. The perquisites and the ability to make rules for everyone but themselves embolden members to disregard the national interest in favor of their own self-interest.

"The ego and the arrogance of some of the members had an impact on me," said John R. Niston, a recently retired Capitol Police officer. "They get to the point where they think the people in the country exist to serve them instead of the other way around."[358]

"It's a disgrace to the American people," said Edward P. Percival, a former Capitol Police officer. "If they knew how they operated, they would get rid of the whole bunch of them."[359]

With his mother, Stephen Mahoney, an eleven-year-old from Stockton, California, was touring the Capitol for the first time. When asked by the author what Congress does, he responded, "Congress works on issues that need to be solved and changed to try to make the country better."[360]

That was the dream of the founding fathers. Today, nothing

could be further from the truth. Rather than consisting of "men of individual honor and personal character, and of absolute independence" who "know no masters," as Daniel Webster claimed, Congress today consists almost entirely of imperious, fractious, mediocre politicians willingly enslaved by special interests.

Reprehensible as it is, the Clinton administration's practice of selling overnight stays in the Lincoln Bedroom and soliciting campaign funds from within the White House are minor abuses compared with the selling of legislation, a real scandal that goes on every day in Congress. Moreover, Congress's purposeful effort to write porous campaign-financing laws contributed to the administration's abuses.

By facing the truth about the present corrupt system and selecting honorable candidates who favor public funding, Americans can throw out sleazy politicans and take charge of their government. America does not need actors and fund-raisers in Congress. It needs honest, decent people like former senator Phil Hart.

To elect such people, voters will have to exercise as much discipline and resolve as the colonists exercised in throwing off the yoke of England. Only then will Americans have the kind of representatives they deserve, a government of which they can be proud, and a country truly free of tyranny.

Capitol Police Memo

★ ★ ★ ★ ★ ★ ★ ★ ★ ★

United States Capitol Police
Office of the Chief
119 D Street NE
Washington, DC 20510-7218

November 27, 1995

MEMORANDUM

TO: The Department
FROM: Chief Gary L. Abrecht
SUBJECT: Recent Phone Inquiries Received at Members' Residences

Recently, I have received complaints from several members of the department regarding telephone calls they received at their residences from a Mr. Ron Kessler.

Mr. Kessler is an author who is in the process of writing a book about Congress. Unfortunately, Mr. Kessler insists on contacting members at home in an effort to encourage them to provide information learned in the course of their duties.

It appears Mr. Kessler has obtained a list of all U.S. Capitol Police personnel from official sources and then uses that information to obtain home telephone numbers. Sergeant Dan Nichols has contacted Mr. Kessler to express our concern about his lack of respect for our members' privacy and to ask him to cease his efforts to call members at home during their personal time. However, it appears Mr. Kessler is continuing his efforts.

I regret that our personnel are inconvenienced at home solely because of their employment with the department. Those who have been called have correctly referred Mr. Kessler to the Public Information Office. As a matter of principle, I hope members who may be contacted in the future continue to refer Mr. Kessler to Sergeant Nichols. If we all do so, Mr. Kessler may cease bothering our personnel and their families at home on their personal time.

Gary L. Abrecht
Chief of Police

Recipe for Senate Bean Soup

Take two pounds of small Michigan Navy Beans, wash, and run through hot water until beans are white again. Put on the fire with four quarts of hot water. Then take one and one-half pounds of smoked ham hocks, boil slowly approximately three hours in covered pot. Braise one chopped onion in a little butter and, when light brown, put in bean soup. Season with salt and pepper, then serve. Do not add salt until ready to serve.

—March 9, 1967, memo from the Architect of the Capitol to the Librarian of the Senate

Congressional Dates

1774 First Continental Congress meets in Philadelphia.

1775 Second Continental Congress meets in Philadelphia.

1776 Richard Henry Lee of Virginia calls for independence by introducing a resolution that "these United Colonies are, and of right ought to be, free and independent states."

Declaration of Independence is approved. It states that governments "are instituted among men, deriving their just powers from the consent of the governed." The signers pledged their "lives," their "fortunes," and their "sacred honor."

1777 Congress adopts Articles of Confederation, the first Constitution, which creates a weak union. Of the few powers delegated to Congress, the most important could not be exercised without the assent of nine of the thirteen states. There is no provision for a chief executive.

1781 Articles of Confederation are ratified.

1787 Constitutional Convention meets in Philadelphia to consider revising the Articles of Confederation. Constitution is adopted.

1789 First Congress meets in Federal Hall at the corner of Broad and Wall Streets in New York. The House adopts the ceremonial mace as a symbol of office for the sergeant at arms.

1790 All thirteen of the original states ratify the Constitution. Congress passes the Residence Act, which provides that the federal government will be located on a permanent site on the Potomac River by 1800.

1791 Pierre Charles L'Enfant proposes a plan for Washington with the Capitol on Jenkins' Hill.

1792 Pierre L'Enfant is dismissed, and a competition is announced for a plan for the Capitol. Dr. William Thornton submits a plan after the deadline.

1793 On the recommendation of President George Washington, Dr. William Thornton is awarded first prize in the competition for design of the Capitol.
George Washington lays down cornerstone of the Capitol, and construction begins.

1794 Senate agrees to open its proceedings to the public.

1800 Congress convenes for first time in the north wing of the Capitol.
When Congress opens its doors, a watchman guards the building. This is the beginning of the Capitol Police.
The Library of Congress is established in the Capitol.

1801 Supreme Court meets for the first time in the Capitol.

1807 The House occupies the south wing of the Capitol.

1810 The Senate occupies the north wing of the Capitol.

1814 The British burn the Capitol. The original House mace is destroyed.

1839 Pages are first mentioned in the *Congressional Globe*, a privately printed predecessor of the *Congressional Record*.

1841 William Adams, a New York silversmith, makes a replica of the original House mace. The copy is used today.

1853 Congress makes it illegal to bribe members.

1860 The Old Senate Chamber is converted for use by the Supreme Court.

1861 The Government Printing Office is established.

1863 The last section of the Statue of Freedom is placed on the dome of the Capitol.

1865 Steam heat is introduced into the Capitol.

1866 Scaffolding is removed from beneath Brumidi's *Apotheosis of George Washington.*

1870 Hiram R. Revels of Mississippi becomes the first black member of Congress when he begins serving in the Senate. Joseph H. Rainey of South Carolina, the first black to become a representative, begins serving.

1873 The Government Printing Office begins printing the *Congressional Record.*

1874 Elevators are installed in the Capitol.

1875 Stables are removed from the Capitol grounds.

1877 Romualdo Pacheco of California becomes the first Hispanic congressman.

1880s Filibustering becomes common in the Senate, which had a cherished tradition of unlimited debate.

1884 Construction begins on terraces designed by Frederick Law Olmsted.

1885 Incandescent lights are installed in the cloakrooms, lobbies, and stairways of the Capitol.

1886 Incandescent lights are installed in the Senate wing of the Capitol.

1888 Incandescent lights are installed in the House wing of the Capitol.

1890 House Speaker Thomas Brackett Reed of Maine tells the House that "the object of a parliamentary body is action, not stoppage of action."
Charles E. Kincaid, a reporter for the *Louisville Times*, fatally wounds Rep. William P. Taulbee of Kentucky, Democrat, in the Capitol after Taulbee attacks him over a story he wrote.

1894 Modern plumbing is installed in the Capitol.

1897 Arc lights replace gas on the Capitol grounds.

The Library of Congress moves from the Capitol to its present main building, now called the Thomas Jefferson Building. It now has more than 97 million items housed in three buildings.

1902 Roofs of old House and Senate wings are reconstructed and fireproofed.

1904 The Senate authorizes construction of the first Senate office building, later named the Russell Senate Office Building.

Congress opens its own power plant at New Jersey Avenue and B Streets SE.

House Speaker Joseph G. Cannon of Illinois orders that bean soup be served every day in the House restaurant.

Sen. Joseph R. Burton of Kansas is convicted of bribery.

1907 Congress bans campaign contributions from banks and corporations.

1908 Construction begins on the first House office building, later named the Cannon Building.

1909 The first subways operate from the Senate wing to what is now known as the Russell Senate Office Building.

1913 The Seventeenth Amendment, providing for direct election of senators instead of selection by state legislatures, is ratified.

1914 The Legislative Reference Bureau, now called the Congressional Research Service, is established within the Library of Congress.

1916 With her election to the House, Jeanette Rankin becomes the first female member of Congress.

1921 Congress establishes the General Accounting Office to audit and investigate the government.

1922 Rebecca Latimer Felton is appointed the first female senator.

1924 Rep. John W. Langley of Kentucky is convicted of violating the National Prohibition Act.

1925 The Teapot Dome scandal results in a new Federal Corrupt Practices Act to limit campaign expenditures.

1931 Rep. Harry E. Rowbottom of Indiana is convicted of accepting bribes.

1933 The Longworth House Office Building, a second House office building, is occupied.

1934 Rep. George E. Foulkes of Michigan is convicted of conspiracy to assess postmasters for political contributions.

1935 The Supreme Court moves from the Capitol to its own building.
Dennis Chavez of New Mexico becomes the first Hispanic senator.

1936 Rep. John Hoeppel of California is convicted of influence peddling.

1937 For the first time, Congress meets in air-conditioned chambers.
Congress begins raising and lowering as many as three hundred American flags a day so members can give them to constituents, who are charged a fee for the flags.

1943 Congress bans campaign contributions from labor unions.

1946 Rep. James Curley of Massachusetts is convicted of mail fraud and conspiracy.

1947 Rep. Andrew J. May of Kentucky is convicted of conspiring to defraud the government and accepting bribes.

1948 Rep. J. Parnell Thomas of New Jersey is convicted of conspiring to defraud the government, payroll padding, and receiving kickbacks from salaries.

1954 Senate censures Sen. Joseph P. McCarthy of Wisconsin for having acted "contrary to senatorial ethics" and for bringing the Senate "into dishonor and disrepute."

1956 Rep. Thomas J. Lane of Massachusetts is convicted of federal income tax evasion.

1957 Dalip Singh Saund of California, the first congressman of Asian ancestry, begins serving.

1958 Dirksen Senate Office Building, the second Senate office building, is occupied.

1965 Rayburn House Office Building, the third House office building, is occupied.

1969 Rep. Hugh J. Addonizio of New Jersey is convicted of extortion, conspiracy, and income tax evasion.

1970 Sen. Jacob Javits appoints the first female page.
Rep. John V. Dowdy of Texas is convicted of conspiracy, perjury, and bribery.
The Legislative Reorganization Act encourages more open committee meetings and hearings and requires that roll call votes be made public.

1971 A bomb explodes in the Capitol, resulting in tighter security precautions.

1972 Congress passes a campaign-finance reform law allowing political action committees (PACs) to flourish.
Rep. Cornelius Gallagher of New Jersey pleads guilty to tax evasion.

1973 Rep. Frank J. Brasco of New York is convicted of conspiracy to receive bribes.
Rep. Bertram L. Podell of New York pleads guilty to conspiracy, bribery, and perjury.

1974 Congress sets contribution and spending limits for candidates in federal elections. The system of choosing committee chairmen by seniority ends when the Democratic Caucus requires that chairmanships be filled by secret ballot at the beginning of each new Congress.
Congress passes the Congressional Budget and Impoundment Control Act, requiring a vote each year to set specific spending, tax, and deficit limits.

1975 Rep. Andrew Hinshaw of California is convicted of bribery and embezzlement.

1976 Elizabeth Ray avers that Rep. Wayne L. Hays of Ohio put her on the payroll solely because she was his mistress.
In *Buckley v. Valeo*, the Supreme Court upholds the limits set by Congress in 1974 on how much individuals and PACs may contribute to candidates. It also upholds public funding of presidential elections. But, on the grounds they violate the First Amendment, the court

rejects campaign spending limits unless they are part of an optional public-funding arrangement.

The *Washington Post* reveals a Justice Department investigation into influence buying by Tongsun Park, a South Korean businessman.

Rep. James F. Hastings of New York is convicted of mail fraud.

1977 Rep. Richard A. Tonry of Louisiana is convicted of receiving illegal campaign contributions and obstruction of justice.

Rep. Richard T. Hanna of California is convicted of conspiracy to defraud the government.

1978 Rep. Charles C. Diggs of Michigan is convicted of mail fraud and perjury.

1980 Rep. Michael "Ozzie" Myers of Pennsylvania is convicted of bribery and conspiracy as part of the FBI's ABSCAM investigation.

Sen. Harrison Williams of New Jersey is convicted of bribery and conspiracy in ABSCAM.

Rep. Raymond F. Lederer of Pennsylvania is convicted of conspiracy and bribery in ABSCAM.

Rep. John W. Jenrette Jr. of South Carolina is convicted of bribery and conspiracy in ABSCAM.

Rep. Frank Thompson of New Jersey is convicted of bribery in ABSCAM.

Rep. John M. Murphy of New York is convicted of bribery in ABSCAM.

Rep. Richard Kelly of Florida is convicted of bribery in ABSCAM.

1982 Hart Senate Office Building, attached to the Dirksen Senate Office Building, opens after plans for a gym are dropped.

1983 A second bomb explodes in the Capitol.

Restoration begins on the west front of the Capitol.

Rep. George Hansen of Idaho is convicted of filing false financial disclosure statements.

1988 Rep. Mario Biaggi of New York is convicted of obstruct-

ing justice, tax evasion, conspiracy, extortion, and accepting bribes.

Rep. Pat Swindall of Georgia is convicted of perjury.

1989 Rep. Donald E. (Buz) Lukens of Ohio is convicted of
contributing to the delinquency of a minor.

1991 Rep. Nick Mavroules of Massachusetts pleads guilty to
bribery and tax evasion.

1993 Rep. Larry Smith of Florida is convicted of income tax
evasion and campaign-reporting violations.

Rep. Albert Bustamante of Texas is convicted of racketeering and accepting an illegal gratuity.

Restoration begins on the Statue of Freedom.

1994 Rep. Carrol Hubbard of Kentucky is convicted of misap-
propriation of funds.

1994 Rep. Carl Perkins of Kentucky pleads guilty to filing a
false financial-disclosure statement.

1995 Rep. Mel Reynolds of Illinois is convicted of having sex
with a minor and obstructing justice.

Sources: *Congressional Quarterly's Guide to Congress, Capital
Confidential,* Architect of the Capitol chronology, *A Compendium of Records and Firsts of the U.S. House of Representatives.*

Notes

1. Interview on January 13, 1996, with Howard R. Ryland.
2. Interview on February 2, 1996, with Gregory M. Lacoss. Carole Tyler died in a plane crash in Ocean City, Maryland, in 1965; also, *Washington Post*, September 23, 1979, C1.
3. Interview on October 5, 1995, with James T. Trollinger.
4. Interview on October 10, 1995, with Charles T. Kindsvatter.
5. Interview on October 25, 1995, with David A. Curry. Conte died in 1991.
6. Interview on September 11, 1995, with Richard Xander. Mills died in 1992.
7. Interview on November 26, 1995, with Wayne N. Beckett.
8. Interview on November 26, 1995, with Jimmy G. Young.
9. Interview on October 15, 1995, with Rodney C. Eades. Nine other former Capitol Police or House officers said Albert was often drunk.
10. Interview on August 1, 1996, with Raymond L. Carson.

Notes

11. In response to a request for comment, a lawyer for Albert said in a letter dated December 17, 1996, that material suggesting that Albert had a drinking problem was "false." The March 6, 1989, edition of *Newsweek* said Albert was one of several members who "reportedly had drinking problems." The article said Albert denies that he "has or ever had a drinking problem."

12. Eades, interview. Kennedy did not respond to a request for comment on November 2, 1996.

13. Interview on December 5, 1995, with Nelson C. Sours.

14. Interview on December 7, 1995, with Richard W. Micer.

15. Interview on October 10, 1995, with Joseph R. Schaap.

16. Eades, interview. Hays died in 1989; Tower died in 1991.

17. *Washington Post*, November 8, 1981, magazine, page 28, and April 20, 1996, D3; *Congressional Quarterly's Guide to Congress*, 69.

18. Eades, interview. *Congressional Quarterly's Guide to Congress*, 788. Ray did not respond to a request for comment made on September 19, 1996.

19. Interview on August 4, 1995, with Martin Lobel.

20. Interview on January 23, 1996, with David S. Kiernan.

21. Carson, interview.

22. Ibid.

23. Interview on November 29, 1996, with Rita Jenrette; *Fall from Grace*, 260.

24. Interview on January 13, 1996, with Linwood T. Binford Jr.

25. Interview on December 17, 1995, with Paul R. McGill.

26. Interview on September 25, 1995, with Talmadge W. Reed.

27. *A Statutory History of the United States Capitol Police Force*, 1; U.S. Senate *Congressional Record*, February 3, 1981, S945.

28. *Legislative Branch Employment, 1960–1995*, Congressional Research Service, November 7, 1995; *Trend of Federal Civilian On-Board Employment for Executive Branch (Non-Postal) Agencies*, Office of Personnel Management, 1960–January 1996; Department of Defense Directorate for Public Communication. Another 191 employees worked for the Office of

Notes

Technology Assessment, which analyzed technological issues; it has since been abolished.

29. Interview on October 14, 1995, with Ernest M. Riddle.
30. Interview on October 14, 1995, with George L. Holmes Jr.
31. McGill, interview.
32. *Washington Post*, April 24, 1992, B3, and March 31, 1992, D3.
33. Interview on November 27, 1995, with Howard F. Pond.
34. Interview on September 25, 1995, with Bruce A. Currie.
35. Curry, interview. On December 7, 1995, former Capitol Police inspector Richard W. Micer confirmed that the incident took place. Powell did not respond to a request for comment made on November 5, 1996.
36. *Washington Post*, July 29, 1983, A9. Ford did not respond to a request by the author for comment made on September 19, 1996.
37. *Washington Post*, July 29, 1983, A9.
38. Interview on November 29, 1995, with Terry D. Coons. The account was confirmed in an interview on February 19, 1996, with David K. Berry, another former Capitol Police officer.
39. Interview on December 4, 1995, with Steven E. Dekelbaum. Kennedy did not respond to a request for comment made on November 2, 1996.
40. Coons, interview.
41. *Congressional Quarterly's Guide to Congress*, 815.
42. Interview on February 3, 1996, with Harper T. Redden. Kennedy, Byrd, and Bonior did not respond to requests for comment made on November 4, 1996.
43. Interview on February 16, 1996 with Mathew H. Moser.
44. Interview on December 7, 1995, with Paul Z. Herman.
45. Dekelbaum, interview.
46. Interview on October 3, 1995, with John A. Gott.
47. *Washington Post*, September 29, 1993, F1.
48. Interview on December 10, 1995, with David L. Coon.
49. Dekelbaum, interview.
50. *Washington Post*, May 18, 1985.
51. Interview on October 18, 1995, with John A. Gott.

52. *The FBI*, 130.

53. *Time*, September 25, 1995, 52.

54. *The Senate: 1789–1989*, 330.

55. Diary of Terry D. Coons, quoted by permission.

56. Gott, interview, October 3, 1995.

57. Interview on January 15, 1996, with Arthur S. Koeller.

58. Interview on January 28, 1996, with James T. Trollinger.

59. Interview on December 1, 1995, with Edward P. Percival.

60. Schaap, interview. On September 20, 1996, Smith confirmed that while in Congress he bought a used red Corvette. He said he did not recall the incident but did not dispute that it took place.

61. Interview on December 2, 1995, with Wayne N. Beckett.

62. *Brief Comparison of Retirement Eligibility and Benefits for Members of Congress and Executive Branch Personnel*, Congressional Research Service, February 8, 1996, CRS2.

63. Interview on January 20, 1996, with Joel C. Raupe.

64. Interview on January 31, 1996, with Steven R. (Rick) Valentine.

65. Ibid.

66. *Congressional Quarterly's Guide to Congress*, 779. The investigation found that Studds had made sexual overtures to two other male pages.

67. Interview on August 6, 1996, with Dr. Bertram S. Brown.

68. Interview on December 17, 1995, with Andrew Kruk.

69. Interviews on January 21, 1996, and on November 4, 1996, with Steven H. Taubenberger.

70. Letter of October 29, 1996, to the author from Rosalynn Carter.

71. *Roll Call*, June 22, 1995.

72. Interview on July 22, 1996, with Amanda Wheeler.

73. Xander, interview.

74. *Investigation of the Office of Postmaster, Pursuant to House Resolution 340*, 14.

75. Carson, interview. Powell did not respond to a request for comment on October 21, 1996.

76. Ibid. On October 7, 1996, Baker said he was not aware of the incident.

77. Interview on April 23, 1996, with James J. Carvino.

78. Xander, interview.

79. *Washington Post,* October 1, 1989, B1.

80. Interview on May 1, 1996, with Frank A. Kerrigan. Ross did not respond to a request for comment made on September 25, 1996.

81. Ibid.; *Washington Post,* March 26, 1992, A1.

82. *Washington Post,* March 26, 1992, A1.

83. *Roll Call,* June 16, 1994.

84. Interview on September 24, 1996, with Frank A. Kerrigan.

85. *Roll Call,* June 13, 1994.

86. Ibid., July 26, 1993, and April 11, 1996.

87. Ibid., July 26, 1993.

88. *Investigation of the Office of Postmaster, Pursuant to House Resolution 340,* 18.

89. Interview on June 8, 1996, with John Cronin Jr. The GAO reports, #B-114854, came out every six months.

90. Interview on January 18, 1996, with Henry F. Arrett.

91. Interview on May 31, 1996, with Rep. Scott L. Klug.

92. Interview on October 9, 1995, with Werner W. Brandt.

93. *Congressional Quarterly Almanac,* 102nd Congress, 2nd session, 1992, 29.

94. *Washington Post,* December 18, 1993, A5.

95. Kiernan, interview.

96. Interview on January 21, 1996, with Charles L. Hoag. Stump did not respond to a request for comment made on September 30, 1996.

97. Interviews on October 8, 1996, with former representative Larry J. Hopkins and on January 3, 1997 with Rep. Bob Stump.

98. Interview on May 29, 1996, with J. Stanley Kimmitt.

99. Interview on September 4, 1996, with Sen. Thad Cochran.

100. Interview on July 16, 1996, with Sen. Ben Nighthorse Campbell.

101. Interview on July 9, 1996, with Sen. Judd Gregg.

102. Interview on June 10, 1996, with William F. Hildenbrand.

103. Interview on May 6, 1996, with former representative Eric D. Fingerhut.

104. FBI background investigation of Sen. John Tower submit-

ted to the White House on December 13, 1988, obtained under the Freedom of Information Act.

105. FBI report of February 7, 1989, obtained under the Freedom of Information Act.

106. Interview on December 19, 1995, with Melvin F. Parker. Nix died in 1987.

107. Interview on April 21, 1996, with Lee A. Schmalbach.

108. Interview on March 10, 1996, with Robert G. Cantor.

109. *Columbia Journalism Review*, September/October 1995, 38.

110. *Washingtonian*, May 1996, 7.

111. Klug, interview.

112. Interview on December 19, 1995, with Donald A. Ritchie.

113. Interview on January 23, 1996, with Eugene J. Kuser.

114. Interview on July 16, 1996, with Scot M. Faulkner; also, *Roll Call*, August 17, 1995.

115. *Capitol Hill in Black and White*, 70.

116. Interview on January 13, 1996, with Kenneth Derreck Cohen.

117. Ibid. Moynihan did not respond to a request for comment made on November 4, 1996.

118. Interview on February 10, 1996, with Jeffrey T. Robinson.

119. Interview on July 16, 1996, with Sen. Orrin G. Hatch.

120. *Boston Globe*, May 16, 1996, op-ed page. The story reported that Kerry's income tax returns show he gave nothing to charity in 1995. Over the past six years, Kerry gave just under 0.7 percent of his income to charity.

121. Cohen, interview.

122. *Washington Post*, October 9, 1991, A23.

123. *United States Capitol*, 24.

124. *Legislative Branch Employment, 1960–1995*, Congressional Research Service, November 7, 1995; *Trend of Federal Civilian On-Board Employment for Executive Branch (Non-Postal) Agencies*, Office of Personnel Management, 1960–January 1996; Department of Defense Directorate for Public Communication.

125. *Congressional Quarterly's Guide to Congress*, 477.

126. Interview on June 20, 1996, with Rep. Collin C. Peterson.

127. *Roll Call*, September 17, 1992.

128. Interview on May 16, 1996, with Bill Tate.

129. Interview on September 23, 1995, with Robert Gellman.

130. Interview on May 14, 1996, with Daniel P. Beard.

131. Interview on July 15, 1996, with Peter D. H. Stockton; also, *Washington Post*, March 1, 1985, A1.

132. *Report of Investigation: The Aldrich Ames Espionage Case*, 46.

133. Interview on October 15, 1996, with U.S. district court judge Charles R. Richey.

134. Interview on June 8, 1996, with Scott M. Waitlevertch.

135. Interview on June 9, 1996, with Douglas B. Loon.

136. Interview on June 17, 1996, with Neal Manne.

137. Interview on June 9, 1996, with Sylvia Nolde. Specter did not respond to a request for comment made on December 12, 1996.

138. Interview on December 13, 1996, with Dr. Bertram S. Brown.

139. *New York Times*, April 12, 1995, A8.

140. Congressional Quarterly's *Congressional Monitor*, October 26, 1995, 5. The story was picked up by the *Wall Street Journal* on October 27, 1995, page A16, the *Washington Post* on December 22, 1995, page A27, and the *New York Times* on January 26, 1996, page A1.

141. Interview on December 24, 1996, with Jamie S. Gorelick.

142. Harry Glenn, a spokesman for Representative Young, said the congressman is extra cautious about dealing with reporters and did not leak the information. The other two members did not respond to a request for comment made on December 9, 1996.

143. Specter did not respond to a request for comment made on December 12, 1996.

144. *Los Angeles Times*, June 7, 1993, A3.

145. Parker, interview. Stevens did not respond to a request for comment made on November 4, 1996.

146. *Hill*, May 8, 1996, 6.

147. *Roll Call*, November 16, 1995, 13.

148. Further background appears in *Newsweek*, May 6, 1996, 36.

149. *Washington Post*, June 19, 1996, A17; also, Associated Press, April 17, 1996.

150. *Los Angeles Times*, June 27, 1996, A5.

151. *Los Angeles Times*, November 13, 1994, A6.

152. *Los Angeles Times*, April 23, 1995, magazine, 16.

153. *Congressional Record*, January 5, 1996, H225.

154. *Progressive*, September 1995, 29; *Washingtonian*, July 1996, 68; *Los Angeles Times*, April 23, 1995, magazine, 16.

155. Young, interview.

156. Kimmitt, interview.

157. Interview on September 28, 1995, with Roy L. Elson.

158. *Wheeling and Dealing*, 48. Kefauver died in 1963.

159. *Congressional Quarterly's Guide to Congress*, 108, 790; and *Washington Post*, January 19, 1995, A9.

160. *Roll Call*, June 5, 1995; *Washington Post*, June 5, 1986, C1; and *Fall from Grace*, page 264.

161. *Congressional Quarterly's Guide to Congress*, 722.

162. *Financing Politics*, 18.

163. *Political Action Committees*, Congressional Research Service, CRS31.

164. Interview on September 6, 1996, with Don Simon.

165. Interview on May 9, 1996, with former representative Romano L. Mazzoli.

166. *New York Times*, September 10, 1995, sec. 4, p. 17.

167. *Washington Post*, October 9, 1996, A1.

168. *Roll Call*, February 8, 1986, 1; also, *Wall Street Journal*, September 20, 1995, A18.

169. *Washington Post*, November 1, 1996, A1; and *Los Angeles Times*, October 20, 1996, A1.

170. *Wall Street Journal*, September 23, 1996, A22; and *Washington Post*, October 26, 1996, A1.

171. *Washington Post*, July 1, 1996, A4.

172. *Washington Monthly*, November 1995, 19.

173. *Washington Post*, March 22, 1996, D1.

174. *New York Times*, September 28, 1996, A1.

175. *Roll Call*, January 20, 1992; also, Federal Election Commission annual report, 1994.

176. *Ethics in Congress*, 103; and *New York Times*, November 29, 1981, 6E.

177. *Fall from Grace*, 258; and *Congressional Quarterly's Guide to Congress*, 769, 796.

178. Interview on July 22, 1996, with Sen. John B. Breaux.

179. Interview on June 4, 1996, with former representative Robert S. Walker.

180. Cochran, interview.

181. Hatch, interview.

182. Interview on September 14, 1995, with Charles (Chuck) Lipsen.

183. *New York Times*, September 10, 1995, A1.

184. *Hill*, November 13, 1996, 1.

185. *Washington Monthly*, November 1995, 19.

186. Interview on May 24, 1996 with Charles Gardner; also, *When the Pentagon Was for Sale*, 321.

187. Interview on May 16, 1996, with Rep. Jim Leach.

188. Interview on May 1, 1996, with former representative Mel Levine; also, *Speaking Freely*, 89.

189. Interview on May 15, 1996, with former representative Anthony C. Beilenson.

190. Interview on May 12, 1996, with Martin Lobel.

191. Interview on May 4, 1996, with former representative Peter H. Kostmayer.

192. Richey, interview; and Richey's opinion in *Animal Legal Defense Fund Inc., et al., vs. Daniel Glickman, Secretary of Agriculture, et al.*, filed October 30, 1996, U.S. District Court, Washington, 6–12.

193. *National Journal*, September 7, 1991, 2143.

194. Interview on July 16, 1996, with Rep. Lee H. Hamilton.

195. Interview on May 30, 1996, with Rep. Bob Inglis.

196. Fingerhut, interview.

197. Interview on July 11, 1996, with Rep. Jim Kolbe.

198. *Speaking Freely*, 3.

199. Interview on January 26, 1996, with former senator William Proxmire.

200. Interview on February 16, 1996, with Richard Cook.

201. Testimony of Ann McBride, president, Common Cause, Senate Rules and Administration Committee, February 1, 1996.

202. *The Politics of Sugar*, Center for Responsive Politics, 1995, 1.

203. *Common Cents*, ix.

204. Interview on August 14, 1996, with Joseph A. Califano Jr.

205. Campbell, interview.

206. Interview on June 19, 1996, with Steven F. Stockmeyer.

207. *Time*, September 11, 1995, 44. D'Amato denied anything improper.

208. Interview on June 13, 1996, with Rep. Christopher Shays.

209. *Washington Post*, January 8, 1995, W18.

210. *Washington Post*, July 14, 1996, C1; also, *Washington Post*, April 22, 1996, A20.

211. *Wall Street Journal*, June 16, 1995; *New York Times*, March 25, 1995; *Washington Post*, April 4, 1995, A1.

212. *New York Times*, December 6, 1995, A1. Solomon said the timing of the fund-raising appeal was a coincidence.

213. *Hill*, July 31, 1996, A1.

214. *New York Times*, October 12, 1996, 37.

215. *Washington Post*, May 11, 1996, A8. Bob Herbert's column appeared in the *New York Times*, May 10, 1996, A33.

216. *Imperial Congress*, ix.

217. *Time*, June 19, 1989, 33; and *Washington Post*, February 26, 1995, W28.

218. *Washington Post*, June 12, 1989, C1, December 19, 1994, A1, and January 3, 1985, B1; *Time*, August 21, 1995, 31; *Vanity Fair*, September 1995, 147; *New Yorker*, October 9, 1995, 50.

219. *Washington Post*, October 13, 1994, A1.

220. *National Journal*, June 24, 1995.

221. Interview on September 19, 1995, with David K. Rehr.

222. *Washington Post*, September 17, 1996, A13, and December 22, 1996, A1; *Wall Street Journal*, November 25, 1996, B8; *Time*, December 30, 1996, 94; *New York Times*, December 28, 1996, 8, 27.

223. Curry, interview.

224. *New York Times*, September 5, 1995, A1.

225. *Wall Street Journal*, July 1, 1968, 1. The article, by the author, was headlined, "Some Medical Experts Contend That Cigarettes Are Truly Addictive." It reported on experiments with humans and animals that showed that cigarettes or pure nicotine produce classic signs of addiction, just like heroin or morphine.

226. *Senator for Sale*, 185.

227. *Wall Street Journal*, October 3, 1996; A15; *Washington Post*, November 16, 1995, D3; and *Omaha World Herald*, November 19, 1995, and February 17, 1996, 1.

228. *Texas Observer*, October 11, 1996, 5.

229. *Roll Call*, October 26, 1995.

230. *FBI*, 426.

231. *Budget of the U.S. Government*, budget aggregates, summary table, 1.

232. *Washington Post*, October 7, 1996, A19.

233. *Washington Post*, March 8, 1996, A1.

234. *Washington Post*, December 22, 1995, A17, December 29, 1995, A1, and January 5, 1996, A19.

235. *Roll Call*, February 8, 1996, 1.

236. *Washington Post*, January 4, 1988, A14; and *New York Times*, January 3, 1988, 1. When the *New York Times* broke the story, Wilson said his budget-cutting efforts were routine, and he had never directly threatened to cut DIA appropriations. But Charlie Schnable, Wilson's administrative assistant, said, "He does want to bust their ass, there's no doubt about it."

237. *FBI*, 217.

238. *Roll Call*, January 22, 1996, B19; and *Washington Post*, July 20, 1995, A8.

239. *Roll Call*, March 23, 1995.

240. Interview on May 12, 1996, with Martin Lobel; also, *A Toothless Tiger: The Lobbying Disclosure Act of 1995* by Martin Lobel; and *Tax Notes*, June 17, 1996, 1699.

241. Stockmeyer, interview.

242. Interview on May 16, 1996, with Amy Rosenbaum.

243. Interview on July 9, 1996, with Scot M. Faulkner.

244. Interview on July 2, 1996, with Scot M. Faulkner.

245. *Office of Inspector General Audit Report*, 27.

246. Interview on May 12, 1996, with Alan S. Novins.

247. Memo of April 14, 1995, from Scot M. Faulkner to Rep. William M. Thomas, chairman, House Committee on Oversight.

248. Faulkner, interview, July 9, 1996. The only hint appeared in the May 25, 1995, *Roll Call*, which quoted Rep. Bill Thomas, a California Republican who was chairman of the oversight committee, as saying vaguely that over the years Democrats had "doled out" parking spaces to lobbyists.

249. Faulkner, interview, July 9, 1996. Rose did not respond to a request for comment made on November 12, 1996.

250. *Federal Personnel: Architect of the Capitol's Personnel System Needs Improving*, GAO, April 1994.

251. Interview on February 25, 1996, with Leroy Tolbert.

252. Interview on October 3, 1995, with John A. Gott.

253. Interview on July 16, 1996, with Scot M. Faulkner.

254. Interview on April 20, 1996, with Terry Eisenberg.

255. *Washington Post*, February 5, 1995, C3.

256. Faulkner, interview, July 16, 1996. Foley did not respond to a request for comment on October 30, 1996.

257. Interview on February 19, 1996, with Steve C. Alder.

258. Interview on March 30, 1996, with Daniel J. Kreitman.

259. Interview on March 31, 1996, with David W. Clements.

260. Faulkner, interview, July 2, 1996.

261. Interview on July 18, 1996, with Matt Raymond.

262. Interview on July 18, 1996, with Sen. Frank H. Murkowski.

263. *Washington Post*, September 12, 1995, B3, and September 13, 1995, B3.

264. *Roll Call*, March 15, 1990, 9.

265. *Washington Post*, February 1, 1994, C3.

266. *Detroit Free Press*, November 13, 1994, magazine, 6; and *Detroit News*, October 17, 1976, 1.

267. *New York Times*, August 14, 1995, A10; and *Washington Post*, September 8, 1995, A1, A16.

268. *Roll Call*, June 5, 1995.

269. *Roll Call*, July 31, 1995; and *New York Times*, November 9, 1996, 9.

270. Leach, interview.

271. *Congress and Its Members*, 124. Figures are based on the 103rd Congress.

272. *New York Times*, September 27, 1996, A18.

273. Klug, interview.

274. Interview on June 5, 1996, with Sen. Russell D. Feingold.

275. Walker, interview.

276. Interview on June 5, 1996, with Rep. Floyd D. Spence.

277. Interview on March 24, 1996, with Robert B. Thomas.

278. Interview on June 10, 1996, with Rep. Constance A. Morella.

279. *Washington Post*, August 7, 1996, A8, and April 29, 1996, A4.

280. Associated Press, December 11, 1996.

281. *Senate: 1789–1989*, 437.

282. *New York Times*, March 11, 1996, D7.

283. Micer, interview.

284. *Washington Post*, May 29, 1981, A18.

285. Curry, interview.

286. Gott, interview, October 3, 1995.

287. Carson, interview.

288. Curry, interview.

289. Gott, interview, October 3, 1995.

290. Micer, interview.

291. Kerrigan, interview.

292. Warrant of arrest, October 7, 1994, Case Number 94-5386, Alexandria General District Court.

293. Interview on May 7, 1996, with John T. Caulfield.

294. Interview on December 12, 1996, with John T. Caulfield.

295. Gott, interview, October 18, 1995.

296. *Narcotics Investigations by the United States Capitol Police*, 4.

297. Micer, interview.

298. Interview on April 27, 1996, with Franklin C. Shelton.

299. *Roll Call*, August 19, 1991, and May 10 and November 11, 1993. Rose did not respond to a request for comment made on November 12, 1996.

300. Interview on December 7, 1996, with Richard W. Micer.

301. Gott, interview, October 3, 1995.

302. Interviews on December 6 and 10, 1996, with Daniel R. Nichols. Abrecht turned down three requests for an interview.

303. Interview on December 7, 1996, with David Curry.

304. Interviews on March 13 and May 21, 1996, with Lisa Wolfington.

305. *Congressional Quarterly's Guide to Congress*, 807.

306. Interview on October 4, 1996, with Frédérique J. Sandretto. On October 16, 1996, Sandretto signed an affidavit prepared by the author stating under penalty of perjury that Bono had sexually harassed her and that the account she gave of his conduct was true.

307. *Hill*, May 29, 1996, 16.

308. *Los Angeles Times*, September 3, 1996, E5; and *Washington Post*, October 10, 1996, D3.

309. Interview on October 10, 1996, with Frédérique J. Sandretto.

310. Two-page memo by Frédérique J. Sandretto. Occasional grammatical errors have been corrected.

311. Sandretto, interview, October 4, 1996.

312. *Congressional Record*, June 20, 1996, H6676.

313. *Roll Call*, May 31, 1993.

314. Interview on October 5, 1996, with Pamela B. Stuart.

315. Interview on December 11, 1996, with Joseph P. Horn.

316. Interview on December 11, 1996, with Frank Cullen Jr.

317. Mazzoli, interview.

318. Brown, interview.

319. *Philip Hart*, 70.

320. *Washington Post*, June 30, 1996, C1.

321. Interview on September 25, 1995, with Patricia Bario.

322. Interview on May 29, 1996, with former senator Gaylord A. Nelson.

323. *Washington Post*, October 13, 1988, A1.

324. *Washington Post*, June 2, 1996, C1.

325. Brooks Jackson, CNN, July 30 and November 5, 1996.

326. *Newsweek*, August 28, 1995, 65.

327. Herbert E. Alexander, *Election Reform and Reality*, February 14–16, 1994.

328. *Washington Post*, August 2, 1983, A1.
329. *Capital Corruption*, 77.
330. *Organization of the Congress: Policy Analysis and Historical Background*, 190.
331. *Hill*, April 17, 1996, 1.
332. *The FBI*, 190
333. CNN *Crossfire*, May 3, 1996.
334. FBI memo of November 4, 1950, obtained under the Freedom of Information Act.
335. *Boston Globe*, October 28, 1986, third section, 27.
336. *Government WasteWatch*, 12, quoting a report by the House Committee on Government Oversight and Reform.
337. *Roll Call*, May 22, 1995. As part of a plea agreement, Agnew pleaded no contest to charges of tax evasion.
338. Interview on November 26, 1996, with former representative John E. Moss.
339. Quoted in *Senator for Sale*, 293.
340. Interview on December 1, 1996, with Frederick Schauer.
341. Fingerhut, interview.
342. Herbert E. Alexander and Lori Cox NyBlom, Citizens' Research Council *Campaign Reform on the Ballots: 1972–1994*; Center for Responsive Politics, *Roundup of State Campaign Finance Reform Ballot Initiatives*, November 1969; and *Financing Politics*, 143–44.
343. *Boston Globe*, January 1, 1996, metro section, 24, and November 1, 1996, A26; Maine Voters for Clean Elections press release.
344. *Christian Science Monitor*, February 28, 1995, 19; and *The World of Campaign Finance*, 3–12.
345. Hildenbrand, interview.
346. *Roll Call*, November 14, 1996, 1.
347. Interview on November 13, 1996, with Don Simon.
348. Interview on November 25, 1996, with Michael R. Lemov.
349. Talk by David Broder and Haynes Johnson at the Federal City Club, December 4, 1996.
350. *Washington Post*, December 3, 1996, A1.
351. *Washington Post*, September 16, 1996, D1.

352. Ibid.

353. Feingold, interview.

354. Hamilton, interview.

355. Further information on the failure of states to regulate the insurance industry properly can be found in the author's 1985 book, *The Life Insurance Game: How the Industry Has Amassed Over $600 Billion at the Expense of the American Public.*

356. Interview on May 16, 1996, with Rep. Martin T. Meehan.

357. *Washington Post*, February 5, 1995, C3.

358. Interview on December 19, 1995, with John R. Niston.

359. Percival, interview.

360. Interview on July 16, 1996, with Stephen Mahoney.

Bibliography

Abourezk, James G. *Advise & Dissent: Memoirs of South Dakota and the U.S. Senate.* Lawrence Hill Books, 1989.

Alexander, Herbert E. *Financing Politics: Money, Elections, and Political Reform.* Congressional Quarterly, 1992.

_____. *Money in Politics.* Public Affairs Press, 1972.

Alexander, Herbert E., and Rei Shiratori, eds. *Comparative Political Finance Among the Democracies.* Westview Press, 1994.

Alexander, John. *Ghosts: Washington's Most Famous Ghost Stories.* Washingtonian Books, 1975.

Alton, Edmund. *Among the Lawmakers.* Charles Scribner's Sons, 1892.

Ashworth, William. *Under the Influence: Congress, Lobbies, and the American Pork Barrel System.* Hawthorn/Dutton, 1981.

Baker, Bobby, with Larry L. King. *Wheeling and Dealing: Confessions of a Capitol Hill Operator.* W. W. Norton & Co., 1978.

Bibliography

Baker, Ross K. *House and Senate.* W. W. Norton & Co., 1989.

Boller, Paul Jr. *Congressional Anecdotes.* Oxford University Press, 1991.

Byrd, Robert C. *The Senate: 1789–1989.* U.S. Government Printing Office, 1988.

Caro, Robert A. *The Path to Power: The Years of Lyndon Johnson.* Random House, 1981, Vintage Books reprint.

Cheney, Richard B., and Lynne V. Cheney. *Kings of the Hill: Power and Responsibility in the House of Representatives.* Continuum, 1983.

Clawson, Dan, Alan Neustadtl, and Denise Scot. *Money Talks: Corporate PACs and Political Influence.* Basic Books, 1992.

Congressional Quarterly's Guide to Congress. Congressional Quarterly, 1991.

Davidson, Roger H., and Walter J. Oleszek. *Congress and Its Members.* Congressional Quarterly, 1994.

Day, Kathleen. *S&L Hell: The People and the Politics Behind the $1 Trillion Savings and Loan Scandal.* W. W. Norton & Co., 1993.

Dickson, Paul, and Paul Clancy. *The Congress Dictionary: The Ways and Meanings of Capitol Hill.* John Wiley & Sons, 1993.

Downs, Anthony. *An Economic Theory of Democracy.* Harper-Collins, 1957.

Elkins, Stanley, and Eric McKitrick. *The Age of Federalism: The Early American Republic, 1788–1800.* Oxford University Press, 1993.

Etzioni, Amitai. *Capital Corruption: The New Attack on American Democracy.* Transaction Publishers, 1995.

Gross, Martin L. *The Political Racket: Deceit, Self-Interest and Corruption in American Politics.* Ballantine Books, 1996.

Hardeman, D. B., and Donald C. Bacon. *Rayburn: A Biography.* Texas Monthly Press, 1987.

Hilton, Stanley G. *Senator for Sale: An Unauthorized Biography of Senator Bob Dole.* St. Martin's Press, 1995.

Jackson, Brooks. *Honest Graft: How Special Interests Buy Influence in Washington.* Alfred A. Knopf, Farragut Publishing reprint, 1990.

Bibliography

Johnson, Haynes, and David S. Broder. *The System: The American Way of Politics at the Breaking Point.* Little, Brown and Co., 1996.

Jones, Gordon S., and John A. Marini, eds. *The Imperial Congress: Crisis in the Separation of Powers.* Pharos Books, 1988.

Jones, Rochelle, and Peter Woll. *The Private World of Congress.* Free Press, 1979.

Kelly, Brian. *Adventures in Porkland: How Washington Wastes Your Money and Why They Won't Stop.* Villard Books, 1992.

Maroon, Fred J. *The United States Capitol.* Stewart, Tabori & Chang, 1993.

Kessler, Ronald. *The FBI: Inside the World's Most Powerful Law Enforcement Agency.* Pocket Books, 1993.

_____. *Inside the White House: The Hidden Lives of the Modern Presidents and the Secrets of the World's Most Powerful Institution.* Pocket Books, 1995.

Lowenberg, Gerald, and Samuel C. Patterson. *Comparing Legislatures.* Little, Brown and Co., 1979.

MacNeil, Neil. *Forge of Democracy: The House of Representatives.* David McKay Co., 1963.

Malbin, Michael J. *Unelected Representatives: Congressional Staff and the Future of Representative Government.* Basic Books Inc., 1980.

Matthews, Christopher. *Hardball: How Politics Is Played—Told by One Who Knows the Game.* Summit Books, 1988.

Michael, M. Luisa. *House for Sale.* Halycon House, 1992.

Miller, Nathan. *Stealing from America: A History of Corruption from Jamestown to Reagan.* Paragon House, 1992.

Miller, William (Fishbait), with Frances Spatz Leighton. *Fishbait: The Memoirs of the Congressional Doorkeeper.* Warner Books reprint, 1978.

Mintz, Morton, and Jerry S. Cohen. *America Inc.: Who Owns and Operates the United States.* Dial Press, 1971.

_____. *Power Inc.: Public and Private Rulers and How to Make Them Accountable.* Viking Press, 1976.

Bibliography

Moore, John L. *Speaking of Washington.* Congressional Quarterly, 1993.

O'Brien, Michael. *Philip Hart: The Conscience of the Senate.* Michigan State University Press, 1995.

Ornstein, Norman J., Thomas E. Mann, and Michael J. Malbin. *Vital Statistics on Congress: 1995–1996.* Congressional Quarterly, 1996.

O'Rourke, P. J. *Parliament of Whores.* Vintage Books reprint, 1992.

Overacker, Louise. *Money in Elections.* Macmillan Co., 1932.

Parker, Robert, with Richard Rashke. *Capitol Hill in Black and White: Revelations of the Inside and Underside of Power Politics by the Black Former Maître d' of the Senate Dining Room.* Dodd, Mead and Co., 1986.

Pasztor, Andy. *When the Pentagon Was for Sale: Inside America's Biggest Defense Scandal.* Scribner, 1995.

Penny, Rep. Timothy J., and Major Garrett. *Common Cents: A Retiring Six-Term Congressman Reveals How Congress Really Works—and What We Must Do to Fix It.* Little, Brown and Co., 1995.

Poore, Ben Perley. *Perley's Reminiscences of Sixty Years in the National Metropolis.* Ames Press, 1971.

Povich, Elaine S. *Partners and Adversaries: The Contentious Connection Between Congress and the Media.* Freedom Forum, 1996.

Rash, Bryson B. *Footnote Washington: Tracking the Engaging, Humorous and Surprising Bypaths of Capitol History.* EPM Publications, 1983.

Reidel, Richard Langham. *Halls of the Mighty: My 47 Years at the Senate.* Robert B. Luce Inc., 1969.

Rienow, Robert, and Leona Train Rienow. *Of Snuff, Sin and the Senate.* Follett Publishing Co., 1965.

Ross, Shelly. *Fall from Grace: Sex, Scandal, and Corruption in American Politics from 1702 to the Present.* Ballantine Books, 1988.

Sabato, Larry J. *PAC Power: Inside the World of Political Action Committees.* W. W. Norton & Co., 1984.

Bibliography

Schram, Martin. *Speaking Freely: Former Members of Congress Talk About Money in Politics.* Center for Responsive Politics, 1995.

Smith, Hedrick. *The Power Game: How Washington Works.* Random House, Ballantine Books reprint, 1989.

Thomas, Bill. *Capital Confidential: One Hundred Years of Sex, Scandal, and Secrets in Washington, D.C.* Pocket Books, 1996.

Thompson, Dennis F. *Ethics in Congress: From Individual to Institutional Corruption.* Brookings Institution, 1995.

U.S. Capitol Historical Society. *We, the People: The Story of the United States Capitol.* 1991.

U.S. Congress, Joint Committee on the Organization of Congress. *Organization of the Congress, final report, policy analysis, and historical background.* U.S. Government Printing Office, 1993.

U.S. Congressional Research Service. *Architect of the Capitol.* March 6, 1995.

_____. *Committee Numbers, Sizes, Assignments and Staff.* February 1, 1996.

_____. *A Compendium of Records and Firsts of the U.S. House of Representatives.* April 3, 1975.

_____. *Decorum in House Debate.* November 24, 1995.

_____. *Legislative Branch Budget Authority, FY 1968–FY 1996.* March 22, 1996.

_____. *Legislative Branch Employment.* 1960–95.

_____. *Pages of the United States Congress.* September 27, 1990.

_____. *Political Action Committees.* April 30, 1984.

_____. *Political Action Committees: Their Evolution, Growth, and Implications for the Political System.* November 6, 1981.

_____. *Salaries and Allowances: The Congress.* July 20, 1995.

U.S. General Accounting Office. *Cost Comparison of House of Representatives Page System Versus Regular Messenger Employees.* September 30, 1983.

Bibliography

_____. *Public Financing of Political Campaigns of Candidates for Congressional Office: Some Constitutional Considerations.* October 15, 1982.

U.S. House of Representatives, Committee on House Administration. *A Statutory History of the United States Capitol Police Force.* U.S. Government Printing Office, 1985.

_____, Committee on House Administration. *Investigation of the Office of the Postmaster, Pursuant to House Resolution 340.* U.S. Government Printing Office, 1992.

_____, Committee on Standards of Official Conduct. *Narcotics Investigations by the United States Capitol Police.* U.S. Government Printing Office, 1983.

_____, Office of Inspector General. *Audits of Administrative Operations,* based on Price Waterhouse LLP audit. July 18, 1995.

_____, Permanent Select Committee on Intelligence. *Report of Investigation: The Aldrich Ames Espionage Case.* Government Printing Office, November 30, 1994.

U.S. Senate, Bicentennial Publication. *The United States Senate: 1787–1801.* U.S. Government Printing Office, 1988.

_____, Senate Committee on Ethics. *The Packwood Report.* Times Books, 1995.

Valentine, Steven R. *Each Time a Man: Family Roots and a Young Life in Politics.* Friends United Press, 1978.

Wolpe, Bruce C., and Bertram J. Levine. *Lobbying Congress: How the System Works.* Congressional Quarterly, 1996.

★ ★ ★ ★ ★ ★ ★ ★ ★

Index

★ ★ ★ ★ ★ ★ ★ ★ ★

A

M

N

Printed in the United States
By Bookmasters